T0309805

Assessing Business Potential
A Biodata Approach

Assessing Business Potential

A Biodata Approach

Barrie Gunter
Professor of Journalism, University of Sheffield

and

Adrian Furnham
Professor of Psychology, University College London

W
WHURR PUBLISHERS
LONDON AND PHILADELPHIA

© 2001 Whurr Publishers
First published 2001 by
Whurr Publishers Ltd
19b Compton Terrace, London N1 2UN, England and
325 Chestnut Street, Philadelphia PA 19106, USA

All rights reserved. No part of this publication may be
reproduced, stored in a retrieval system, or transmitted in any form or by any means, electronic,
mechanical, photocopying, recording or otherwise,
without the prior permission of Whurr Publishers
Limited.

This publication is sold subject to the conditions that
it shall not, by way of trade or otherwise, be lent,
resold, hired out, or otherwise circulated without the
publisher's prior consent in any form of binding or
cover other than that in which it is published and
without a similar condition including this condition
being imposed upon any subsequent purchaser.

British Library Cataloguing in Publication Data
A catalogue record for this book is available from the
British Library.

ISBN: 1 86156 175 X

Printed and bound in the UK by Athenaeum Press Ltd,
Gateshead, Tyne & Wear

Contents

Chapter 1
Assessing Potential

Introduction

Among the most important and vital ingredients of any successful organization are its employees. For any business to perform well, it must acquire and maximize the deployment of people with talent. Identifying the right talent to fill particular positions and roles is critical to an organization's effective functioning. All too often, though, businesses fail to devote sufficient attention to this issue. Instead, attention tends to be directed more towards the external deliverables of the business (or internal deliverables when considering a department that provides a service in an organization). Such concerns may involve the development of a new process or product or the introduction of a new system or structure. In so doing, senior executives and their managers analyse market trends, anticipate political, economic and technological changes and innovations that have implications for their business, and try to respond appropriately. Much of this activity is concerned with assessing opportunities and risks.

Although not always thought of in these terms, the practice of employee development, recruitment, selection and succession planning is also about the assessment of risks and opportunities. The recruitment of new employees entails a degree of risk, because new recruits may not always work out — they may fail to perform or may decide to leave after only a short period of employment with the organization. Meanwhile, that person has incurred certain costs (salary, office space, administrative support, business expenses, training) for the organization. And if they have to be replaced, the entire process (and cost) of recruitment and induction has to be gone through all over again. The higher the level at which recruitment takes place (and included in this consideration is 'internal recruitment' into a new position as a result of promotion), the greater the potential risks and costs. However, failure to reduce the risk of poor recruitment often stems from a failure to invest sufficiently in the process in the first place.

Although initial recruitment is important, successful organizations also need successful strategies and procedures for the identification and realization of potential among their current employees. This process is about the 'strategic intent of organizations to utilize and realize their employees' potential and in-company tacit knowledge' (Iles and Foster, 1994; Tillema, 1998). Recognition of the significance of this issue is reflected in current interest in development centres and assessment centres. Assessment centres have a long history and have been popular as performance evaluation methods that are regarded as supplying sensitive and accurate measures of actual competence. A developmental centre can assess employee performance, and has a number of other applications as well. It can provide a workplace-related and learning-oriented tool for performance assessment that simultaneously can be used to:

- Enable organizations to audit who of their current employees is fit for specified work performance;
- Determine training needs;
- Match assessment with appropriate career, development and learning plans.

Ideally, developmental centres assess and encourage potential by providing realistic, accurate and timely feedback on personal talents, skills and knowledge that could be better realized.

Assessing the potential of an individual to succeed, even flourish, in a demanding and crucial job, and in a series of more senior jobs thereafter, is essentially an actuarial-type decision. The assessment of managerial potential has three fundamental issues to consider:

- First, what are you looking for? What personal characteristics need to be assessed and why? This essentially means having some idea of the predictors of success. Just as actuaries have a clear idea of risk factors for insurance (what they are, their respective weights, how they interact and how common they are), so people assessors need first to have some idea of the characteristics that predict success in a particular job or series of jobs.
- Second, it is important to know how to gather the data. The range of possible methods used to gather such data include self-report (questionnaire, interview, biodata), observation data (references, assessment centre data, 360° feedback) and test data (ability tests, intelligence tests). Each has characteristic advantages and disadvantages and costs and benefits that need specific consideration.
- Third, how can you help a person fulfil their potential? After potential has been identified the question remains as to how to realize that potential, rather than waste or frustrate it.

Few people disagree about the usefulness of spotting those with high potential. It helps identify those who are ready for promotion, and focuses attention on optimal developmental job moves. Identifying employees with special talents can assist with high-level succession planning and targets training efforts for senior positions.

As organizations mature and grow, they tend to develop selection and recruitment strategies based on particular ideas. Some employee selection philosophies place the responsibility for talent screening on to others. At the initial stages of recruitment at the lower levels, there may be a tendency to prefer candidates from particular schools or universities in the belief that if they attended such institutions, then they must have ability. This naturally puts the onus on others to choose the selection criteria and apply them, but presumably if an organization has been pleased with 'products' from these institutions, they will continue to use this cost-effective method. Another widely held view is that even if people turn out not to be ideal after the selection process, they can be trained to become well fitted to the job. Although this may be true in certain instances with certain skills, employee development research paints a rather depressing picture of this strategy. There is much evidence to reinforce the view that it is better to invest more in selection and less in training rather than the other way around (Cook, 1998).

The criteria for identifying 'high potential' among external applicants, or those already in an organization, usually include the identification of job skills and future needs of the organization through processes such as job analysis and person specification. The fundamental questions posed by the process include:

- What will future executive jobs be like? What requirements do future staff need to have? What knowledge base will be an essential requirement? In short, can we specify what skills, abilities and knowledge sets will be needed to perform all the major tasks in any job?
- What sort of people will be required to fill these jobs? What will be their demography (sex, age), typical educational background, skill-set and personality traits? Will they be able to adapt to changing circumstances? Can they cope with stress and do they welcome change?
- What are the best methods to identify high potential? How can one best evaluate the usefulness of these different methods? What particular biases and limitations do different methods have? Is the collection of biographical data about applicants and current employees more cost-effective and accurate than having an assessment centre? Are interviews of any validity at all?

The assessment of potential means not only attempting optimally to match people for jobs, but also deciding how people and competency or skills requirements may change in the future. Some organizations use the concept of a 'fast stream' of young, recently hired individuals who have been labelled as those with potential to 'go far' — meaning that they have the potential to get rapid, but deserved, promotion. They are usually sought after for their intelligence and temperament, and most of all for their motivation and flexibility. Given that the future is unclear, but notably different from the present, the successful employee must, potentially, be able to anticipate, adapt to and thrive in a different working situation from the one they were originally chosen for.

Speculating on the nature of future job requirements is an important yet problematic issue in the selection of high-flyers and those with potential. This may be done by an examination of current management jobs and plotting historical trends. Another method may be to look at generic lists of identified managerial competencies or capabilities. In this case, a schema exists that embodies all that is believed to be central, in terms of capabilities, to a particular position in the organization. Organizations then seek out those individuals whose measured competencies (knowledge, experience, skills and so on) most closely match the specified requirements of the post for which they are being recruited, or the requirements that are anticipated for that position in the future.

The problem of using the past and the present to evaluate and predict the future is nicely summarized by Spreitzer et al. (1997):

> '...executive identification and selection systems based on end-state competencies alone are likely to be double edged. When they are carefully developed and connected to the business strategy, the resulting set of defined and internally accepted competencies can be invaluable. However, because the origins of competencies are based on past success rather than future challenges, their value for the early identification of executives may be limited. We risk choosing people who fit today's model of executive success rather than the unknown model of tomorrow. The competencies that get attention today may not be enough to ensure that a person will master requisite competencies for the future. Given that future demands may include some skills that are different from the skills values today, the ability to learn from experience may prove to be more important in the long run than a high rating in a currently valued competency. Thus, to the degree that executive leadership skills are learned from experience, any improvement in identifying people who can learn more from their experiences is likely to aid in the early identification of international executives'. (1997: 6)

Even with the observation that people are increasingly less likely to have jobs for life and may therefore experience multiple job changes, and even dramatic career changes, organizations are still committed to assessing the potential of those they recruit and those already working for them. It is more important than at any time hitherto that organizations are able quickly and effectively to identify individuals who will be good performers in the short to medium term and those who may have the potential to go to the top.

Central Questions

This book is about the assessment of potential in employees. A basic premise is that business potential is built on recruiting, promoting and developing the right people in the right way. As a management objective, however, this is a difficult target to achieve. It requires an integrated and holistic approach to analysis of the entire organization. Effective recruitment to an organization and effective development of employees in the organization depends on a detailed analysis and understanding of the required aptitudes and competencies for different jobs in the organization. Any such system of organizational analysis must also be flexible enough to acknowledge that job requirements may change over time as business environments change.

The assessment of individuals is based on a number of assumptions, such as how much people change over time naturally, how easy it is for them to change and how best to create an environment that ensures talented people with 'the right stuff' achieve their potential. An equally important and central question is what characteristics seem to predict success; and which methods are most sensitive, robust and reasonable in doing so. In this book, we shall examine the importance of the information obtained about people during their initial contacts with an organization to effective recruitment of employees and subsequent development plans for those individuals. This chapter takes a broad view of assessment of potential, by examining biographical data (or 'biodata') alongside other types of personal data on job applicants and employees (for example, measures of abilities or personality). It also considers whether it is possible to collect data on stable characteristics of individuals at one point in time that can be expected to continue to serve as sound predictors of future performance. As an opening question, then, to what extent can organizations expect their employees to change? Is there any way of coping with this process when attempting to devise instruments or techniques for the assessment of employee potential?

1. How Much do People Change over Time?

This is a central question to the personnel assessment process, because if people change a great deal in terms of their personality, preferences and predilections, and one cannot control factors that cause these changes (or indeed understand the process of change itself), then the practice of predictive employee assessment will be extremely difficult to achieve.

There is little doubt that people can and do change over time, mainly as a result of life experiences. Among the major factors that drive changes in individuals are *traumatic experience* (death of loved ones, personal death scare, failure of marriage), undergoing *therapy* (aimed at radical cognitive behavioural change) or *personal motivation* (a determination to improve oneself or to change one's circumstances).

Intriguingly, evidence from one profession designed to assist or instigate personal change, namely therapy, has shown that achieving radical changes to a person's character is extremely difficult and relatively rare. It is by no means easy for adults to change their habits and outlooks once these have become established. One explanation of this phenomenon is that many behaviour patterns are closely linked to personality traits or skill and ability sets that are themselves genetically based. Indeed, the more we discover about behaviour genetics, the more obvious it is that a great deal of variance can be explained by genetic factors that are themselves not much open to change.

The issue of character stability is central to trait psychology, particularly the stability of individual differences over time. Analysts have concluded that mean trait levels alter little after the age of 30 (Matthews and Deary, 1998). We know that there are small reductions in neuroticism and increases in conscientiousness, and that after the age of 50 activity level decreases, but many of the research data support the view that behaviour patterns are stable over time. This is good news for the assessment of employee potential.

A body of research evidence has accumulated from a group of studies that tested people's psychological characteristics over reasonably long periods of time, such as 24 years (Costa and McCrae, 1994) and 45 years (Conley, 1984). Perhaps the most impressive data come from Conley (1984) who followed up 300 middle-class couples tested in 1935–8, again in 1954–5 and then in 1980–1. Four personality traits were measured by using different methods over three different occasions. The results were dramatic: first, the four traits (neuroticism, extroversion, impulse control and agreeableness) were distinct and surprisingly stable over long periods like 20 years, even when measured by different people. Thus, a person's self-estimates of, say, extroversion in 1935 correlated highly significantly with his/her partner's estimates of the same trait in 1954.

In a meta-review of several studies Costa and McCrae (1994) found an average stability coefficient over time (typically 3–8 years) to be about 0.64 (where 0=unstable, 1=totally stable). Conley (1984) looked at the data for three traits over 40 years and estimated that the reliability index was 0.45. Matthews and Deary (1998: 54) conclude: 'Large-scale reviews and large single studies, therefore, offer overwhelming evidence for the stability of personality traits over many years. Extraversion appears to be particularly stable, with good evidence for the high stability of neuroticism, openness and conscientiousness. Agreeableness would appear to be less stable'.

In a subsequent study, Soldz and Vaillant (1999) followed up 163 men for 45 years. They showed that their traits were stable over time and also that they were clearly related to 'life course variables' such as career success, social relations, mental health, substance misuse and political attitudes. The most powerful predictor was conscientiousness. Maximum income was best predicted by extroversion; and smoking was predicted by neuroticism and low conscientiousness. Overall, conscientiousness at university was the best predictor of what happened to men in their futures, whereas neuroticism in late midlife was the best indicator of life course (dys)function across a variety of domains.

What these findings suggest is that for an adult of 25 years or older, 'what you see is what you get'. That is, basic personality structure and functioning does not alter appreciably. Although their jobs may change dramatically over time, individuals do not.

2. What is the Cost-effectiveness of Change?

If personality traits and abilities are fairly stable over time, how easy is it to change them or a style of working directly related to them? Is it possible through training, developmental centres and experience to acquire skills, change preferences and work in radically different ways?

The process of change and learning to adapt, at any age, is often stressful. Learning new skills, or how to treat staff and customers differently, or how to face the ruthlessness of market forces, naturally induces anxiety. It also causes problems for those who have to, or choose to, bring about change. 'Adapt or die: change or decay' is not just a rallying cry for the senior manager. It is a reality. The question is how to bring about successful change to maximize effectiveness and minimize pain (Shapiro, 1995).

There are many trainers dedicated to personal change. Often, therapy is dedicated to changing beliefs and behaviour patterns to make people happier and more functional. This process refers to counselling and psychotherapy. Training is dedicated to instilling skills and knowledge, so that people can be more effective at work. This is training and education. It is quite legitimate to distinguish between various types of strategies for change. One broad distinction can be made between counselling and psychotherapy (see Table 1.1).

Table 1.1: Differences between counselling and psychotherapy

Counselling	Psychotherapy
Caring, enabling, facilitating, supporting	Con-/de-/re-constructing, interpreting, intervening, treating
Explore, discover, clarify issues	
Find solutions to problems/deal with crises	Develop new ways of solving problems
Alleviate suffering	Improve functioning
Focus on here and now	Focus on past and present
Evolutionary change	Revolutionary change
Short term/clients seen frequently	Long term/clients seen frequently
Therapy low on theory	Therapy high on theory
No need for personal therapy	Usually need for personal therapy
Everyday, average, 'mundane' problems	Abnormal, serious, chronic/acute problems
Person-centred	Problem-centred

All sorts of reasons have been given for the weak or non-existent evidence for the effects of psychotherapy. Exactly the same is true of attempts to instil change through training programmes at work. The myth of patient and therapist uniformity – the idea that patients (and therapists) are more alike than they are different at the start of therapy – has quite rightly been pointed out (Vincent and Furnham, 1997). In other words, there is too much variation (random and systematic) in the psychotherapeutic process to effectively measure change.

More than 45 years ago, Eysenck's (1952) findings electrified and infuriated the placid, self-contained world of psychotherapy by concluding from an analysis of 25 studies and 7,293 patients that: 'The figures fail to support the hypothesis that psychotherapy facilitates recovery from neurotic disorders' (1952: 324). The findings seemed to suggest that two-thirds of neurotics recover or show considerable improvement without the benefit of systematic psychotherapy. Eysenck certainly accepted the need for better quality research, but pointed out that the strong feelings regarding the usefulness and effectiveness of therapy need to be substantiated with facts. The same applies to management training that attempts both to change attitudes and instil skills. What Eysenck did, however, was to seriously encourage attempts to investigate this issue.

After examining 475 studies of psychotherapy's effectiveness, Smith, Glass and Miller (*The Benefits of Psychotherapy*, 1980) concluded:

> Psychotherapy is beneficial, consistently so, and in many different ways. Its benefits are on a par with other expensive and ambitious interactions such as schooling and medicine. (1980: 183)

> Psychotherapy benefits people of all ages as reliably as schooling educates them, medicine cures them, or business turns a profit. (1980: 183)

> Psychotherapists have a legitimate, though not exclusive claim, substantiated by controlled research, on those roles in society ... whose responsibility it is to restore to health the sick, the suffering, the alienated and the disaffected. (1980: 185)

They concluded, as others have done before, that all therapy works for similar reasons, which are:

(a) *The therapeutic alliance*: Through therapy, patients and clients get acceptance, attention, care, respect and support. It is this sense of being understood and assisted that is essential to cure.
(b) *Self-examination*: The whole therapeutic process encourages greater self-monitoring and self-analyses, which often in, and of, themselves suggest solutions.
(c) *Morale*: Clients often report being happier and more optimistic because they believe that their coping mechanisms and strategies have improved and that the overcoming of their personal difficulties is possible.
(d) *Commitment to change*: Agreeing to and indeed attending therapy voluntarily and paying for that therapy is a reaffirmation of commitment to change, which is the best predictor of change.

In other words, because many types of therapy offer and require the above four crucial processes, they seem to lead to similar outcomes. Exactly the same could be said of business training, particularly of the one-on-one type that is now fashionable.

A recent innovation in the USA has been the use of consumer reports to examine the outcome of therapy. In 1995, a US publication called *Consumer Reports* published a short article entitled 'Mental health: Does therapy help?' In all, 22,000 people responded and answered 26 questions, including how long therapy lasted and their level of satisfaction. Among other things, it concluded:

- Patients benefit substantially from psychotherapy;
- Long-term treatment did considerably better than short-term treatment;
- Psychotherapy alone did not differ in effectiveness from medication *plus* psychotherapy;
- No specific modality/type of psychotherapy did/does any better than any other for any disorder;
- Psychologists, psychiatrists and social workers did not differ in their effectiveness as treaters, but all did better than marriage counsellors and long-term family doctors;
- Patients whose length of therapy or choice of therapist was limited by insurance or managed care did worse.

The conclusion to all this is that personal change is possible, but at some cost and investment of both the agent of change (therapist, trainer) and the client of change. People can change – although the prognosis for some forms of psychological problems remains very poor. As any dieter or ex-smoker will tell you, it takes willpower, support and perseverance to change personal habits. Personal preferences and pathology are closely linked to work style, productivity and outcome. Neurotics manifest lower morale, greater absenteeism and often lower productivity. It is possible, but difficult and costly, to 'cure' or dramatically alleviate neurosis. Training is often little different from therapy in its aims to change attitudes and behaviour. Yet the research on therapy and its effectiveness is far superior to that on training.

The established fact that fundamentally, or even modestly, changing individuals' beliefs, preferences and behaviour is difficult emphasized the important point of choosing the best person in the first place.

3. Is Talent What Is, or What Could Be?

The issue of identifying precursors or predictors of employee success are one stage of the bigger issue of maximizing business potential. Once recognized, potential has to be realized. The fact that an individual is judged to have certain potential when first recruited into an organization does not mean that that person will blossom into a high flyer or even prove to be moderately effective at lower levels in the organizational hierarchy. It may be important to create conditions under which an employee's likelihood of realizing their potential is increased.

The fundamental question that is being considered in this context is a variant on whether managers are born or made. McCall (1998: 118) believed that 'even if talent's origins are biological, bringing it to fruition requires years of hard work and conscious developments'. He lamented the fact that so many organizations strive so hard to develop a list of exclusive, and essential, competencies (a pot-pourri of traits, motives, values, behaviours and attitudes) that drive all their human resource systems, including selection. This approach has several shortcomings in that it can erroneously assume that:

- the job will not change significantly in the short term;
- the job has an identity separate from the incumbent and will not be shaped by him or her;
- the requirements for effective performance in the job are exclusively described by the list of competencies;
- the incumbent's actions, rather than the organization-wide forces, control the outcome;
- the list of competencies can be found in one individual;
- the competencies interact with each other to change the outcome.

In short, talent (ability and motivation) alone is not enough to ensure competent, if not excellent, management. What is also required is appropriate learning experiences.

McCall (1998: xii) argues that 'leadership ability can be learned, that creating a context that supports the development of talent can become a source of competitive advantage, and that the development of leaders is itself a leadership responsibility'. He rejects the assumption that a shortlist of generic qualities can be drawn up to describe all effective leaders; that those qualities are stable over the course of a person's career; and that through survival of the fittest the best survive, requiring only a minor polish and refinement. He stresses that continual growth, transition and transformation are as much associated with success as 'natural ability'. According to McCall (1998), dealing with adversity may be a better predictor of success than the seamless career of a wunderkind. In short, he believes that 'leaders are both born and made, but mostly made', (1998: 51); and that organizations need to strengthen and polish what already exists, but also bring potential into being. He distinguished between two models:

The Darwinian Model, which attempts to differentiate less/more successful executive traits, search for the latter, then give people tests/experience to polish these skills. On-the-job challenges reveal actual talent.

The Agricultural Model, which attempts to identify strategic challenges likely to occur and to search for people who can learn from the experiences, and then help them to succeed.

In a sense, he argues from *survival* of the fittest to the *development* of the fittest: from being a corporate Darwinist to a managerial developer. A number of experimental criteria are thought to be good for development. These include job transitions (taking on unfamiliar responsibilities), implementing change strategies, taking on higher levels of responsibility and being influential in non-authority relationships. Developmental opportunities can arise from being given *new assignments* (project, task force), dealing with *hardships/setbacks* (business failure), *other people* (who are role models) and *other events*. Clearly, people who take on continuous modest challenges with occasional change of function learn most. International assignments and training can all justify this process. Some organizations choose to have company schools and universities. Whether deliberate or serendipitous, organizations provide powerful experiences that give an opportunity to learn.

Ultimately, the Darwinian and developmental approaches are not opposites. McCall's (1998) preference is to focus on the range of developmental experiences that talented people should have to develop their abilities, rather than finding those people who currently show these desired qualities. It has been argued that leadership is a journey of personal development and that derailment is the result primarily of talented people not learning from experience; or of course not having the experience.

The question remains about how organizations provide the learning experience their potential leaders need. Most companies insist that managers are accountable for results and not development and hence ignore the development aspects of job assignments. Job rotation focuses on exposure rather than task. Managers need incentives, resources and support to change. What one needs, according to McCall (1998) is a model for developing talent. This is an explicit, systematic and comprehensive attempt to take the developmental model seriously.

McCall's (1998) research suggests that it is the capacity to learn that is most important. Successful managers have to *draw attention to their talent* which results in better opportunities to develop it. They need to have a *sense of adventure* to take on challenges and to *create a context* for their own learning. They also need to be able to learn from experience, respond to feedback and bounce back after setbacks (see next section). In this sense, you can pick people with potential by looking at certain characteristics that predict that their potential will be realized.

4. Conclusion

The answer to the three central questions posed above seems to be: generally, adults do not change much over time. Their preferences, abilities, personalities, and even their attitudes and values remain fairly stable. But people try to, and indeed do, change with the help of professionals or through particular circumstances (therapists, trainers). However, as noted by most psychological and organizational agents of change, radical change is unlikely and the costs in terms of time, effort and money are high. Finally, people can be developed to maximize their potential if it is spotted and the situation is carefully arranged to exploit and realize that potential.

The three central questions lead to the inevitable conclusion that the assessment and development of potential are of fundamental importance to every organization. Recruiting, selecting and retaining adaptable, stable, conscientious staff who learn from experience is perhaps the most important thing companies must do if they are to survive all the changes of the new millennium.

Three Research Methods

Those interested in the assessment of potential go about research in rather different ways, even though they have a common aim – namely, to understand the best predictors of work success. The three most common methods are the *high-flyer approach*, which attempts to identify business high-flyers (successful entrepreneurs) and discover commonalities between those individuals that may have accounted for their success. A second approach is the *psychometric approach*, which examines large databases to find statistically significant and replicated relationships between traits and abilities and work outcome measures. The third approach is the *biodata approach*, which is a mixture of the previous two approaches in that it is retrospective in analysis like the high-flyer approach, and relentlessly empirical like the psychometric approach. The first two approaches may be considered to be particularly important as they relate to identifying the enduring characteristics of business success. The main focus of this book is an examination of the biodata method.

1. The High-flyer and Business Elite Approach

One obvious way to look at determinants and correlates of business success, as well as success in specific jobs, is a biographical approach based on the lives of recognized success stories. This is not the same as the biodata method, as we shall see. The method that adopts a historical approach is fairly well established. The principal task is to identify a number of individuals who fall into a predefined group of business successes. These cases are then assessed from a variety of perspectives to try to identify common themes that may explain the origin of their success.

One area that has attracted considerable research within this tradition is the characteristics of an 'entrepreneur'. Attempts to define the salient features of entrepreneurs differ widely. Some see entrepreneurs as people assuming risks associated with uncertainty, and allocating resources among alternative uses.

Others see entrepreneurs as individuals who supply financial capital, and still others see them as contradictions, arbitrageurs or innovators (Herbert and Link, 1988).

Chell (1986) has argued that there are three psychological models of the entrepreneurial personality. First, the *psychodynamic*, neo-Freudian approach sees the entrepreneur as someone whose family background has been particularly formative in shaping a deviant personality – one who is unable to operate effectively in an imposed and structural environment. The entrepreneur is hostile, aggressive and impulsive and the entrepreneurial behaviour is a sublimation activity that enables entrepreneurs subconsciously to resolve their inner conflicts and tensions by creating an environment with which they can cope. However, there is limited empirical support for this position and the evidence that does exist seems to describe unusual extreme cases. Second, the *social development* model stresses that changing social contexts and groups are as much a source of entrepreneurial activity as anything else. It suggests that situational, opportunistic features are important in the origin of entrepreneurship. Once again, the extant literature in support of this position is limited. Third, the *trait* approach has identified various stable traits (anxiety, need for achievement, persistence, instrumentalism). Chell (1986) argues that traits seem to account for too little of the variance, and that the model ignores other relevant factors and overemphasizes consistency among cases. She advocates an interactive model where personal factors (abilities, skills, constraints, expectations, values, plans) allow certain people to act in particular entrepreneurial ways, which show their desires, enhance their reputation and create successful output. Alas, the model does not expand on the person factors by explaining what they are or where they come from. Without such understanding it becomes difficult to predict which individuals are likely to become successful.

Casson (1982) offered an economic insight into the successful entrepreneur and came to 10 conclusions about 'Jack Brash' the successful entrepreneur. To summarize his conclusions:

1. Information about profit opportunities needs to be synthesized from different sources. Entrepreneurs come up with novel ideas through insight or personal experience (being a migrant).
2. The family is a potentially valuable source of information. Families provide help, skill and labour at crucial points in the process.
3. Feedback or learning from past activities is crucial to the long-term success of an enterprise. Analysis of experience means adversity can be turned to advantage.
4. Personal wealth is a major contribution to entrepreneurial activity because it must be strongly influenced by attempts to maximize the impact of this constraint – namely, rapid successful growth. The lessons learnt through early attempts to survive and grow in a capital-constrained environment are essential.

5. Clubs and societies are the most important non-profit institutions to establish contacts and disseminate information. The socially disadvantaged entrepreneur therefore has more challenge.
6. Educational qualifications permit entry to established institutions, and capital may be used as a screening device to recruit managers. Many entrepreneurs have to succeed despite poor qualifications.
7. Negotiation tactics are one of the most important elements of entrepreneurial activity.
8. Organizational skills are important for the entrepreneur, particularly people management and delegation during periods of growth. With little or unhappy work experience as an employee, many entrepreneurs make poor managers and can be unwilling to delegate and uncertain about motivation.
9. Product innovation through product versatility (using multi-component designs and mass marketing) is crucial.
10. Market making depends less on advertising and salesmanship as on invention management and quality control.

In this analysis, Casson (1982) pointed to the paradoxes in the high-flying entrepreneur. These include the idea that personal wealth may be a disadvantage; that entrepreneurs buy academic distinction by endowing institutions as revenge, so placing academics in demeaning roles because they have to accept patronage from whom they previously rejected.

Some of these studies have concentrated on the stresses and problems of success (Jennings, 1989), but most have focused on the correlates of those people known to succeed. They focus on personality traits and attitudes rather than situational factors. Thus, Cox and Cooper (1988) identified 'key person characteristics' that are related to success. These were:

1. Determination: a characteristic often derived from childhood experiences where people had to take personal responsibility for themselves.
2. Learning from adversity: using adversity and setbacks to learn better coping strategies and new skills.
3. Seizing chances: not the same as opportunism but enthusiastically taking on difficult decisions early in life.
4. Being achievement orientated: being ambitious and positive and going after long-term big prizes.
5. Internal locus of control: being a self-confident instrumentalist, not a fatalist.
6. Having a well-integrated value system: having a clear, integrated and lived-by value system (valuing integrity, independence, initiative and so on).
7. Effective risk management: moderate but calculated risk-takers.
8. Having clear objectives: having both long-term and short-term objectives and striving constantly for them.
9. Dedication to the job: feeling the job was the most important aspect of life yet not being a workaholic.

10. Intrinsic motivation: finding energy and enthusiasm in the job, not simply being motivated by extrinsic reward.
11. Well-organized lifestyle: preventing conflicts between work and home life.
12. A pragmatic rather than intellectual approach: having practical interests and pursuits rather than intellectual ones.
13. Analytic and problem-solving skills: perhaps seeming intuitive rather than rational.
14. Exemplary people skills: being socially skilled, open and consultative and also being authoritiative.
15. Being innovative: not being constrained by procedures, current systems and assumptions.
16. Having a competitive, hard-driving lifestyle and sometimes called the type A personality.

Although the above list is impressively long and fairly commonsensical, it has the traditional drawbacks of such an approach. The data are based on self-report (interviews and questionnaires) and it may be that beliefs and behaviour patterns are ignored or 'repackaged' to make them seem more attractive. Certainly, many high-flyers have a reputation for being egotistical, ruthless and amoral, although this is not how they present themselves to the world.

Next, the list is long, but it is not rank ordered. Are some characteristics more important than others? And if so, which? Third, what relationship exists between the different characteristics? Can they be reduced to a more parsimonious and clearer list?

In a later, similar work, Jennings, Cox and Cooper (1994) investigated numerous famous 'élite entrapreneurs' (people who built and control companies) and 'élite intrapreneurs' (people who have worked themselves up to the CEO position in a single organization). As before, they examined a variety of attributes of these individuals, including early childhood experiences, socio-demographic origins, education, specific support from others, their approach to work and their work ethic, their personality traits and their philanthropic interests. They focused on three spheres of life – work (education and work history), personality with developmental history, and non-work/family environment. Their results were surprisingly similar to those of the earlier study.

Borrowing heavily on other explanatory systems, Cox and Cooper (1988) also presented a *developmental model for managerial success*. First, they noted the importance of parental attitudes and values, and also of early trauma associated with separation of one kind or another. Next, they found that schooling at primary, secondary or tertiary level was not particularly influential or important. Indeed, choice of institution may well reflect parental values, which represent the really important function here. Early experience at work is regarded as most important, particularly having a helpful early mentor or role model and succeeding when early 'make-or-break' opportunities presented themselves. Their conceptual model is shown in Figure 1.1.

Figure 1.1: Factors contributing to high-flyer performance

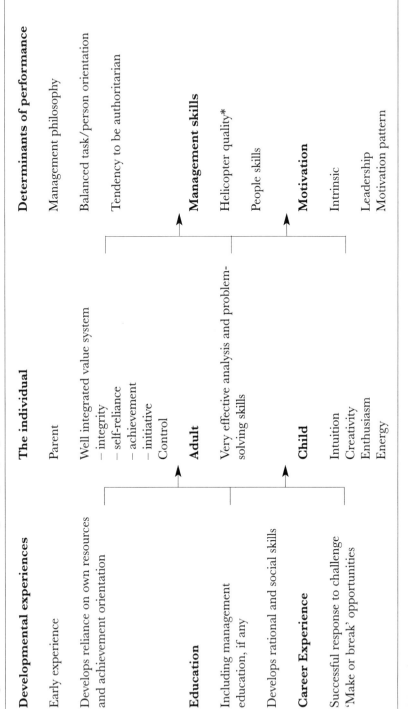

Developmental experiences	The individual	Determinants of performance
	Parent	**Determinants of performance**
Early experience	Well integrated value system	Management philosophy
Develops reliance on own resources and achievement orientation	– integrity – self-reliance – achievement – initiative	Balanced task/person orientation
	Control	Tendency to be authoritarian
	Adult	**Management skills**
Education	Very effective analysis and problem-solving skills	Helicopter quality*
Including management education, if any		People skills
Develops rational and social skills		
	Child	**Motivation**
Career Experience	Intuition	Intrinsic
Successful response to challenge 'Make or break' opportunities	Creativity Enthusiasm Energy	Leadership Motivation pattern

Note *Seeing the 'big picture' from above.
Source: Cox and Cooper (1988)

There are three major problems with the high-flyer biographical method. The first is specifying what constitutes a high-flyer. No single criterion – amount of money made, a 'business' award (knighthood), or the size and success of the organization that one creates – suffices. Almost inevitably, luck and chance play a part – hence, particular characteristics of high-flyers may be little more than spotting opportunities and exploiting entrepreneurial chances faster and more successfully than others. The business of defining a high-flyer or a member of a successful business élite is by no means simple. Ideally, researchers would specify objectively and explicitly a range of criteria that would explain the principle by which certain people are included and others excluded from the sample.

The second problem is actually getting the nominated high-flyers to take part in the study by agreeing to an interview or completing a survey. High-flyers soon get 'over-researched', receiving little personal benefit from being research participants. Indeed, many are advised by cautious public relations people not to answer in-depth 'psychological' questions of dubious validity. Hence, many of those carefully selected for investigation refuse to take part, forcing researchers to weaken their criteria, which in turn undermines the quality of the study as a whole.

Third, these studies almost never have a control group of individuals matched on a number of criteria, who simply did not 'make it'. Thus, you can never really say whether the special characteristics of high-flyers identified by researchers are unique to the individuals or indeed played any part in their success.

There are two quite specific and unique high-flyer approaches that are both conceptually rich but that also suggest possible hypotheses for those eager to select potential. Each will be briefly discussed.

(i) GAM Theory, Creative Genius and Success

GAM theory attempts to provide an explanation for the frequently observed, and indeed carefully documented, observation that many eminent (particularly creative) people had had personal experience of early parental death. Therivel (1998) has argued that the combination of three things – G=Genetic Endowment, A=Assistances of Youth (help from parental substitutes (teachers, relatives)), M=Misfortunes of Youth (parental death/absence, physical infirmity, uprootedness, parental professional failure) – gives rise to the *challenged* personality.

According to this model, Therivel (1998) constructed a simple two-by-two matrix with 'misfortunes' on the y axis and 'assistances' on the x axis. Thus, those high on misfortune and low on assistance are described as *crushed*, and those high on assistance and low on misfortune are called *dedicated*. His interest was in the *challenged*, who were high on both axes. His argument insisted that misfortunes of youth 'reduce the acquisition of regular scripts' or habitual ways of thinking and behaving. Parental death removes role models; failure changes family life and how one interacts with other families. The challenged young therefore have to develop their own scripts. Furthermore, they become alert, even hypersensitive, to the clash of scripts between themselves and others, particularly while growing up. They thus become divergent thinkers capable of fusing ideas and seeing linkages, but without feeling that they are infringing norms or taboos.

GAM theory is not strictly a theory of personality. It is a psycho-historical attempt to discover similarities in the lives of those considered eminent or geniuses. Although there have been few attempts to 'test' the theory, there seems to be impressive evidence that childhood experiences, along with pure ability, are crucially important in determining success in life.

The assistance of youth plus genetic endowment ensures self-confident, driven, visionary adults. These resilient children can grow into eminently successful adults. Therivel (1998), in his careful autobiographical work, identified 14 types of families of challenged youth (Table 1.2).

(ii) Learning from Experience

In a series of studies, McCall and colleagues have attempted to identify executive potential, or executive competences (also known as end-state skills) (McCall, Lombardo and Morrison, 1990; McCall, 1994; 1998; McCall, Spreitzer and Mahoney, 1994; Spreitzer, McCall and Mahoney, 1997). To a large extent this team argued that the *ability to learn from experience* is the fundamental key to managerial potential.

They argued that a review of the diverse literature on the early identification of executive success through the assessment centre work shows five themes or areas of importance:

1. General intelligence: IQ or cognitive ability is clearly linked to business-related issues such as analytic agility, reasoning, incisiveness, and synthetic and visionary thinking.
2. Business knowledge: this is an understanding of the company and the sector's products, markets and policies, as well as a breadth of awareness and interest in trends of the market as a whole.
3. Interpersonal skills: social skills are important in handling relationships, team building, and in the capacity to motivate and inspire as well as align people behind particular strategies.
4. Commitment: this can be expressed in various ways, such as a passion for success, personal drive and perseverance. These characteristics all refer to extreme interest in and commitment to work.
5. Courage: to a large extent this means non-risk-averse and willing to take actions to ensure that things happen. It is related to self-confidence but not arrogance.

Table 1.2: The GAM Dedicated and 14 Challenged Personality Families: Causes and Results

	The dedicated	
	Causes	*Results*
	Good parental assistance, no major misfortune	Enlightened conservatives; sociable, realistic, mature; many have old and new friends; strong family and community ties; in academe, science and the arts, they work within the system
The challenged (14 families)		
Universalists	Early parental death or much parental absence coupled with love and good assistance from the remaining parent or relatives; good assistance from school and a stable socioeconomic status	Fond of moral concepts that are logical and prescriptive; have penchant for vast, nonrelativistic, theoretical thinking, fond of higher/intellectual pursuits such as religion, philosophy, mathematics, science and law
Architects	Causes same as universalists, but are raised; involved from an early age in an aristocratic, upper-class, military, professional or business environment	Show vision and great enterprise; give priority to the institution they are part of or have created (many of the greatest statesmen, founders of great enterprises and of great families were architects)
Seekers	Physical infirmity, coupled with much parental love and assistances	Seek escape from this world by putting emphasis on intellectual or spiritual matters; search for answers, especially from religion or philosophy, or from mathematics, science or engineering (many mystics are seekers)
Alchemists	Parental professional/character failure, coupled with quality assistances	Self-confident, courageous, protean; perpetually shaping and creating; often moving to new grounds in their love for variety or pantheistic synthesis

(contd)

The challenged
(14 families)

	Causes	Results
Leadsmen	Rootlessness or uprootedness (for example, forced conversion or assimilation of parents to religion or ethnic ways of majority; major changes of abode; major religious or cultural differences between parents); good assistances	Detached; critical thinkers; relativism; often hold cosmopolitan and pragmatic attitudes
Reformers	Mild paternal domination (for example, a successful father wants too much to guide and help, makes heavy use of the power of the purse to achieve his aims)	Loathe any kind of personal or social tyranny; want to stop abuses, malpractices, and corruption; often despise money for its corruptive power; want to make the world better by removing defects and demolishing oppressive superstructures
Fishers	Parental aloofness	Loners who often compensate by escaping into their own world of imaginary excitement; avoid emotional involvement; patient; sharp observers of people and of the ambiguities of loyalties; often hold a negative view of the world
Brewers	Incompatibilities between father and mother; arguments, fights, lies, infidelities	Disillusioned with the possibility of a meaningful dialogue; critical of society; often cynical and disconcertingly remote; sharp observers of the contrast between appearances and reality
Miners	Lack of love (for example, lack of love from remaining parent after one died, is divorced or was pushed aside)	Sceptics with a tendency towards pessimism and satire; sharp eye for hypocrisy (many great poets are miners)
Swatters	Strong maternal domination	Mostly indolent, forgetful, procrastinating; moody, with strong fluctuations of temper; sometimes bitingly satirical; mixture of passive and aggressive; resist demands of others

The challenged
(14 families)

	Causes	Results
Tankers	Strong paternal domination	Complex, tortured, introverted, outwardly cool, self-controlled; concerned to appear in the best light, while inwardly harbouring feelings of insecurity and repressed rebellion; often detached, reticent, seemingly unemotional; small remnant of the *reformer's* zeal
Radiologists	Painful or humiliating physical infirmities	Keen eye for anything that is sick in people and society, may have some religious or mystical interests (like *seekers*), but permeated with pessimism
Critical jesters	Early parental death or parental separation with subsequent downfall of family fortunes and status, in which society is seen as the main culprit of their suffering and humiliations	Understand and identify with the oppressed, the partisan, and the clown; humour is preferred weapon of attack and defence; vitriolic social criticism
Trappers	Conditions that say child is not as 'legitimate' as other siblings or peers and that child is stained inferior	Feel bitterly uprooted; without illusions; little respect for parenthood, marriage, family and society; ambitious realists

Source: Therivel (1998: p 206)

A theme identified strongly by this team is the ability to learn from experience. Those with the potential take a proactive approach to learning, learn from their mistakes, adapt well to difficult circumstances and seek and use feedback in order to make sense of their work environment. McCall identified 11 dimensions that he believed are related to being a high-flyer (Table 1.3).

The high-flyer approach has a number of fundamental problems, of which the greatest is the identification of these people in the first place. There are both conceptual and methodological problems in this fascinating but restricted area of research. The criteria for being considered a high-flyer are rarely explicit or consensually agreed on. Worse still, it is not unusual for an identified high-flyer

Table 1.3: Eleven dimensions of early identification of global executives

1. Seeks opportunities to learn
Has shown a pattern of learning over time. Seeks out experiences that may change perspective or provide an opportunity to learn new things. Takes advantage of opportunities to do new things when such opportunities come along. Has developed new skills and has changed over time.

2. Acts with integrity
Tells the truth and is described by others as honest. Is not self-promoting and consistently takes responsibility for his or her actions.

3. Adapts to cultural differences
Enjoys the challenge of working in and experiencing cultures different from his or her own. Is sensitive to cultural differences, works hard to understand them and changes behaviour in response to them.

4. Is committed to making a difference
Shows a strong commitment to the success of the organization and is willing to make personal sacrifices to contribute to that success. Seeks to have a positive impact on the business. Shows passion and commitment through a strong drive for results.

5. Seeks broad business knowledge
Has an understanding of the business that goes beyond his or her own limited area. Seeks to understand both the products or services and the financial aspects of the business. Seeks to understand how the various parts of the business fit together.

6. Brings out the best in people
Has a special talent with people that is evident in his or her ability to pull people together into highly effective teams. Is able to work with a wide variety of people, drawing the best out of them and achieving consensus in the face of disagreement.

7. Is insightful: sees things from new angles
Other people admire this person's intelligence, particularly his or her ability to ask insightful questions, identify the most important part of a problem or issue, and see things from a different perspective.

8. Has the courage to take risks
Will take a stand when others disagree, go against the status quo, persevere in the face of opposition. Has the courage to act when others hesitate and will take both personal and business risks.

9. Seeks and uses feedback
Pursues, responds to and uses feedback. Actively asks for information on his or her impact and has changed as a result of such feedback.

10. Learns from mistakes
Is able to learn from mistakes. Changes direction when the current path isn't working, responds to data without getting defensive and starts over after setbacks.

11. Is open to criticism
Handles criticism effectively: does not act threatened or get overly defensive when others (especially superiors) are critical.

Source: McCall, Spreitzer and Mahoney (1994).

to 'fall to earth' not long after a study is complete. Given that the whole approach attempts to find out what is unique to the psyche of the high-flyer, the issue of establishing the key judgmental criterion is a most fundamental one

2. The Psychometric Approach

Although the psychometric approach is more than 100 years old, it was not until comparatively recently that it had been used extensively for recruitment selection and attempts to assess potential. Furnham and Heaven (1999) have noted:

> It is self evident to any manager, if not to all psychologists, that the personality of employees, along with their ability, has a powerful influence on their work output and satisfaction. Indeed, many people assume that they can be 'understood' from their (chosen) occupations – 'you are what you do'. Absenteeism, productivity and morale, lying and cheating are all seen to be a function of characteristics of individuals, not especially of organisational factors (such as supervisor style or corporate culture). More recently, it has been suggested that career change, innovation and creativity in the workplace and work-team performance are also logically related to personality traits, as well as to such factors as training outcomes. The studies are of a highly variable quality, but where the traits are theoretically expected to relate to a particular work behaviour, and where that behaviour is reliably measured by aggregated data, it does seem clear that personality traits are one important factor in determining work outcome. (1999: 205),

Psychometricians attempt to show that personality (and ability) variables predict work outcomes. Hough (1998) has listed eight 'outcome measures' or measures of potential:

1. *Overall job performance:* overall job performance ratings, promotion vs demotion, overall suitability, fired vs not fired.
2. *Technical proficiency:* measures of technical competency, knowledge of one's line of work.
3. *Irresponsible behaviour:* poor attendance, counter-productive behaviour, number of disciplinary actions, not following directions, being absent without authorization, use of drugs (including alcohol) on the job.
4. *Sales effectiveness:* amount sold, sales goals attained, supervisory ratings of sales effectiveness.
5. *Creativity:* number of patents, peer and/or supervisory ratings of sales effectiveness.
6. *Teamwork:* ratings of co-operativeness with other co-workers/team members, ability to work with others in joint efforts, quality of interpersonal relationships, constructive interpersonal behaviour.
7. *Effort:* measures of hard work, initiative, work energy, extra effort, working long hours under adverse conditions.
8. *Combat effectiveness:* survival in combat, reaction to life-threatening situations.

Consider three examples of studies in this area. Rothstein, Paunonen, Rush and King (1994) set out to examine personality and cognitive ability predictors of performance in master's degree students. They had two outcome measures – grade point average and a rating of class participation. They had various predictor measures including two GMAT scores (verbal and qualitative) as well as a personality questionnaire that measured 20 traits. They found, fairly predictably, that ability test scores were good predictors of written work performance, but poor in class performance measures, whereas the opposite was true for personality variables. Judge, Cable, Boudreau and Bretz (1995) obtained objective (pay, ascendancy) and subjective (job/career satisfaction) data on 1388 US executives. Education was a good predictor of financial success, and motivational and organizational variables predicted job satisfaction.

Spreitzer, McCall and Mahoney (1997) tried to predict the current performance, executive potential and on-the-job learning in 838 managers from six US firms. They found four factors of significance: first, the manager has to be noticed by people in the organization and thought to be a good investment. Qualities that predicted this were: being committed to success, being insightful, having the courage to take a stand, having broad business knowledge, and taking risks. Next, the manager with potential needs a sense of adventure, characterized by three dimensions: seeks opportunities to learn, is cross-culturally adventurous and seeks feedback. Following this, the young manager with potential needs to be responsive in learning contexts, which is predicted by: acts with integrity, brings out the best in people, is sensitive to cultural differences and is open to criticism. Finally, the manager needs to change as a result of experience and this is predicted by being flexible and using feedback.

More recently, Seibert, Grant and Kraimer (1999) looked at the relationship between personality and career success. They developed a 17-item personality scale that attempts to identify people who are highly proactive, who identify opportunities and act on them, and who show initiative and persevere until they bring about meaningful change. People who score low on this scale tend to be passive and reactive, and adapt to circumstances rather than change them. They found a correlation of this personality trait with self-report objective indications of career success (salary, number of promotions) and subjective indications such as career satisfaction. Even when they controlled for all sorts of other variables including personal (demographic) and sector (industry) measures they found that this personality trait predicted success. A one-point (out of 17) increase on the personality scale was associated with an $8677 (£5785) increase in yearly salary, after controlling for all other variables. They speculated on various behaviours that may mediate the relationship between proactive personality and career success, including the effective use of influence tactics, building social networks, active career planning and initiating new projects. They concluded:

These findings contribute to the understanding of both career success and the proactive personality construct. Our results extend models of career success by adding a dispositional variable to the array of variables associated with career success. This is important because the interactional perspective suggests that dispositional variables should influence career processes and outcomes, yet previous work within the organizational behavioural literature has largely ignored dispositional influences on career success. Our findings suggest that dispositional variables have the potential to explain variance in career success in addition to that accounted for by other individual, organizational, and structural variables (1999: 423).

Historically, there have been various meta-reviews of research that attempted to ascertain whether personality could predict work success. Ghiselli and Barthol (1953) reviewed 113 studies reported between 1919 and 1953. The validities ranged from 0.13 to 0.36, the mean being 0.22. Although the authors wisely attempted to exclude data for measured traits that were clearly unrelated to the job, it seems that no thorough job analysis was performed, and hence some of the weaker correlations may well be a result of traits that are not relevant to specific jobs. Second, and most importantly, it is likely that many of the personality questionnaires that were being used at that time were psychometrically poor, with few reliability or validity statistics.

The first thorough report on the validity of personality tests was made by Ghiselli and Brown (1955) more than 40 years ago. They were interested in the prediction of occupational success by means of various types of tests (intelligence, spatial, motor and personality). Intelligence tests correlated r=0.37 and personality r=0.18 for managerial staff. About 10 years later, Ghiselli (1966) undertook a second review, which provided evidence of the validity of personality measurement. Personality tests correlated r=0.27 in executives. This analysis used aggregated data and it showed that the best predictor of work-related behaviour was r=0.24. The reviewers only considered studies in which the personality trait measure seemed relevant to the work variable. However, other reviews up until the late 1980s were much less positive about the role of personality traits in predicting job/work performance.

Between 1965 and 1985, there were 8–10 meta-analyses using different tests and outcome measures. Validities ranged from 0.10 to 0.60, with most being in the range 0.15–0.25. The review of Guion and Gottier (1965), like others published in the 1960s, seemed gloomy and damning. Their conclusion was often repeated: 'it is difficult in the face of this summary to advocate, with a clear conscience, the use of personality measures in most situations as a basis for making employment decisions' (Guion and Gottier, 1965: 160). However, many subsequent reviewers have pointed out serious flaws in their review method (Tett, Jackson and Rothstein, 1991).

Early meta-analyses could be criticized on various grounds. First, all of the results were collapsed across personality dimensions, occupations and work outcome criteria, obscuring possibly important relationships. Second, situational factors such as organizational culture, management style and job content were neglected. These factors can and do impact powerfully on an individual's ability to fulfil their potential. Third, the criteria of success were often problematic, being based primarily on supervisor ratings. In other words, what was thought of as 'success' was often poorly measured.

Schmitt, Gooding, Noe and Kirsch (1984) found a mean correlation of 0.21 between personality and performance, which compared favourably with measures of general cognitive ability (0.22) and special aptitude scales (0.16). Because of increasing interest in both the structure of personality dimensions (in particular, the five-factor model) and the validation of personality tests through work-related criteria, a number of important and comprehensive reviews and meta-analyses appeared in the 1990s. The first of these was by Barrick and Mount (1991), who looked at the relationship between the Big Five personality variables and job proficiency, training proficiency and personnel data in widely varying occupational groups (police, sales and so on). The Big Five are widely accepted now as *the* fundamental unrelated personality traits (Matthews and Deary, 1998). These are: extroversion, neuroticism, agreeableness, openness-to-experience and conscientiousness. They expected to find at least two correlates in all jobs – namely, *conscientiousness* (because it assesses persistent, planful, careful, responsible and hardworking traits important in all jobs) and *neuroticism* (because it assesses worrying, nervousness, self-pity and so on, which tend to inhibit rather than facilitate work-task performance), and other dimensions that they thought would predict performance in particular jobs. For example, in management and sales ('people-type') jobs, extroversion and agreeableness would be important. Furthermore, some dimensions of personality were thought to be related only to particular aspects of the job. Thus, openness to experience was thought to relate more to training than to performance criteria.

Barrick and Mount (1991) reviewed 117 studies, which were carefully selected to fulfil exact criteria. As predicted, they found that conscientiousness – a manifestation of a strong sense of purpose, obligation and persistence – was strongly predictive of work proficiency across all of the data. On the whole, the other predictors were confirmed, although they found less evidence that neuroticism was a good predictor of poorer work, notably for technical reasons.

They also distinguished between objective and subjective work criteria, the former relating to such factors as sales figures, productivity counts and so on, and the latter usually involving ratings by others. Personality tests seem to predict ratings better than objective measures, either for methodological reasons (item overlap) or else because ratings measure replication, which is a good summary of a person's personality.

Using a different type of meta-analysis, Tett, Jackson and Rothstein (1991) identified higher average correlations between personality and job efficiency than the Barrick and Mount (1991) review. They included 494 studies that together examined more than 13,000 people, and they found a corrected mean personality scale validity of 0.29, and an even higher validity (0.38) when examining studies that conducted a job analysis to attempt to determine which personality dimensions should actually be related to the particular job. According to their careful analysis, personality traits were clearly better predictors of work-related behaviour under the following conditions:

1. In confirmatory rather than exploratory studies – that is, when the expected relationships (in terms of theory) were examined, as opposed to all of those available;
2. Where job analysis was used to select predictions – that is, where jobs were examined in detail and the requirements linked logically to personality theory;
3. For recruits rather than incumbents, doubtless because there are greater number of variables in recruits, and the effects of socialization and non-retention have not operated;
4. In military rather than civilian samples, possibly because it is easier to define the job requirements in the former;
5. In published articles rather than doctoral dissertations, no doubt because of the quality of research.

This review has been subject to criticism on methodological grounds (Ones, Mount, Barrick and Hunter, 1984), which of course demanded and received a reply (Tett, Jackson and Rothstein, 1991). Reanalysis showed slightly lower correlations, but they were still respectably high (r=0.24).

In a UK study, Robertson and Kinder (1993) were also concerned with the poor validity of 0.15 reviewed by Schmitt, Gooding, Noe and Kirsch (1984). Following the critique of others, they used confirmatory criterion-related measures – that is, they examined the correlations they expected would be related to 12 different work judgements (for example, decision-making ability, managing staff and so on). They found the mean sample (based on 20 samples) of about 1500 people to be 0.20 for the personality variables, but with higher values (up to 0.33) for specific work-related criteria such as creativity and judgement. They also found that ability measures were unrelated to the trait measures, and accounted for similar amounts of variance to the personality tests.

Looking exclusively at studies done in the European Community, Salgado (1997) conducted a meta-analysis of 36 studies on the relationship between personality and job performance. He found that conscientiousness (true validity 0.25) was the best predictor, followed by emotional stability (true validity 0.19). Openness to experience and agreeableness were valid predictors of training proficiency, and extroversion was a good predictor in certain professional groups.

The psychometric method is probably the approach most favoured by 'scientific' researchers in the area. It has the advantage of being theoretically based with careful multivariate statistical analysis of large data banks. Furthermore, there seemed to be consensus in the results of studies, which suggests that for all jobs good predictors of success are intelligence, stability and conscientiousness. Other traits such as extroversion and other specific abilities may be important for particular jobs but the above triumvirate will go a long way to explaining success.

What the psychometric approach does not do is take into consideration social and occupational factors that lead to an individual's success and ability to realize his or her potential. Thus, it does not take into consideration the role of reputation, which can have a powerful effect on the lives of individuals. It also often takes little cognizance of person–organization fit. More importantly, success at work is often related to market forces and economic conditions, which may, for the individual, be as much a matter of chance as of personality or ability. Nevertheless, it is to the psychometric approach that both organizations and social scientists turn most often to attempt to assess potential in selection, assessment and developmental exercise centres.

3. The Biodata Approach

The biodata approach is the main topic of this book and will only briefly be introduced here. To a large extent, the biodata approach is the most common-sensical to those in business and fits logically into nearly all selection methods that use application forms and curricula vitae and that interview candidates about their past performance.

Biodata are biographical data: traditionally, they include comprehensive information about a person's past life and work experience. The Jesuits, the psychoanalysts and many others have stressed the importance of early life experience, whereas the neo-psychoanalysts and some organizational psychologists have pointed to the relevance of adolescent and early work experience. The idea is straightforward – certain life experiences, such as going to particular educational institutions, geographically moving, being voted into positions of leadership and so on, are statistically and logically related to certain specific work criteria.

The approach is strong on verification but weak on theory in that most biodata researchers are happy to entertain any ideas, hunches or hypotheses about which factors are correlated with demonstrable success at work. However, they are most insistent that these relationships are empirically validated on one sample and confirmed in another. What the biodata research aims to do is to establish empirically which biographical factors are predictive of which work outcomes so that they can devise biodata items used and scored in selection settings.

Nearly all meta-analyses have shown biodata to be among the best methods for selection. Thus, in one review that included 23 studies of biodata (n=10,800), Hunter and Hunter (1984) found that the average mean validity coefficient was 0.37. As Cook (1998: 96) notes: 'Biographical methods have to be taken seriously because they achieve consistently good results'. Chapters 2 to 5 will consider this method in greater detail.

Conclusion

The problem for all organizations is how to select, develop and retain the best people with the most potential to face the business challenges and opportunities of the future. They are all seeking bright, hard-working, motivated, adaptable staff who are happy and whose work will provide maximum returns to the many stakeholders in the organization.

The idea that one can train or develop all staff to maximum potential has proved unsuccessful. On the other hand, the finding that adults do not change fundamentally over the lifespan means the business of prediction is possible. What is problematic is trying to understand what the working world of the future performance will look like and how this will impact on individuals. Will face-to-face interaction between employees decline in favour of teleworking and electronic communication? Will companies be able to outsource most of their functions to subcontractors and freelance workers, who are perhaps in different countries where workforces are cheaper? Will demographic changes mean that the workforce and the organization's customers will have different needs?

Some organizations spend a lot of time, effort and money assessing their potential employees before hiring them. They have to. If there are issues of security involved, most organizations recognize that one unstable, bitter or incompetent worker can do considerable damage. Hence, they take care through assessment centres, advance testing, interviewing, reference gathering and various other selection methods to gather data on the current (and future) state of the individuals they hire. Employers also need to train their staff well and thoroughly and think carefully about where to place them in the organiza-tion and when.

It is not clear why all organizations do not spend more 'up-front' rather than rely on training or Darwinian wastage methods. It could be that they simply do not believe the money is well spent. Some are more concerned with *selection out than in*, in the sense that their assessment is only about negative rather than positive success. If it is true that people do not change dramatically over time, that attempts at change and development are costly, and that individual differ-ences well nurtured in the organization play a major part in overall organiza-tional success, it is surprising that more time is not spent on the business of assessing employee potential.

Chapter 2
A History of Biodata

Definition and Description

Biodata – biographical accounts of past events or, more specifically, data on personal biographies – are information concerning an individual's personal life history and experience. Biodata refer to the various sorts of information that individuals are frequently required to provide when writing their curricula vitae (résumés), filling out application forms for jobs, insurance companies and government offices, and answering questions at interviews. To be effective in a business potential context, however, biodata should include information about aspects of a person's earlier life and experiences that give a clear insight into aptitudes, skills and competencies that are relevant for the job. In essence, the term refers to the biographical details of a person's life: the individual's conception (and hopefully accurate and truthful recall) of his or her own personal history. In giving such biographical information, individuals are required to recall not just static details, such as their qualifications or previous jobs held, but also to report on how they might have behaved in different situations. References are made to earlier events in their lives in situations that are relevant to current job requirements (Mumford and Owens, 1987).

Many people assume that, for individual behaviour, the best predictor of the future is the past. That is, the sorts of experiences that a person has had and the ways they have coped with them best predict their future behaviour. There is therefore nothing new in the concept of biodata; they refer to objectively scored and validatable items or samples of biographical behaviour that are systematically gathered, scored, compared and assessed against specific, usually work-related, criteria.

Biodata have been found to have high predictive efficiency in relation to a wide range of criteria covering career choice, job performance, organizational loyalty, staff turnover, management or leadership potential, absenteeism and employee theft (Owens, 1976; Reilly and Chao, 1982; Hunter and Hunter, 1984; Mumford and Owens, 1987; Russell, 1990; Brown and Campion, 1994).

Measures of biodata have been deployed across a wide range of occupations in the public and private sector, from the lowest clerical grades through to higher management (Nickels, 1994).

For many years, the use of biographical details in employment, organizational and management research was frowned on in psychology. Among the reasons given for this were that biodata instruments lacked objectivity, reliability and validity. There was no grand theory driving biodata research – it has comprised exploratory empiricism. It was frequently argued that biodata were susceptible to error and bias in the ways they classified or measured individuals. Psychologists have also been traditionally interested in comparing and contrasting individuals on the same criteria, and data revealed from autobiographies simply does not allow for this.

A universally agreed definition of biodata does not exist. Among the most frequently cited, and probably the best definition, is:

> scored autobiographical data which are objective or scorable items of information provided by an individual on previous experience (demographic, experiential, attitudinal) which can be presumed or demonstrated to be related to personality structure, personal adjustment, or success in social educational or occupational pursuits. (Owens, 1976: 162)

Thus biodata encompass wider aspects of personality and motivation than behaviour alone. Furthermore, this definition emphasizes a predictive, classical model of selection. In other words, since biodata are said to be items that can be shown to be related to success in occupational pursuits, they can be regarded as the 'predictors' of specific 'criteria' of success.

Typically, biographical items tend to be selected from the kinds of categories listed below (Glennon, Albright and Owens, 1966):

- classification or simple demographic data;
- habits and attitudes;
- health;
- human relations;
- money;
- parental, home, childhood, teens;
- personal attributes;
- present home, spouse and children;
- recreation, hobbies and interests;
- school and education;
- self-impressions;
- values, opinions and preferences;
- work.

Thus, biodata items have been classified under different categories, such as 'background' data (for example, parents, social class, types of school attended), 'commitment' data (for example, leisure activities) and 'achievement' data (for example, school and work performance) (Drakeley, 1989). Perhaps the easiest way to describe biodata is to examine various examples of questions used. Table 2.1 presents a random list of biodata items by way of illustration.

Biographical items may therefore be found in measures that are variously referred to as application blanks (forms), biographical information blanks, individual background surveys and life history questionnaires. Exactly what items should be classified as biographical, however, has been a source of controversy (Henry, 1966). For example, a biographical item may vary on any of the following dimensions:

- verifiable–unverifiable;
- historical–futuristic;
- actual behaviour–hypothetical behaviour;
- memory–conjecture;
- factual–interpretive;
- specific–general;
- response–response tendency;
- external events–internal events;
- strictly biographical–attitudes.

If only historical items that are verifiable are included as biodata items, then questions such as the following would not be asked: 'Did you ever build a model airplane that flew?' Cureton (see Henry, 1966: 913) commented that this single item, although it cannot be easily verified for any specific individual, was almost as good a predictor of success in flight training during the Second World War as the entire US Air Force Test Battery.

Other researchers feel that any person-type question that describes the individual may be classified as a biodata item. This would include items such as personality, motivation, aspiration, attitudes and values. From this enlarged classification, any item is included that answers one of these questions:

- What have I done?
- Where have I been?
- What do I believe?
- What do I want to be?
- What do I feel?
- What am I apt to do?
- What interests me?
- What relationships have I had with others?

Although the enlarged classification of biodata items obviously expands the amount of personal information collected, a more constrained classification may reduce a tendency towards fictionalization. Biodata items that are historical and verifiable may result in a narrow, yet representative set of data about

Table 2.1: Examples of biodata items

In how many different cities, towns, or townships have you lived?
1. 1 to 3.
2. 4 to 6.
3. 7 to 9.
4. 10 to 12.
5. 13 or more.

Have you been in the armed forces?
1. Yes, as an officer.
2. Yes, as an enlisted man.
3. Yes, both as an officer and as an enlisted man.
4. No, but you were a civilian employee of the government.
5. None of the above.

How often do you tell jokes?
1. Very frequently.
2. Frequently.
3. Occasionally.
4. Seldom.
5. Can't remember jokes.

How do you regard your neighbours?
1. Not interested in your neighbours.
2. Like them but seldom see them
3. Visit in each others' homes occasionally.
4. Spend a lot of time together.

About how many new friends have you made in the past year?
1. No need to make new friends.
2. One or two.
3. Three or four.
4. Five or more.
5. Can't remember exactly.

Before you were 18 years of age, how many times did your family move from one house to another?
1. Never.
2. Once.
3. Two or three times.
4. Four or five times.
5. Moved every year or so.

In what section of town did your family live longest while you were growing up?
1. Lived in one of the most exclusive sections of town.
2. Lived in a good but not the best section.
3. Lived in an average section of town.
4. Lived in one of the poorer sections of town.
5. Lived in a rural area.

(contd)

Table 2.1: (contd)

While in school, how often did your father or guardian seem to take an interest in how you were doing in your classes?
1. Never.
2. Once in a great while.
3. Frequently.
4. Always.

While in high school, about how many evenings a week did you go out?
1. Less than one.
2. One.
3. Two.
4. Three.
5. Four or more.

How creative do you feel you are?
1. Highly creative.
2. Somewhat more creative than most in your field.
3. Moderately creative.
4. Somewhat less creative than most in your field.
5. Not creative.

As you grew up, how did you feel about school?
1. Liked it very much.
2. Liked it most of the time.
3. Just accepted it as necessary.
4. Was often a little unhappy with it.
5. Cordially disliked it and was glad to finish.

How many times did you change schools before you were 16 year of age other than by graduation?
1. Never.
2. One or two times.
3. Three to five times.
4. Six or more times.
5. I can't remember.

How do you compare with your friends in athletic ability?
1. You are very much better than most.
2. You are a little better than average.
3. You were about average.
4. You are a little poorer than most.
5. Your friends are very much better than you.

How do you feel about the time you have to do your job?
1. Have time for everything without feeling pushed.
2. Wish you had a little more time to plan and to think.
3. Necessary to keep pushing to get everything done.
4. Very hard to do what is expected of you in the time available.
5. Never seem to have enough time to do everything.

(contd)

Table 2.1: (contd)

Is the type of work that interests you most that which ...
1. Has much fine detail involved.
2. Has some fine detail aspects.
3. Very seldom requires fine detail work.
4. Would never require you to bother with fine details.

How do you feel about travelling in your work?
1. Would enjoy it tremendously.
2. Would like to do some travelling.
3. Would travel if it were necessary.
4. Definitely dislike travelling.

the individual, whereas the enlarged classification may be quite unrepresenta-
tive. For example, even when respondents are inclined to respond honestly,
items calling for conjecture, interpretation and supposition may have enough
ambiguity to enable individuals to respond with a sort of leniency rating error
(giving a falsely positive impression) about themselves.

Ten attributes of biodata have been identified in a more recent analysis
(Mael, 1991). The dimensions used to classify biodata items in this scheme are
history, externality, objectivity, first-handedness, discreteness, verifiability,
controllability, equal accessibility, job relevance and invasiveness. Important
criteria for biodata are that they should reflect established patterns in an individual's personal history; they should address observable events as far as possible
(externality); they should be based on fact (objectivity); and they should be based
on information that is directly available to the respondent (first-handedness).
Each biodata item should deal with a specific piece of information about an
individual (discreteness) and it should be possible to check its accuracy (verifiability). The final set of criteria concern legal and moral issues related to employment opportunities. Biodata should measure aspects of a respondent's past over
which he or she had personal control (controllability). The events or experiences
asked about must have been equally possible for all candidates. In other words,
including a measure that unfairly excludes certain categories of applicant should
be avoided (equal accessibility). Items on a biodata scale should be included only
if they deal with matters of relevance to the job (job relevance). Finally, biodata
scales should respect a respondent's right to privacy. Items dealing with religious
affiliation or marital status, for example, may be of dubious relevance in many
job selection contexts and represent sensitive issues for some respondents.

Biodata have been used in a variety of industrial and business settings since
the early part of the twentieth century. As we shall see in this book, one characteristic of biodata that is little challenged is their ability to predict a variety of
work-related criteria. In this sense they may be uniquely useful in predicting or
assessing potential.

The History of Biodata: Application Forms

Biodata have a long history of use in industry, but it was not until the 1950s that biodata became widely used (particularly in the USA) as a formal part of selection systems. The term 'biodata', as used here, encompassed a broad range of information including items that were objective and verifiable (for example, age) and those that were based on unverifiable self-reports (for example, one's favourite hobby), covering a respondent's life and work history. Typically, biodata were collected from job candidates through written forms, such as an application blank or a special biographical information form. Regardless of what the form was called, biographical items were usually in a multiple-choice or short-answer format which lent itself to objective scoring.

The earliest recorded use of biodata was at a meeting of the Chicago Underwriters in 1894 (see Ferguson, 1961) when Colonel Thomas L. Peters of the Washington Life Insurance Company of Atlanta, Georgia, proposed that one way to improve the selection of life insurance agents 'would be for managers to require all applicants to answer a list of standardised questions'. Thus, it was not a group of psychologists, as many have believed, but a group of businessmen who created the prototype of the scorable application form.

A few years later, Goldsmith (1922) investigated the usefulness of biodata in selecting people who could endure selling life assurance. He took 50 good, 50 poor and 50 middling salesmen from a larger sample of 502, and analysed their application forms. Age, marital status, education, (current) occupation, previous experience (of selling insurance), belonging to clubs, whether the candidate was applying for full- or part-time selling, whether the candidate himself had life assurance, and whether (not what) candidates replied to the question: 'What amount of insurance are you confident of placing each month?' collectively distinguished good from average and average from bad (Table 2.2).

Goldsmith turned the conventional application form into what was called a 'weighted application blank' (WAB). The WAB works on the principle that 'the best predictor of future behaviour is the past behaviour', and the easiest way of measuring past behaviour is what the applicant writes on his or her application form. The principle is familiar to anyone with motor insurance, and is the basis of the actuarial profession. By the end of the 1930s, the WAB technique was well developed; ready-made tables had been drawn up from WAB construction.

Biodata instruments come in more than one variety, as we shall see later. Allport (1942) reviewed the use of personal documents in psychological science. He listed them as including autobiographies, questionnaires, verbatim recordings, diaries, letters, and expressive and projective productions. He also noted that biographical data had been used in studies of attitudes and this had given rise to early debate about the kinds of items that technically qualified as indicators of life history.

WAB construction is entirely empirical. A biodata 'score' therefore may have various meanings and implications which depend on the nature of the

Table 2.2: Early biodata scoring scheme: weighted application blank

Age		Marital Status		Service	
18–20	−2	Married	+1	Full-time	+2
21–22	−1	Single	−1	Part-time	−2
23–24	0				
25–27	+1	**Occupation**		**Insurance**	
28–29	+2				
30–40	+3	Social	+1	Carried	+1
41–50	+1	Unsocial	−1	Not carried	−1
51–60	0				
Over 60	−1				

Education		Experience	
8 years	+1	Previous life assurance experience	+1
10 years	+2		
12 years	+3	**Confidence**	
16 years	+2		
		Replies to question: 'What amount of insurance are you confident of placing each month?'	+1
		Does not reply	−1

performance variables to which it has been empirically linked (Guion, 1965). It never matters why an item differentiates successful estate agents from unsuccessful – only that it does. Among the criteria that WABs have been used successfully to test are:

- job turnover;
- oil company executive progress;
- military promotability;
- sales performance;
- length of tenure;
- salary progression;
- employee theft.

The classic WAB is 'invisible' and hard to fake. It is invisible because the applicant expects to complete an application form and does not realize that it is to be scored and used in selection. Rarely do individuals apply for a job without being asked to fill out some type of application form. The amount of required information in such applications may vary from simply name, age, address and phone number to a 10-page document covering all aspects of previous education, work history and private life. It is considered inappropriate to fake because most of the items *could* be verified independently, if the employer and others could afford the time and the expense to do so. Such vetting of job applicants' background is vigilantly conducted by some employers, such as government departments, the police force and the military.

The classic WAB has tended to have been supplanted since the 1960s by BQs – biographical questionnaires or inventories containing a more extensive list of life history data. BQs tend to use a more recognizable questionnaire format with multiple-choice answers and have been used successfully to predict job performance among research engineers, oil industry research scientists, pharmaceutical industry researchers, bus drivers, 'custodial officers' and police officers (see Chapter 6). Biodata are used for selecting professional, clerical, sales, skilled labour and unskilled labour; in short, all socioeconomic groups. Biodata have been used extensively among recruiters in the military. Biodata seem to be used most frequently for selecting sales staff, and least often for managerial occupations, although research emerged in the 1990s to show that biodata instruments can be developed specifically for management selection (Wilkinson, 1993, 1994, 1995).

Most modern researchers use a mixture of the classic WAB and biodata. The success of the classic WAB depends on respondents never suspecting that application forms have any function other than a mundane bureaucratic purpose. In fact, such forms can yield valuable data that, when designed and used properly, can contribute towards enhanced organizational performance and business potential.

Application forms, with weighted biodata predictors, provide specific and predictive information about the employee that the organization may need if the individual is hired. Examples are age, sex, number of dependants, national insurance number, age of marriage, living accommodation, location of address and so on. In addition, such application forms are designed to gather information about job applicants which the human relations specialists have found to be pertinent to the hiring process and interview. A carefully designed application form is like a highly structured interview in which the questions have been standardized and determined in advance. Unfortunately, it is far from clear that all organizations have specific reasons for gathering the information that they do on application forms. Many routinely collect biographical information on personnel that is never seriously processed. Often historical accident, rather than careful research and planning, determines what goes into application forms.

The major problem with application forms is that, more often than not, they are designed rather haphazardly, perhaps by having one to two individuals make up the kinds of questions they feel 'ought to be asked' or by including questions known to be asked by most other organizations. Such a procedure can result in lengthy and inappropriate application blanks that contain questions of dubious relevance or predictive capability in that particular selection context. The central issue in designing biodata instruments concerns which questions to ask and how to interpret the answers and relate them to something worth trying to predict.

The problem of what items need to be included on an application form is crucial. However, this can be answered only by considering the related question of what use will be made of the information obtained – that is, how is it to be used? For example, it is of little value to have an application form ask for information if the personnel office is only going to give the application a quick scan and use it simply as general background information preliminary to the employment interview.

Used properly as an aid to selection, the application form can be, and sometimes is, one of the better selection devices at the disposal of the personnel or human resources expert. Just as with any other selection device, though, only *valid* informational items should be included on the form and this requires that *all* the items on an application form should be checked to see if they are in any way indicative of future successful job performance. Only items that have been carefully checked for their ability to predict some aspect of performance should be included. This, of course, means that different application forms have to be designed for different jobs. The process of designing and printing these non-standardized forms in an organization may indeed account for the fact that forms are rarely designed to fulfil proper criteria of biodata research. The most common method of ensuring predictive validity of a biodata tool is simply to compute the correlation between an item on the application form (for example, number of previous jobs in the past five years) and some later measure of job success (for example, job salary, promotion, appraisal data). If a significant relationship is found, that item can then be used to select future job applicants – otherwise it should be dropped. However, because of the various possible causes of error (such as sample size, or other factors relating to the dependent variable) it is wise to replicate biodata validation studies in an organization at least once, and more frequently if the organization is in a state of change.

It is thus possible to construct 'keys' for each of a number of different jobs in a plant, where a key consists of a list of those items on the application form that best predict success on that particular job. It remains essential that cross-validation of these keys is a prerequisite to their actual use in a selection situation.

One advantage of the application form over the interview or tests of personality is that response bias does not usually play as great a role. Even if applicants do 'bias' their answers on the application form in a concern to be seen to give the desired answer (even if it is not honest), in many cases such data are subject to rather easy verification from other sources, such as the candidate's previous employer, educational establishment and so on. Intuitively, most people would probably expect that many questions on an application form *should* be related to job success. Certainly, a person's previous work history should provide some sort of clue to the probability of successful performance on the job under consideration. Similarly, past personal life history and family data ought to give some indication of the emotional and personality characteristics of the applicant, which may have some bearing on eventual job adjustment. Many WAB items are familiar to any personnel manager or human relations expert: (absence of) 'job-hopping'; being born locally; being referred by existing employee; owning a home; being married; belonging to clubs and organizations; playing sports or physical games. Others are less obvious, such as coming from rural or small-town homes, being religious or family size. Some items make sense when you know they work, but would need an insightful mind to predict – for example, 'doesn't want a relative contacted in case of emergency' as a predictor of employee theft. Some items are bizarre, such as no middle initial given (employee theft again). Physique is often mentioned: extremes of height or weight are usually bad signs and are related to poor work performance.

Suffice it to say that there is no list of WAB or biodata items that is exhaustive or inclusive. Whereas some studies have found the same items (for example, parental divorce, educational experiences) predictive of different occupational behaviours, others have been unable to replicate the results. Many researchers, either because of experimental constraints, poor imagination or little knowledge of psychological theories or processes, have not really explored a full range of questions that might be highly predictive. The recent renewed interest in biodata, both in applied and research settings, probably means that this state of affairs will change. What psychological theories, then, are relevant to biodata?

Developmental and Personality Psychological Theories

Most psychological theories emphasize how developmental experiences shape the personality of individuals. Any theory of development must describe the process through which development occurs and must outline the reasons for various patterns of growth. Among the most significant environmental determinants of personality are experiences that individuals have as a result of membership in a particular culture. Each culture has its own institutionalized and sanctioned patterns of learned behaviours, rituals and beliefs. Thus, most members of a culture will have certain personality characteristics in common. Even in complex developed societies, the importance of cultural forces in shaping personality functioning is considerable. These forces influence needs and the desired means of satisfying them, our relationships to authority, self-concept, experiences of major forms of anxiety and conflict, and coping strategies. They affect what people think is funny and sad, what they view as healthy and sick, and how successful they are at work. C. Kluckhohn wrote:

> Culture regulates our lives at every turn. From the moment we are born until we die there is, whether we are conscious of it or not, constant pressure upon us to follow certain types of behaviour that other men have created for us. (Kluckhohn, 1949: 37)

Although certain patterns of behaviour develop as a result of membership in a culture, others are developed as a result of *membership in some group*. Few aspects of an individual's personality can be understood without reference to the group to which that person belongs. Social class factors help determine the status of individuals, the roles they perform, the duties they are bound by, and the privileges they enjoy. These factors influence how individuals see themselves, how they perceive members of other social classes, and how they earn and spend money. Like cultural factors, social class factors influence the ways in which individuals define situations and how they respond to them. There is evidence that social class factors in a population are related to the prevalence of mental illness and to the types of mental disorders found.

Beyond the similarities determined by environmental factors such as membership in the same culture or social class, specific environmental factors lead to considerable variation in the personality functioning of members of a single culture or class. The peculiar, individualistic relationships in families are crucial to personality development. Parents may be warm and loving or hostile and rejecting, overprotective and possessive or aware of their children's needs for freedom and autonomy. Each pattern of parental behaviour affects the personality development of the child.

Some theories of personality attach particular importance to early social interaction between infant and mother. During infancy the developing self-perception is influenced by the amount of anxiety the mother communicates, often in a subtle way, to the child. In later years, the person's self-concept is influenced by reflected appraisals – how the individual perceives others as perceiving and responding to him or her.

Parents influence their children's behaviour in at least three important ways:

1. Through their own behaviour they present situations that elicit certain behaviour in children (for example, frustration leads to aggression).
2. They serve as role models for identification.
3. They selectively reward behaviours.

Along with environmental factors, genetic factors play a major role in determining personality, particularly in relation to what is unique in the individual. Although many psychologists historically have argued the relative importance of environmental and genetic factors in shaping personality as a whole, recent theorists have recognized that the importance of these factors may vary from one personality characteristic to another. Genetic factors are generally more important in characteristics such as intelligence and temperament, and less important in regard to values, ideals and beliefs. Psychologists have also begun to explore possible interactions between genetic and environmental factors. Although heredity fixes a number of possible behavioural outcomes, environment ultimately determines the behaviour. Heredity may set a range *within which* the further development of the characteristic is determined by the environment. However, the relationship may be even more complicated than this since genetically influenced characteristics may lead the person to act on, and in return be influenced by, the environment in a particular way. Thus, rather than a simple cause–effect relationship, there is an ongoing interaction or reciprocal process involving person and environment.

Psychologists argue that personality is determined by many interacting factors, including genetic, cultural, social class and familial forces. Heredity sets limits on the range of development of characteristics; within this range, characteristics are determined by environmental forces. Heredity provides the potential that a culture may or may not reward and cultivate. It is possible to see the interaction of these many genetic and environmental forces in any significant aspect of personality. Theories of personality differ in the importance attributed to questions of growth and development, in the relative weight given to genetic and environmental factors, and in interpretations of the mechanisms through which personality development occurs. Ultimately, however, it is the task of any personality theory to account for the development of structures and patterns of behaving. A theory of personality should explain what is developed, how it is developed, and why it is developed.

Consider one classic example of a theory that emphasized the importance of biographical experiences. Like Freud, Erikson (1958, 1975) attributed considerable psychological importance to the unusually long period of human childhood. Erikson also agreed that childhood conflicts exert a significant influence on the adult personality, and that some of these concern the repressed issue of infantile sexuality; and he concluded that the prolonged inequality of adult and child leaves us with a lifelong residue of emotional immaturity, which inevitably conflicts with our more rational and ethical aims. Nevertheless, Erikson specifically rejected Freud's efforts to explain personality wholly in terms of the first four or five years of life. Instead he stressed that personality development continues throughout the whole life cycle, and he posited eight stages that extend from infancy to old age.

Another approach is provided by De Waele and Harré (1979), who concentrated on the importance of a person's autobiography in understanding his or her adult behaviour. They argued that autobiographical data can be as objective, reliable, valid and thoughtful (particularly the last) as all other data. They further argued that psychology is too synchronic rather than diachronic (historical) and stressed that autobiography offers a way of rendering life events intelligible. They devised a time-oriented and topic-oriented method, using an in-depth interview with reflexive and direct questions as well as putting people into 'problem and conflict' situations to elicit their autobiographies. Interestingly, the former author used this approach later to help him decide whether to release murderers from prison out into the community. Perhaps the most relevant aspect of these authors' method in the current discussion is the biographical inventory. This had three sections including the micro-sociological situation in which people were living, social psychological life patterns and individual characteristics.

The final section (IIIA) is given in detail below to give an idea of this approach:

A. Self-description and interpretation
1. The body
   (a) The subject is asked to rate thirty-eight aspects of the body (a) as to their subjective importance, and (b) as to the satisfaction experienced concerning them.
   (b) Reasons for complaints about some part of the body and about one's physical characteristics.
   (c) Indication of that part of the body which is experienced as the centre of one's person.
   (d) Body Focus Questionnaire (Fisher). (Parts of the body are presented in pairs; the subject is asked to indicate the part of which he is actually most conscious.)
   (e) The Body Distortion Questionnaire (Fisher). (A list of eighty-two perceived distortions has to be checked.)
2. Personal appearance. A series of questions is asked concerning (a) situations in which one was laughed at, (b) nicknames, (c) physical defects and diseases, (d) valued characteristics of a beautiful person and of a beautiful woman, (e) evaluation of physical characteristics shown during certain life periods (puberty, adolescence, adulthood, old age).
3. Peculiar habits. Enumeration of peculiar mannerisms and ticks (picking one's nose, sucking, nail-biting, for example) performed in public or in private.
4. Questions concerning subject's physical development, after birth, during early childhood and first years of life (description of conditions, hygiene, speech development, lateralization, peculiar habits with mention of source).
5. Health. A chronological enumeration of illnesses, hospitalizations and surgical interventions. Furthermore the subject has to relate (a) his personal experience with medical staff during these periods, (b) possible effect of the illnesses, hospitalizations and interventions on his personality, and (c) role definitions of members of medical staff.
   (a) Descriptions of one's play activities and their evolution in time.
   (b) Description of one's sleeping habits and dreams, and their evolution in time.
   (c) Description of one's eating habits and of their evolution in time.
   (d) Description of one's drinking habits and their evolution in time.
   (e) Description of one's evacuation habits and their evolution in time.
   (f) Cleanness of body and clothes. Information is gathered on personal hygiene and on clothing habits, as well as on their evolution in time and their variations in different settings.

(g) Description of subject's sexual experiences and attitudes towards sexuality (Eysenck-Wilson questionnaire on sexuality).

6. Emotional reactions and sentiments: The subject is asked to give detailed descriptions of situations in which he experienced: fury, rage, joy, sadness, fear, guilt, remorse, inferiority, pride, jealousy, envy, superiority, admiration, disapproval, compassion, indignation, resentment.

7. Self-description by means of (a) the enumeration, (b) classification, and (c) exemplification of one's important personal characteristics (modification of the 'Who Am I' technique).

8. Self-description focused on elementary school period, indicating the sources of information.

9. Self-description focused on adolescence period, indicating sources of information.

10. A description of oneself within ten years from 'now' (or at another future moment).

11. Imaginary self-description at the age of sixty-four.

12. Description of other persons: most similar to the subject; most dissimilar to the subject.

13. Subject's description as he imagines it would be given by his best friends; by his enemies.

14. A series of questions is asked concerning one's opinions about (a) one's name, (b) favourite objects, environments and animals.

15. Family relations.
    (a) Names and occupations of all members.
    (b) For each member a series of questions is asked in order to gather information on major events in their lives, date of birth, present address, date of death, physical condition, disease, medical and psychiatric care, hospitalizations, accidents, physical weaknesses, alcoholism, etc.
    (c) Important personality traits of each family member.
    (d) With respect to the subject's parents questions are asked concerning the evolution of their marriage, also concubines, divorces, and their relations within the rest of the family.
    (e) Interpersonal relations. Questions are asked about (a) preferences for certain members of the family, (b) interpersonal importance of each member, (c) similarities and differences within the family.
    (f) Role definitions. The subject is asked – for each role mentioned in the list below – to give a general opinion about a good/bad father, mother, etc.; a description of the corresponding members of his own family; and a self-description as a father, etc.
    (g) Role list: a father, a stepfather, a mother, a stepmother, a grandfather, a grandmother, an aunt, an uncle, a brother, a sister.

16. The 'Self and Others' questionnaire (Berger). Sixty-five items concerning self and other acceptance are to be rated on a five-point scale according to their applicability to oneself.

17. Personality description. Thirty short personality descriptions are presented and the subject is asked to indicate which individuals personally known to him fit the descriptions. The subject is also asked to describe for each person the circumstances of their first contacts and to describe the evolution of their relationship.

18. Profile of mood scales (POMS by Lorr and McNair). Sixty descriptions of mood states are rated on a five-point scale as to their applicability to (a) the real self, (b) the ideal self, (c) the father, (d) the mother, and (e) the girlfriend or wife.

19. Two hundred and sixty items concerning personality characteristics are rated on a five-point scale as to their applicability to: (a) self, (b) ideal self, (c) subject's father, (d) subject's mother, and (c) subject's girlfriend or wife.

20. Psychological rating. Three hundred and sixty-three items concerning psychopathological characteristics are rated as to their applicability to the self.

21. Leary's checklist. One hundred and twenty-eight personality characteristics are checked so as to yield a description of subject's real and ideal self.

22. Adjective checklist (ACL) by Gough. Out of three hundred adjectives those that are descriptive of the self are to be checked (one global scale; eight sub-scales, two factor scores).

23. Buss's questionnaire on Aggression (Seventy-five items).

24. Estimate of various abilities and skills (physical, technical, economical, leadership ability, social, erotic, intellectual, aesthetic and artistic). The subject is asked to give an estimation of his real ability in each of these fields, and to indicate his desired ability level. Besides, the subject has to mention the family members who had (in a particular field) manifested an ability above average.

25. Inventory of the subject's reference persons. A list of role titles is given and the subject is asked to fill in the name of the person he knew who best matched the role title in question. Furthermore, he is asked to describe the person mentioned, to indicate their most salient characteristics, and to describe the circumstances under which the person mentioned and the subject became acquainted.

The following titles are given: (a) Most peculiar or interesting persons ever met, (b) the most peculiar or interesting person ever heard of or read about, (c) persons whose advice would be asked, (d) the best friend(s) one had, (e) a friend (role definition), (f) admired public figure (sports, music, painting, etc.), (g) disliked public figures, (h) important persons one would like to meet. (De Waele and Harré, 1979: 22)

Although there are a large number of quite different personality theories – trait/types; psychodynamic/genetic; physiological/experiential – all attempt to categorize people along specific delineated dimensions. All personality theories have a unique nomenclature and ideas about how and why people come to have a trait, or be a type. Personality measurement is, therefore, about devising sensitive yet robust psychometric measures of trait or type that allow people to be categorized. This can be done both for applied or research reasons. For instance, employers would want to know if their employees were hypochondriacal; and researchers would like to test various theories by comparing and contrasting introverts and extroverts. In the study of personality, measurement usually follows theory.

Much more effort has gone into developing personality theory and research than biodata and yet its impact has been limited. This may be because, as Guthrie (1944: 50) stated:

> An individual's past affiliations, political and religious, offer better and more specific predictions of his future than any of the traits that we usually think of as personality traits. When we know how men adjust themselves through learning to their situation, and also know the situations to which they have been exposed ... we know the men themselves and there is no need to speculate concerning the deeper reaches of the soul until we can explore these with similar knowledge.

This seems to imply that we do not need to know *why* people do as they do, only that they will do it. Nevertheless, there are clearly advantages of being driven by theory and devising measures that allow one to compare people on the same criteria. Theories can be tested and extended, and the scientific enterprise tends to be programmatic and cumulative rather than piecemeal.

Biodata may have been less appealing to the academic psychologist and management scientists precisely because it tends to be atheoretical. If anything, theory flows from measurement in the sense that people try to derive a theory to explain their results, such as why do some biodata and not others predict occupational behaviour. Biodata research is rarely driven by theory and the WABs or biodata questionnaires are infrequently developed to measure highly specific behavioural traits. They are thus less frequently scrutinized by psychometricians. The level of abstraction at which personality researchers often work makes theorizing more satisfactory. This is not to say that there are no dangers in over-elaborate theoretical construction and debate. For many, personality research has progressed precious little over the past 50 years.

Despite the relative inattention to theory developments in biodata research, evidence has emerged for a strong relationship between background data measures of life history and personality (Mumford, Snell, Reiter-Palmon, 1994). This evidence derives from studies examining the relationship between background data items and scores on established personality inventories. Nearly 30 years ago, Mokesel and Tesser (1971), for example, showed that background data items were effective predictors of scores on the California F Scale.

Mumford and Stokes (1982) correlated background data items with scores on measures of positive and negative emotionality for a sample of nearly 2000 men and women. Again, many relationships emerged between biographical details and personality. Reviews of the personality literature and background data literature have identified common factors that consistently emerge in each case. In personality research, the five most frequently appearing factors have been: neuroticism, extroversion, openness or cultural differences, agreeableness, and conscientiousness (Eysenck and Eysenck, 1985; McCrae and Costa, 1987; Zuckerman, Kuhlman and Camac, 1988). In the biodata literature, factors such as adjustment, extroversion, cultural interests, social leadership and social maturity have been commonly seen (Mumford and Owens, 1987).

Indeed, biodata items may be used as indicators of personality. Biodata may provide instruments through which personality constructs can be assessed (Mumford, Snell and Reiter-Palmon, 1994). In fact, personality constructs as measured through biodata may yield better predictions of beliefs about future behaviour than when measured through standard personality items. This trend might be attributable to the advantageous psychometric characteristics evidenced by background data items such as freedom from response biases (Ames, 1983; Shaffer, Saunders and Owens, 1986), high reliability (Cascio, 1975; Shaffer et al., 1986), the non-transparent nature of item content (Lautenschlager, 1985) and relative item independence (Owens, 1976).

The substantive relationship between personality and biodata may be cemented by the construct of self-esteem. Self-esteem is known to be important in determining people's behaviour in, and reactions to, various situations, in that it underpins the motivation to perform challenging tasks, emotional reactions to situations, and what situations you choose to put yourself in (Bandura, 1986, 1989). The self-esteem construct has also been identified in a number of factorings of background data items. Furthermore, background data measures of self-esteem seem to be effective predictors of real-world performance criteria (Morrison, Owens, Glennon and Albright, 1962).

A number of biographical characteristics have been found to show links with personality traits such as extroversion and neuroticism (Smernou and Lautenschlager, 1991). Perceived environmental conditions associated with family background, such as parental pressure to succeed, were associated with neuroticism. The style of parental discipline was another important factor. Parents of those individuals who scored high on the neuroticism scale were reported as being more authoritarian, more likely to refrain from reasoning with them, and inconsistent in their reward giving. Relationships in such families were often described as harsh and problematic. High neuroticism scorers disclosed a negative impression regarding their own attractiveness, tended to avoid physical exercise and had poor health during their school years. They also recalled wanting to be alone, daydreaming a lot and playing fantasy games as children.

Extroversion was associated with memories of a warm, supportive family background in which parents encouraged their children to engage in various activities and paid them plenty of attention. Satisfying relationships with parents and other family members were important to extroverts. They also found mixing with other people a rewarding experience. Extroverts tended to engage in individual and team sports and started dating early. This personality type showed interest in creative activities from an early age and the most highly valued activities were those that brought them into contact with other people.

Conclusion

Interest in the use of biodata as a psychological method for classifying individuals goes back to the beginning of the twentieth century. Throughout this period researchers and practitioners have been trying to relate biographical events to work-related behaviours. For the lay person, it is self evident that early experiences have a long-term and profound effect on individuals for the rest of their lives, and that they must affect their working lives as well. Yet, much more research has gone into personality theory and research compared with biodata. How does personality research and assessment differ from biodata research and measurement? Are there any lessons to be learnt from personality research for the biodata enthusiast?

Although there are a large number of quite different personality theories – trait/types; psychodynamic/genetic; physiological/experiential – all try to categorize people along specific delineated dimensions. All personality theories have a unique nomenclature and ideas about how and why people come to have a trait, or be a type. Personality measurement is, therefore, about devising sensitive yet robust psychometric measures of trait or type that allow people to be categorized. This can be done for applied or research reasons. For instance, employers would want to know if their employees were hypochondriacal; and researchers would like to test various theories by comparing and contrasting introverts and extroverts. Usually, in personality theory measurements follow theory.

Biodata may be less appealing to the academic psychologist and management scientist because it tends to be atheoretical. If anything, theory flows from measurement in the sense that people try to derive a theory to explain their results – namely, why some biodata predict occupational behaviour and not others. Biodata are not driven by theory, and the WABs or biodata questionnaires are rarely developed to measure highly specific behavioural traits. They are thus less frequently scrutinized by psychometricians.

There are clearly advantages to being theory-driven and devising measures that allow you to compare people on the same criteria. Theories can be tested and extended, and the scientific enterprise tends to be programmatic and cumulative rather than piecemeal. Also, the level of abstraction at which personality researchers often work makes theorizing more satisfactory. But there can be dangers in theoretical construction and debate. For many, personality research has progressed precious little over the past 50 years.

Whatever the advantages and disadvantages of biodata over personality testing, the former does have its special uses. Twenty-five years ago Owens (1976) wisely and correctly pointed out seven reasons why the industrial utility of what he called 'background data' has lead to its increased usage in all sectors of society.

To turn to a more eclectic view, biodata seems likely to be employed to serve many of the following purposes in the years immediately ahead.

1. With Equal Employment Opportunity Commission (EEOC) and Office of Federal Contract Compliance (OFCC) applying substantial deterrent pressures to industrial testing, biodata may be used either to predict test scores, and indirectly their criterion correlates, or to directly predict the criterion variables, themselves.
2. Under the pressures recognized in point 1 above, biodata may come into increasing prominence as a relatively race- and culture-fair predictor.
3. In view of the fact that there are numerous biodata correlates of differential age changes in mental abilities, it seems reasonable to expect a longitudinal study of cause and effect relationships. If the biodata-appraised characteristics are antecedent to the intellective changes, biodata could be used to predict which management candidates could be expected to display most intellectual growth, or at least decline, subsequent to selection.
4. Because biodata have proven to be excellent predictors of measured interests, job tenure, and choice behaviour, they seem likely to find increasing use in the prediction of an expanded range of motivation-saturated criteria.
5. Biodata devices will undoubtedly continue to be particularly useful in discriminating among persons whose status argues that they must be relatively homogenous with respect to mental ability, for example, scientists, executives, the creative, etc.
6. If subjects with similar biodata-defined backgrounds are of greater than average compatibility, then the efficiency of the workforce may depend to a very important extent on discovering who should work with whom.
7. Because biodata scales tend to be of high validity, and because biodata items and both cluster and factor scales are characterized by very low intercorrelations, it is apparent that the substance of biodata lends itself uncommonly well to the construction of devices to fit the personnel classification function.

In summary, the predictions of Galton and Guthries have been amply fulfilled. Past behaviour, as recorded in background data, is indeed an excellent predictor of future behaviour. What is new, strangely enough, is our recognition that it *is* precisely this past behaviour or prior experience that scored autobiographical data primarily measures. Given this recognition, many new perspectives are possible. We can build conceptual models, and we can envision the role and place of biodata devices in the area of measurement and in the broader domains of psychology and the behavioural sciences. It is too early to definitely predict the shape of research to come, but it is not too early to note that the vistas are intriguing and the effort of great promise.

Chapter 3
Different Approaches
to Biodata

So far we have established that biographical information, or 'biodata', has a long history in the context of employment selection – longer perhaps than that of personality testing. Biodata comprise discrete, often verifiable, details about a person's background which can be used to predict future performance in a particular work situation, or, more widely, in terms of general success (or failure) at work. Biodata are also to be distinguished from measures of personality, even though in their 'softer' form they may seem similar. Biodata may nevertheless show relationships with certain personality factors. Biodata can be most readily differentiated in terms of content classifications, and by the format in which they are presented. Three well-known distinctions are: biodata versus personality data; hard versus soft biodata; and biodata versus background investigations.

Biodata Items Versus Personality Items

Many 'biographical' items look remarkably like personality inventory items. What is the conceptual difference between personality inventory questions and biodata questions? First, biodata questions allow a definite specific, unique answer, whereas personality questions often do not. Most biodata questions could be argued about sensibly (notably, whether they actually occurred), which many personality questions cannot be. Second, personality inventory questions are carefully phrased to elicit rapid, unthinking replies, whereas biodata items often sound quite clumsy in their desire to specify precisely the information they want. Third, personality inventories have fixed keys, whereas biodata items are rekeyed for each selection task.

The distinction between a personality inventory and a biodata inventory, however, can often be a very fine one. Some biodata questionnaires contain items that 'look' like personality items. Indeed, some biodata inventories have actually taken items from established personality inventories, thus making the distinction between them even cloudier. Consider, for example:

It is often impractical to involve other people when decisions have to be made.
1. Strongly disagree.
2. Disagree.
3. Unsure.
4. Agree.
5. Strongly agree.

Whenever I have made important decisions ...
1. I usually involved other people.
2. I involved other people only if it was practical to do so.
3. I usually made up my own mind.
4. I haven't made any important decisions.

The first item is taken from the Occupational Personality Questionnaire (Saville and Holdsworth, 1984) and the second is a 'biodata-ized' version. Apart from asking a more concrete question about *experience* of decision making rather than decision-making in the abstract – hence the need for an 'opt-out' option in the second example – it is a moot point whether or not the two items are really measuring the same thing. Certainly, a high correlation between the two should be expected. In this case, the biodata-ized version of the item also represents an example of the second distinction – that between 'hard' and 'soft' items.

Hard Versus Soft Biodata

Despite the claimed advantage of biodata – that they largely comprise verifiable items of information about individuals – the inclusion of questions that depart from being simply questions about life history or past experiences and background, and that concern themselves more with matters of belief or opinion, undermines the benefits that are claimed for the technique.

The distinction has been drawn, for instance, between 'hard' and 'soft' biodata items. The former represent historical and verifiable information about an individual, whereas the latter are of a more abstract or private nature and cover value judgements, aspirations, motivations, attitudes and expectations. Some writers have argued that *only* an individual's historical experiences, events or situations that are verifiable should be classified as biographical information. Using this system, most items on the usual application form would be classed as biodata, but not those typical of an extended biographical questionnaire. However, research has shown that there may be some value also in including softer items. While 'they may be open to distortion' and could lead individuals to 'fictionalize' their past lives (Asher, 1972: 252), they may be useful to tap into success-related constructs not readily measured by hard biodata, particularly 'motivation saturated' job performance criteria (Owens, 1976). Although research comparisons of the two have generally shown that hard items are superior to soft items in predicting job performance criteria, questions about 'soft' issues can nevertheless be useful if used in the appropriate way. In short, both types of item can go some way towards predicting job performance.

Whatever the nature of the individual items in the questionnaire, there is one fundamental difference between biodata and conventional application forms: with biodata the respondent's answers are combined to produce a score analogous to that produced from a test. It is this score, rather than the value-judgements of individuals reading the questionnaire, that is used for selection purposes. Thus, the critical factor with biodata items, whether 'hard' or 'soft', is ultimately that they have predictive value. The validity of biodata in this sense is linked closely with the way in which biodata forms or questionnaires are constructed and biodata can be further differentiated in terms of the method used to construct or derive the items. Before turning to the subject of how biodata are derived there is another distinction that should be drawn.

Biodata and Background Investigations

Information about an individual's background is typically sought on job applicants by prospective employers, on the premise that an individual's past behaviour and experience are useful predictors of future behaviour. The results of hundreds of studies testify to the effectiveness of background data in predicting particular performance in a variety of occupational contexts. A distinction has been drawn between biographical data and personality data. We have also seen, however, that some forms of biodata – notably 'soft' biodata – can sometimes be almost indistinguishable from personality-type items. A further subtle distinction can be made between *biodata inventories* and *background investigations*. Both techniques are designed to elicit historical data about individuals which are deemed to be relevant to judging their suitability for a specific employment position. There are differences between them, however, which it is important to be clear about in defining the range and variety of forms of biodata.

One writer outlined certain features for distinguishing between biodata inventories and background investigations (McDaniel, 1988). One difference between them relates to the type of occupation for which they are used as part of the applicant screening process. Biodata inventories have been used for a variety of occupations, involving unskilled, semi-skilled and skilled labour, and professional and managerial positions. Background investigative data are used mostly when screening people for positions of trust, in which integrity and positive psychological adjustments are important (for example, law enforcement, private security, nuclear power security). One example of this form of checking out job applicants is to examine their credit history. This would generally focus on whether they have a negative credit history. Another example might be to check out any record of criminal arrest.

Another distinction is concerned with the way data are assessed. Biodata inventories are scored in an empirical fashion, whereas background investigation data are dealt with more judgementally, often using a rationally developed standard. Thus, on biodata inventories the respondent's score is added up and a pass–fail assessment is made on the basis of whether or not the obtained score exceeds or falls below an empirically defined threshold. With background investigation data, if information comes to light that the applicant has used drugs, then that might be sufficient to exclude him or her from further consideration.

Little research has been dedicated to testing the efficacy of background investigation data, as defined here. There have, however, been closed-coded background investigation-type items included in biodata inventories, one example being the Educational and Biographical Information Survey (EBIS; Means and Perelman, 1984). This self-report inventory contains questions that deal with educational experiences, drug and alcohol use, criminal activities and driving record. It thus taps many of the content areas found in background investigations. Several studies have used the EBIS (Means, Laurence and Waters, 1984; Means and Perelman 1984; Means and Heisey, 1986; Means and Laurence, 1986; McDaniel, 1988).

Two studies, in particular, have used the EBIS to examine the structure of background data as obtained through an empirically keyed biodata inventory. Steinhouse (1988) examined relationships between EBIS variables and military attrition during the first 20 months of service. Using a factor analysis with EBIS data, Steinhouse produced a six-factor solution reflecting the following groups of characteristics: general non-conformity and getting into trouble; alcohol use and illegal drug use; history of criminal offences; quitting behaviour (failing to finish courses and so on); high school achievement; and employment experience.

McDaniel (1989) subsequently extended the previous study, once again using the EBIS with military personnel. A similar factor structure emerged, this time comprising seven factors rather than six (see Table 3.1). In a regression analysis, scores on these factors and on a test of cognitive ability were related to the occurrence of early discharge from service. All seven factors were statistically significant predictors of unsuitable discharge from the armed forces, with the quitting school and school suspension scales yielding the highest validities.

Although background investigations may be justifiable in the military or for sensitive occupations, their use by other organizations for more traditional types of employment is highly questionable. Hence this is another reason for regarding them as distinct from biodata.

'Rationally' or 'Empirically' Derived Biodata

Biodata measures depend on retrospective self-report data from respondents about past experiences deemed relevant to the particular job selection exercise

Table 3.1: Factor analysis and reliability results for the EBIS data set

Factor label	Description	No. of retained items	Reliability: Alpha	Test–retest reliability
1. School suspension	Suspended from school; fought in school	7	0.81	0.80
2. Drug use	Frequently used drugs; began use at early age	9	0.79	0.46
3. Quitting school	Considered quitting school; reasons for wanting to quit school; years of schooling	8	0.49	0.86
4. Employment experience	Worked outside the home; reasons for leaving jobs	9	0.60	0.75
5. Grades and school clubs	School grades; participated in school clubs	8	0.67	0.82
6. Legal system contacts	Arrested or convicted for offences as juvenile or adult	7	0.51	0.55
7. Socioeconomic status	Parents highly educated; high family income when teenager; father's discipline strict; father in home	5	0.63	0.82

Source: McDaniel (1989). Reproduced with permission.
Note: EBIS = Educational and Biographical Information Survey; descriptions depict attributes for high scores on factor scales.

in which the methodology is being used. The predictive power of a biodata instrument depends on the ability of its constituent items to represent past events of most relevance to the job role under consideration (Mumford and Owens, 1987). The techniques that are deployed to compile biodata items are therefore very important. More than one type of technique has been used in this context. A broad distinction has been made between rational and empirical techniques for biodata item selection (Owens, 1976; Mumford and Owens, 1987). Each of these approaches has its own idiosyncratic advantages and disadvantages (Mitchell and Klimoski, 1982; Schoenfeldt, 1992).

Until the mid-1970s, the most popular method for developing a biographical inventory was through a strictly empirical approach. This meant that biodata items were selected on the basis of their capacity to discriminate between people according to certain criteria such as their performance at work. The empirical keying approach is thus founded on item-criterion relationships, and it is intended to maximize the prediction of an external criterion such as tenure or job performance. By the mid-1930s, empirical keying methods for weighting application forms had become so commonplace that Long and Sandiford (1935) could review 23 different methods. According to England (1971: 10), the intelligent development of a weighted application form can be outlined as follows:

1. Personal history information such as age, years of education, previous occupations, and marital status represent important aspects of a person's total background and should be useful in selection. The major assumption is that how one will behave in the future is best predicted by how one has behaved in the past or by characteristics associated with past behaviour.
2. Certain aspects of a person's total background should be related to whether or not he will be successful in a specific position. Numerous studies have shown that information contained in application forms is predictive in selecting employees for certain types of positions. Personal factors such as age, years of education, previous occupations, and marital status have been found to be correlated with indicators of desirable employee behaviour (length of service, supervisory ratings, sales volume, and average salary increase).
3. A way is needed of determining which aspects of a person's total background are important for a given occupation. The WAB (Weighted Application Blank) technique identified those items on an application form that differentiate between groups of desirable and undesirable employees in a given occupation.
4. A way of combining the important aspects of a person's total background is needed so we can predict whether or not he is likely to be successful in a given occupation. By determining the predictive power of each application blank item, it is possible to assign numerical weights or scores to each possible answer. Weights for these items may then be totalled for each individual and a minimum total score established, which, if used at the time of hiring, will eliminate the maximum number of undesirable candidates with a minimum loss of desirable candidates.

The WAB technique, then, provides one systematic method for determining which personal factors are important in specific occupations and how to use them in selection. Use of the WAB technique in the employment process permits rapid screening of applicants by means of a simple scoring of the application blank. WAB results also can be used in combination with test and interview information to further improve screening and placement.

Although the empirical approach frequently yielded significant results, its very nature presented some problems (Mitchell and Klimoski, 1982). It has been attacked on several fronts. For instance, it has been argued that the non-job relevance of scoring procedures could violate the spirit, if not the letter, of employment legislation (Pace and Schoenfeldt, 1977). Additionally, it has been suggested that the validity and usefulness of the WAB technique may be substantially overstated in the literature (Schwab and Oliver, 1974). For example, the empirical keying capitalizes on chance variation. It frequently uncovers relations that do not hold up over time. It has been argued that the predictive power of empirically derived biodata items is limited by the nature of the criterion used to define it (Thayer, 1977; Mumford and Owens, 1987). Transient applicant pools may also distort the predictive validity of biodata items where the characteristics of the item development sample become radically altered as the population is replaced with significantly differing types of people (Wernimont, 1962; Schwab and Oliver, 1974). More generally, the empirical keying approach has been criticized for its basic empiricism (Dunnette, 1962; Baehr and Williams, 1968). The approach has been challenged for failing to advance any theoretical understanding of just *why* biodata would predict the criteria of interest (Mitchell and Klimoski, 1982).

Thus, critics of the technique advocated a rational approach to biodata analysis (Owens, 1976). In such an approach, a conceptual framework or theory guides instrument construction. Inventory items are selected *a priori* to measure constructs that are thought to be related to the criterion. Procedures such as factor analysis are used to derive scores that are then related to the criterion of interest. Thus, when significant relations are obtained, they can be interpreted and understood. As early as 1951, however, exploratory work had begun on devising a more rationally based strategy for scoring biographical data (Levine and Zachert, 1951). Within the next few years several examples of *personal history construct* approaches to the development of 'rational' scoring systems for biographical data emerged (Loenvinger, Gleser and Dubois, 1953; Morrison, Owens, Glennon and Albright, 1962; Baehr and Williams, 1967; Matteson, Osborn and Sparks, 1969; Klimoski, 1973).

It should be added perhaps that the 'rational' school of biodata construction does not usually go in for very elaborate theories. Indeed, by the standards of personality research, rational biodata inventory construction is still very empirically minded. Rather than isolate and examine the predictive effectiveness of single biodata items, this perspective tends instead to refer to the predictive capacity of composites of such items derived through correlational or derivative forms of statistical analysis. Such constructs are regarded as representing psychologically meaningful personal history variables (Mitchell and Klimoski, 1982). Advocates of rational biodata approaches have claimed that their method will result in less shrinkage, an assertion that has received some support (Clifton, Kilculan, Reiter-Palmon and Mumford, 1992; Schoenfeldt, 1992), but it has also been challenged (Mitchell and Klimoski, 1982). According to some writers:

> Because the rational approach typically attempts to measure unitary constructs, items that can be clearly related to a single construct, and then combined into homogeneous scales, are preferred. In turn, this should generally lead to a preference for subjective, temperament-like items which can be focused on one, and only one, construct. By contrast, performance of heterogeneous, objective behaviours often draws on multiple individual characteristics, and responses to items about these behaviours are difficult to assign to the influence of a single construct. (Mael and Hirsch, 1993: 720)

The same writers noted that one difficulty with the rational approach stems from the assignment of individual biodata items to categories or constructs. It is possible to conceive of items that could quite reasonably and legitimately be allocated to more than one construct. An example here would be having served as head pupil at school. This could signify self-confidence or dominance or possibly be indicative of high intellect or good interpersonal skills.

The rational approaches have generally relied on the theoretical interpretability of internal variance analyses (results of factor analysis or internal consistency analyses). Rational approaches attempt to quantify composites of items that measure an interpretable set of constructs. Most typically in biographical inventories, the component model of factor analysis is used to compute personal history scores on each of several obtained dimensions. These scores are then related to some criterion of interest.

Matteson (1978) proposed item analysis of biographical data to find sets of closely related facts; his target was a group of four items that were homogeneous in item content and highly correlated. Analysis of 75 items in successful and unsuccessful applicants for oil refinery maintenance and construction work produced 12 keys. Each key contained at least six items, which was believed to make the scores derived from them more reliable and less subject to chance fluctuations. Matteson also predicted that such keys would suffer less 'shrinkage' and be more 'transportable'.

In their simplest form, then, biodata items reflect performance outcomes – that is, knowledge of previous event outcomes can be used to predict future event outcomes, though the causal influences are unknown. At a more complex level, biographical information may focus on the personal characteristics and behaviour behind a particular performance outcome. That is, predictors that reflect any individual's values, attitudes and beliefs, and that capture developmental processes associated with some prior life event, are related to the criterion of interest (Guion, 1965; Ferguson, 1967; Mitchell, 1986).

Theoretical Developments in Biodata Measurement

Owens (1968, 1971) took this idea further and used biodata to classify people. Building on this notion of meaningful prior life experiences, Owens developed a theoretical framework for biodata – the Developmental/Integrative (DI) Model. Underlying the DI model is the notion that 'different kinds of individuals undergo differing patterns of experiences as they develop, and that, if this is true, then identifying these experiential patterns also identifies the kinds of person who have them' (Owens, 1976: 571). In other words, although people are influenced by their experiences, by virtue of their nature (traits and values) they seek or avoid many experiences and situations on the basis of perceived compatibility with their self-perceptions (Owens, 1976; Owens and Schoenfeldt, 1979). Hence the DI model is developmental in that it emphasizes antecedent life experiences that represent fundamental inputs at critical stages in a person's development. The model is integrative in that such past experiences need to be described not only in terms of their outcomes, but also in terms of the values, traits and behaviours of the individual.

To develop the model, Owens and Schoenfeldt (1979) reported a procedure in which an initial pool of 2000 items was generated which represented a wide range of behavioural and personal history categories. 'Rational screening' reduced this number down to 659, which were then administered to 1700 male undergraduates. Through a process of further division of items and factor analyses of responses, further item reductions were achieved until a core of 142 items was arrived at, which clustered statistically into nine groups.

The item pool was again extended by adopting a more lenient statistical criterion for inclusion of some of those criteria that had previously been dropped. This newly extended set of items was given to a further sample of more than 1000 undergraduates. Following further statistical analyses, a 118-item short form was developed which was composed of those items that best accounted for variation in response. This short form was subsequently used with further samples of undergraduates, with factor analyses yielding 13 categories of items for men and 15 categories for women.

These instruments were used to develop a classification system to identify subgroups of individuals with internally homogeneous and externally heterogeneous patterns of input and prior experience variables. The assertion made by Owens and Schoenfeldt that subgroup membership should determine a wide range of behaviours has found considerable support from other researchers.

Empirical support for the DI model has been found in stable factor structures (Eberhardt and Muchinsky, 1982a, 1982b; Lautenschlager and Shaffer, 1987) and scoring keys for biodata items (Brown, 1978) over long periods of time, as well as in its usefulness in differentiating groups and aiding in the interpretation of concurrent measurement and field studies (Rychlak, 1982; Mumford and Owens, 1984).

Sub-group membership seems, for example, to be related to academic achievement (Klein, 1972), dropping out of college (Nutt, 1975), voting behaviour (Golembiewski, Billingsley and Munzenrider, 1970), drug misuse (Strimbu and Schoenfeldt, 1973) and even interpersonal attraction (Bowditch, 1969; Jones, 1971). Owens and Schoenfeldt's approach has been deservedly influential and their classification of persons has proved extremely compelling. Nevertheless, it is essentially a *measurement* model. It does not yield a great insight into how particular developmental experiences influence behaviour, as it is not sufficient to link specific biodata items to specific job performance criteria. The model does not yet indicate *how* particular developmental experiences influence behaviour; in other words, the level of understanding of *why* biodata inventories predict future performance has not kept pace with the development of different types of biodata items. Again, the premise of DI theory is that different individuals have different patterns of meaningful life experiences. With DI theory as a launching point, one might ask whether knowledge of individuals' past meaningful life experiences can be used to generate biodata items with high predictive validity and strong explanatory power.

Stokes, Owens and other members of the University of Georgia's Institute of Behavioral Research (Stokes, Mumford and Owens, 1989b; Stokes, Jackson and Owens, 1990; Stokes and Reddy, 1992) have taken up the challenge and attempted to refine their model to overcome its original limitations. While conducting perhaps the most extensive longitudinal study of the subgroups identified by the Biographical Questionnaire (BQ), Stokes, Meechan, Block and Hogan (1989a) noted both continuity and discontinuity in subgroup membership over a 6–8 year period. In the case of six out of 23 male and five out of 15 female subgroups there was no significant pathway between the adolescent and the adult subgroups. This discontinuity was attributed to various intervening life experiences, such as individuals being successful in their attempts to gain entry into their chosen profession on graduation. These and other results led Stokes and colleagues to propose a general theoretical framework they called the 'Ecology Model' (Mumford, Stokes and Owens, 1990). The following account of the model is taken from a review of the area by Stokes:

> Basically, the model suggests that individual development proceeds as a result of the ongoing interchange between individuals and their environments. Individuals bring to any situation their pasts, including their intellectual resources, personality resources, and social resources, which have been formed on the basis of their heredity and early environments and which are influenced continuously by interactions and experiences throughout their lives. Because individuals' time and energy are inherently limited, they must make choices throughout their lives regarding their activities. Presumably, they will select certain activities for their potential value for advancing their long-term adaptation to the environment. This choice behaviour results in a process of channelled differential development whereby differential characteristics initially emerge, and then, are maintained. Future activity selections and their outcomes lead to a further refinement of the individuals' characteristics. Over time, individuals create an interpretable developmental trajectory which can be predicted.
> (Stokes and Reddy, 1992: 288)

The value of the model is that it provides a *causal* framework for understanding how individual characteristics and experiences lead to criterion performance. The ecology model's general precepts can be used to develop biodata items that address causal and developmental influences – manifest measures of the social, personality and intellectual resource domains, the filter and choice process – which can be related to specific occupational outcomes through individual choice of actions. The ecology model thus has implications for generating items with strong predictive power – the problem with the DI approach discussed earlier. Test of the model have so far been encouraging (Caspi, Bem and Elder, 1989; Stokes, Meechan, Block and Hogan, 1989a; Wesley, 1989). Such tests have also begun to explain why a biodata key developed in one group will not necessarily predict the same criterion in another group. If the 'developmental trajectories' of the two groups are different because of cultural or environmental influences affecting personal choice, or even the situations that an individual may encounter, the biodata key can hardly be expected to generalize from one group to another.

The Validity of Rational Versus Empirical Methods

Although each perspective has its proponents who espouse its inherent advantages and disadvantages in assessing the predictive value of life history data, there have been few direct comparisons of the efficacy of each technique. Except for a comparison of empirical item keying versus rational approaches to analysing a psychological climate questionnaire (Hornick, James and Jones, 1977) and a military study (Berkeley, 1953) that compared rational and empirical approaches for keying a biographical inventory, a field test of the usefulness of these two approaches had not been reported in the organizational behaviour literature before the 1980s.

In an effort to fill this gap, Mitchell and Klimoski (1982) conducted a study among nearly 700 job entrants into real estate sales in which biographical and criterion data were collected on a longitudinal basis. The cross-validities and predictive accuracies of empirical and rational approaches to biodata scoring were compared.

Biographical items were selected from existing item pools (for example, Glennon, Albright and Owens, 1966), and generated through interviews with real estate brokers and associates and a review of existing salesperson job analyses. Using the empirical approach (which will be discussed in more detail in Chapter 4), scores on biodata items were compared between employees who fell into high-performing and low-performing groups in organizations. In this case, the criterion was to obtain a licence to sell real estate in the US state in which the study took place. Biodata items were therefore weighted according to the extent to which they differentiated between individuals who had obtained a licence and those who had failed to do so.

The rational approach emphasizes the identification of items that measure a theoretically meaningful set of constructs. In the present study this analysis involved: (a) an examination of the tasks performed by the real estate sales associate, (b) a perusal of the literatures on career counselling and career development, and (c) a review of psychological and sociological theories regarding the influence of background factors on career success. This, in turn, led to a proposed set of four *a priori* life history constructs: (a) drive, (b) conventional success, (c) social orientation, and (d) real estate involvement.

Each of the items was initially viewed as a hypothetical continuum on which its multiple-choice alternatives could be positioned. Unit weights were then assigned to alternatives as a function of ordinal position on the continuum. The biographical dimensions produced by Mitchell and Klimoski are shown in Table 3.2.

The amount of shrinkage (that is, loss in validity from derivation to cross-validation) was compared for the rational versus empirical approaches using a test of the difference between correlation coefficients obtained on two

Table 3.2: Obtained life history dimensions

Components

I. *Financial ascendance.* High expectation for future financial success, self-confidence in a variety of situations, energetic, desire for authority over others, an early financial orientation, and positive values for financial achievement.

II. *Economic establishment.* Financially established and secure, most likely married, tending to be older, active in community and civic affairs, socially ascendant, professional knowledge and contacts beyond what would be expected of a younger person.

III. *Real estate professional identification.* Real estate career plans, realistic outlook regarding the actual demands of the profession, sales knowledge, active in real estate in some capacity in the past, high expectation for real estate career success, friends and family involved in real estate.

IV. *Educational background.* History of academic success, socially active in school years, participation in extracurricular activity, stimulating experiences in school, early leadership, a stable childhood environment, and secure family situation facilitating educational achievement.

V. *Social enthusiasm.* Strong social confidence, enjoyment in meeting and introducing oneself and others to new people, resistant to social rejection, interpersonally perceptive, socially oriented, socially supportive, healthful, and emotionally positive.

VI. *Sales personality.* History of success in sales pursuits, early financial independence, competitive nature, early sales contacts and knowledge, commission sales experience, and a tendency to ask favours of others.

Source: Mitchell and Klimoski (1982).

separate samples. For the rational approach, shrinkage was not substantial (in fact, validity was slightly higher in the cross-validation sample). On the other hand, shrinkage for empirical approaches was appreciable. The validity coefficients for the rational versus empirical methods were also compared in each of the derivation and cross-validation samples. It was found that the derivation validity for the empirical method was significantly greater than the derivation validity for the rational method. More importantly, the cross-validity for the empirical approach was significantly greater than the cross-validity for the rational approach.

In an effort to assess the practical differences between the two methods, cutting scores were derived on the basis of the derivation sample and applied to the cross-validation sample. This procedure determined the point of greatest differentiation between high and low criterion groups based on differences in mean response frequencies for each group at each predicted WAB value. This was done for the rational and the empirical approach. These scores were then used to sort members of the cross-validation sample into either (a) high or (b) low predicted criterion groups. These same individuals were also cross-sorted into high versus low groups by known criterion status (that is, licensed versus unlicensed).

The empirical approach resulted in a cut score that eliminated 59.4% of the failures while retaining 80.5% of the successes in the cross-validation sample. The rational approach was somewhat less effective, but none the less managed to eliminate 62.4% of the failures while retaining 68.8% of the successes. On comparing the percentages of individuals correctly classified by each of the two approaches, it was found that the rational approach correctly classified 232 people, whereas the empirical approach correctly classified 245 people, giving the latter a net 6% advantage over the other approach. If the primary purpose of using biodata is prediction, then, as Mitchell and Klimoski note, it is indeed 'rational to be empirical' – a topic to which we return in Chapter 5.

Conclusion

This chapter discussed different types of biodata. Essentially, there are three sorts of major differences: the criteria by which items are admitted and/or excluded as biodata questions; the way in which biodata items are combined into subcategories; and the sorts of biodata factors/clusters that emerge. At present there remains no agreed set of items making up an interpretable multi-dimensional scale that is widely used. To some extent, this is a pity and reflects the non-cumulative nature of the research. It would be interesting if there were various factor-analytic studies of rather different databases, but using the same questions, to check the factor solutions. Once an agreed, interpretable and limited number of factors were forthcoming, it might be useful again to test across studies the predictive power of various of these factors.

The various life-history taxonomies that exist seem eminently sensible and useful. But there still seems to be a reluctance to build on other research in using the same instrument. Certainly, there is also a resistance to using too many 'soft' items in biodata research, no doubt because then the difference between biodata and personality research is considerably reduced and the former simply becomes an atheoretical type of the latter.

However, there is a constant struggle between those empirical biodata researchers who want the 'numbers to speak for themselves' by doing atheoretical multivariate analysis on their data, and those more concerned with meaning and theory who try to make sense of their data at every stage of analysis. Most biodata practitioners are not extremists: many attempt to interpret their findings but are happy to rely on the statistical results for their predictions. Both researchers and practitioners want to be better at assessing potential in people at work. They strive to understand why biographical factors relate to business success and failure.

Chapter 4
Why Use Biodata?

Personnel and human resources managers are frequently called on to give advice as to which person to recruit into the organization, select for promotion, send on particular training courses, provide counselling to or remove from the organization. Effective decisions on all of these issues are based on valid, reliable and predictive information about the person with regard to their skills and experience, their past and current performance, and how they are likely to perform in the future.

Personnel and human resources officers can obtain information about job applicants and current staff through a variety of methods. In selection and recruitment, in particular, the job interview together with information supplied by candidates on an application form, have represented the core techniques for assessing applicants.

Over the past decade or so, the standard interview has been supplemented in increasing numbers of organizations by the use of psychological tests of many kinds. Psychological tests of ability and personality have been especially popular and are characterized by a number of specific advantages and disadvantages.

Among the main advantages of psychological testing are:

1. Tests provide numeric information that means individuals can more easily be compared on the same criteria. In interviews, different questions are asked of different candidates, and the answers are often forgotten.
2. With data-based records one can trace a person's development over time. In fact, by going back to test results in a person's file one can actually see if, and by how much, the tests were predictive of later success.
3. Tests give explicit and specific results on temperament and ability rather than the vague, ambiguous, coded platitudes that are often found in references. A percentage of a sten score (a standardized statistic measuring an aspect of a person's character), provided, of course, that it is valid, makes for much clearer thinking about personal characteristics than terms like satisfactory, sufficient or high-flyer.

4. Tests are fair because they eliminate corruption, favouritism, old-boy, mason or Oxbridge networks from self-perpetuating. That is, if a person does not have the ability or a 'dangerous' profile, they will not be chosen irrespective of their other 'assets'.
5. Tests are comprehensive in that they cover all the basic dimensions of personality and ability from which other behaviour patterns derive.
6. Tests are scientific in that they are soundly empirically based on theoretical foundations – that is, they are reliable, valid and able to discriminate the good from the mediocre and the average from the bad.

Many, often related, objections are made to psychological testing. Among the most common and sensible objections are:

1. Many of these tests are fakeable – that is, people like to put themselves in a good light and receive a good score so that they may be accepted, but, in a way, this reflects their real personality (some tests have lie scores to attempt to overcome this).
2. Some people do not have sufficient self-insight to actually report on their own feelings and behaviour – that is, it is not that people lie, but that they cannot, rather than will not, give accurate answers about themselves (some tests look only for simple behavioural data to overcome this).
3. Tests are unreliable in that all sorts of temporary factors, such as test anxiety, boredom, weariness, a headache, period pains, all lead people to give different answers on different occasions (although this is partly true, it is only a minor factor).
4. Most importantly, tests are invalid – they do not measure what they say they are measuring and those scores do not predict behaviour over time. For many tests this is indeed the Achilles heel and they are lamentably short of robust proof of their validity.
5. They might be able to measure all sorts of dimensions of behaviour but not the crucial ones to the organization like trustworthiness and likelihood of absenteeism. Buying personality tests is like having a set menu, and what many managers want is an à la carte menu where they can select only what they want.
6. People have to be sufficiently literate or articulate to do these tests, not to mention sufficiently familiar with North American jargon. Many organizations therefore believe that their workforce could not do the tests properly, they would take too much time or would cause needless embarrassment.
7. There are not good norms for the population they want to test and comparing them to white US students can be dangerously misleading.
8. The tests are unfair and biased towards WASPs (White Anglo-Saxon Protestants); hence white males tend to do better or get a more attractive profile and therefore get selected. They therefore fly in the face of anti-discriminatory legislation by being meritocratic, which to some people is unethical.

9. Interpretation of the tests takes skill, insight and experience and this is either too expensive or not available. In the wrong hands they are dangerous because profiles are given either inaccurate or too literal interpretations.

10. Freedom of information legislation may mean that candidates would be able to see and hence challenge either the scores themselves, their interpretation or the decisions made based on them. The less objective the recorded data, the better.

11. As tests become known, people could buy copies and practise so that they know the correct or most desirable answers. This happens extensively with ability and personality testing and when it does happen results may have more to do with preparation and practice than reflecting true ability.

Because the above 'objections' or 'disadvantages' seem to outweigh the advantages, many organizations have turned to biodata as a supplement or even as an alternative to other selection procedures. It is worth noting, however, that many of the problems identified with other selection techniques apply to biodata also. In this chapter, we look at both reasons for, and objections to, biodata in the selection process.

Reasons for Using Biodata

Biodata represent *one* objective and systematic way of making use of information about past events to predict future job success. This objectivity brings certain advantages. The same questions are asked of everyone who completes the weighted application blank (WAB) or biodata form, and the answers given are often assessed in a consistent way. In this sense a biodata questionnaire is probably a fairer means of selection than more conventional procedures. It is also possible to monitor candidates' responses to individual questions and to eliminate items that show evidence of discrimination against some social groups. This is a far more difficult proposition with the traditional interview, for example, where the overall decision can be monitored quite easily, but not so the questions that led to the decision.

When developed properly, biodata devices are demonstrably related to job performance because this is the basis on which items are selected for inclusion in the first place. This is important in terms of most countries' equal opportunities employment legislation, since job relatedness is usually regarded as the acid test of the appropriateness of a selection procedure.

As we saw earlier in this book, biodata can be collected in two principal formats, the WAB and the extended biodata questionnaire or inventory. From the candidates' point of view, the only real difference between these two formats is length. The application form is a much shorter instrument than the questionnaire and takes much less time for the candidate to fill out. Whichever format is used, research has shown that either can provide effective predictive information provided that the items included have been appropriately selected and validated. We shall return to the subject of validity of biodata in Chapter 6; suffice to say that it is the one area where there is least debate. Most researchers would agree that biodata are valid for a wide range of occupations. Asher (1972), for example, examined a series of studies that had explored the predictive value of biodata with a large number of different occupational groups (including architects, college students, door-to-door salesmen, engineers, clerical workers, hospital aides, insurance salesmen and research scientists). He laid down certain criteria according to which the studies were selected. In each case, cross-validation of their biodata items had been expressed as a correlation statistic, biographical items were used in combination as predictors rather than as single items and the definition of biodata items was judged to be historical and verifiable throughout.

On comparing biodata with other test predictors, Asher reported favourable results for biodata. In connection with prediction of job proficiency, biographical items were better than the intelligence test by two to one, were better than spatial relations measures by 18 to one, and stayed ahead of a range of other psychometric tests at varying validity coefficient levels. As we shall see in later sections, empirically keyed background data measures yield cross-validated validity coefficients in the low 0.40s against performance and attendance criteria, and they have been shown to be capable of predicting a range of criteria from managerial progress to theft behaviour. A number of researchers have concluded that the predictive power of background data measures is sufficient to consider it one of the few legitimate alternatives to standardized testing for personnel selection (Reilly and Chao, 1982). Finally, biodata forms can be developed in multiple-choice formats which are amenable to machine scoring or direct entry to a computer terminal. Thus, processing large numbers of applicants can become a routine clerical activity, freeing up valuable personnel professionals' or line managers' time.

Other Advantages: Theoretical Issues

A number of theoretical reasons have been put forward to explain why biodata can provide better predictive accuracy than other test data. According to the 'non-fiction theory', one explanation for the better accuracy and predictive value of biodata in relation to a range of specific work behaviours is that these weighted items are representative of an individual's history whereas other predictors, especially the unstructured interview, may be a caricature. In an interview, for instance, the individual can present a fictionalized concept of him/herself, whereas the biodata form, whether a WAB or more extensive questionnaire, is more apt to be a systematic, comprehensive collection of factual information about the individual.

The 'relevant-item theory' makes the point that the validity of any test may be dampened because it is a set of 'relevant' and 'irrelevant' items (Lykken and Rose, 1963). The predictive value of many psychometric tests may be undermined because they contain items of dubious validity in the context of predicting specific job-related behaviour. Biodata instruments pose less of a problem in this respect because only job-relevant or performance-relevant items are selected for inclusion in the first place.

The 'point-to-point theory' explains that biodata tests work because they escape the fallacy of attempting to make predictions by measuring general mediators. For instance, a classic strategy in testing is to assume that criterion behaviour (behaviour to be predicted) is controlled or determined by generalized mediators such as traits, aptitudes or intelligence. The problem then is to measure the general mediators. The more accurate the measurement, the higher the probability that criterion behaviour can be estimated with precision. This approach is based on the behavioural consistency model. Wernimont and Campbell (1968) suggested, for instance, that good predictors of job performance should be 'samples' of future job-related behaviours. This implies that individuals succeed to the extent that they already perform some of the behaviours required for successful job performance, and that this is indicated by their biodata.

While this is certainly true of some items, such as previous work experience or educational attainment, this explanation copes less well with 'soft' biodata (which could be regarded as 'signs' rather than as 'samples') and not at all for some items cited in the literature. A rationale for those kinds of item can nevertheless be found in the DI model (Owens and Schoenfeldt, 1979) introduced earlier.

Practical Advantages

As we have already seen, biodata represent another format for the traditional selection or employment interview, with the advantages that (a) every interviewee is asked the same questions in exactly the same way, and (b) the value judgements made by the 'interviewer' are standardized, relevant and of known validity. This format can be used as an extension and revision of the existing and accepted application blank or as a more extended inventory to elicit detailed background information from job applicants or employees.

Studies by Mosel and Cozan (1952) and by Keating, Paterson and Stones (1950) suggest that correlations between information provided by the applicant and that obtained from previous employers are very high; virtually all correlation coefficients were in the range 0.90–0.99. This is impressive accuracy of reporting *for these selected sorts of verifiable items*.

Biodata are useful in appraising significant, non-cognitive characteristics among employees at levels such that substantial and relatively homogeneous abilities can be inferred from prior performance and/or academic record (for example, Smith, Albright, Glennon and Owens, 1961; Laurent, 1962; Taylor, Ellison and Tucker, 1965). Biodata represent an appealing exploratory device. For example, if good and poor foremen are discriminated by an item dealing with amount of education, the presence of a mental ability test in a subsequent selection battery may well be justified.

The biodata item has both intuitive and intrinsic validity, probably based on the fact that it speaks directly to a central measurement axiom – namely, that how a person will perform in the future can be predicted from how they have performed in the past. Biodata items make it possible to uncover real underlying attributes and experiences that are related to future behaviour. An examination of discriminating item responses can tell a great deal about what kinds of employees remain on a job and what kinds do not, what kinds sell a lot of insurance and what kinds sell little, or what kinds are promoted rapidly. Insights obtained in this fashion may serve anyone from the initial interviewer to the manager who formulates personnel policy.

The usual empirical derivation of both items and scoring keys tends to assume that only job-relevant questions will be asked, and that answers will be evaluated only in terms of their relationship to subsequent job success. There can thus be no justified complaints of wilful discrimination against minority groups. Nor is there any 'hidden exploration of the psyche' in the sense belaboured by Gross (1962). In academic and industrial contexts, biodata have proven themselves at least as good a criterion predictor as cognitive measures, and are less highly correlated with race.

With tests in general and personality questionnaires in particular being the subjects of some rather scathing criticism from time to time, biodata may well enjoy better acceptance than the former, and will almost certainly be more valid than the latter. Since the measurement practitioner is often unsure of the antecedents of what he or she measures, it may be noted that causal-type inferences can be approached by relating biodata-based patterns of prior experience to scores on tests or questionnaires of concern (Chaney and Owens, 1964). Biodata are an efficient, robust and highly valid predictor of a broad spectrum of very practical concerns.

Organizational Advantages

The use of biodata can offer a range of advantages to an organization of a commercial, voluntary or even political nature, and there are distinct cost benefits to be gained as well. The same questions are asked of everyone who completes the form and answers given are assessed in a consistent way. In this sense, a biodata questionnaire is probably a fairer means of selection than more conventional procedures. It is also possible to monitor candidates' responses to individual questions and to eliminate items that show evidence of discrimination against some social groups. Although there may be fairly extensive research and development costs at the outset, once criteria are known, biodata are cheap to use.

The process of developing the scoring key yields further benefits to the organization. Discovering the selection criteria can be useful in itself. Many organizations have never really examined their selection criteria in detail. The criteria have just grown up over time or reflect the personal preferences of recruiters. The process of diagnosing clear selection criteria in advance of setting up a biodata system will have considerable benefits for the whole of the selection process.

The standards set in using biodata are objective and consistent. Reading through application forms is an extremely tedious activity. It is often shared by a number of managers, who may not set precisely the same standards or use the same criteria. This is especially true where similar jobs are being filled across a number of locations or offices, or when recruitment takes place only at specific times of year. The biodata approach allows for basic standards to be set objectively and with total consistency.

Minorities can be identified and treated fairly. In setting up a biodata form, the link between the information on the form and suitability for the job needs to be established. This, in itself, tends to ensure that any other elements are excluded from the selection process. In addition, the research necessary to set up the form can provide the basis for setting up and monitoring an equal opportunities programme. Biodata forms, especially when scored by computer, are completely blind to incidental items such as personal names, which might indicate ethnic background.

Finally, although biodata forms have not always delivered the same level of accuracy in practical use as has been obtained in academic experimentation, their track record is still good. Compared with the normal unstructured interview, which is a typical alternative, or to reading an application form in an unstructured way, they can produce increases in accuracy of many orders of magnitude.

Objections to Biodata

Any method used to select, promote or fire employees naturally attracts a great deal of examination and criticism. The biodata method is no exception. For some, the raw, naked empiricism of the technique is the major failing, whereas, for others, this is its strongest appeal. Critics and reviewers of the biodata method have come up with standard objections. The following are the most common.

Homogeneity versus Heterogeneity

If many biographical items are used in selection, the organization inevitably becomes more homogeneous over time, which has both advantages and disadvantages. Heterogeneity may occur across divisions with different criteria but not within them. A biographical homogeneous organization may be a time bomb if, for some reason, the criteria on which all are chosen no longer predicts success; indeed, may predict the opposite.

Cloning the Past

The biodata method works on the idea that past behaviour predicts current performance, but if current criteria are unstable (say, in a rapidly changing market), one is perpetually out of date. Biodata may be best in stable organizations and environmental conditions, which are becoming increasingly rarer.

Atheoretical

The major disadvantage of biodata being entirely empirical and non-theoretical is that you can never know which of myriad biographical factors to choose from. Theory-based approaches can explain and indicate which factors predict, and can help choose which ones to use in different situations.

Time-consuming

In a predictive design, the questionnaire is intended to be used for applicants – hence it is developed using data from applicants. This can be very time-consuming if an organization does not have a regular intake of new staff. It might, for example, take at least 12 months to obtain reliable, meaningful criterion data on new employees. There could even be a delay of several years between sending the research form out to applicants, waiting until sufficient numbers of applicants have joined the organization and been in post long enough to gather job performance data, and then completing the development of the scoring key.

Content Validity

One common criticism is that biodata items often lack the content validity required in industrial selection. This critical issue has been examined in at least two sets of investigations. One found that managerial assessment centre performance was predicted only by background data (Quaintance, 1981). Elsewhere it has been found that content valid background data items could be formulated on the basis of job requirements that showed substantial predictive validity (Mumford, Cooper and Schwimmer, 1983).

Faking

Biodata have been shown to be fakeable. Goldstein (1971) checked information given by applicants for a nursing aide post with what previous employers said. Half of the sample overestimated how long they had worked for their previous employer. Overstating previous salary and describing part-time work as full-time were also common. More seriously, a quarter gave reasons for leaving their last job the employer did not agree with, and no less than 17% gave as their last employer someone who had never heard of them.

Biodata Do Not Travel Well

The same criteria do not have the same predictability across jobs, organizations or time periods. Biodata instruments developed to predict performance of employees in one organization may be ineffective in another organization. Instruments based on one set of employees who have been cultivated into their organization's value system may be affected by that idiosyncratic organizational culture. If fresh validation criteria have to be established every time, the development of biodata can be expensive and tedious. However, limited successes have been recorded – for example, a biodata instrument that was developed for use in one national division of an international corporation being effectively applied in another division of the same company based in a different country (Laurent, 1970).

Criterion Specific

Biodata items may not only be organization specific, but also criterion specific. This means that a particular set of biodata items may be tied to specific kinds of performance that they can predict well, but that they are less able to predict performance on other job criteria with any degree of accuracy.

Shrinkage Over Time

Biodata scoring keys do not seem to hold up indefinitely. There is evidence that the validity of biodata shrinks over time, and that periodic revalidation and reweighting may be necessary. This can be costly and time-consuming. Furthermore, one cannot predict what items 'hold up' over time or why. In general, the evidence suggests that the 'shelf-life' of biodata is between three and five years. It should be noted, however, that most of the studies that have reported large amounts of shrinkage have used turnover as the criterion. Turnover is more readily affected by labour-market conditions than performance measures and where the latter are used the outlook may not be as bleak. In this context, however, it is important to be sure that it is the validity of the biodata instrument that has changed and not that of the criterion variables against which its predictive capacity is validated (Wilkinson, 1993).

Fairness in the Law

If biodata items are shown to be major biographical determinants, such as sex, age, race and so on, is there a temptation to select in and select out particular groups? This would be illegal. Items such as age, sex and marital status may in fact be challenged in the courts, if such items are included in inventories for the purpose of personnel selection. In that event, whatever gains in predictive power that are derived through the inclusion of these items must be weighed against the possible costs of legal action.

Some of these objections to biodata are discussed in other parts of this book. In the remaining sections of this chapter we want to take a closer look at the last four: faking, the generalizability problem, shrinkage and fairness.

Fakeability and the Accuracy Problem

Evidence is mixed regarding the accuracy of information obtained by biodata inventories and the extent to which social desirability influences responses to biodata items. As was suggested by Annis (1967), the type of information provided by the biography not only depends on the kind of instruction given by the investigator, but also on the instructions the person has given himself or herself in responding to the task, the kind of relationship existing between the investigator and the writer, the institutional situation in which a personal document is being collected, and the degree of motivation and the ability of the individual to divulge information about himself or herself.

Obviously, the veridicality, personal involvement and degree of self-disclosure in the autobiography will be a function of the combination of operative motives. Knowledge of these motives will place the reader in a better position to view the autobiographical communication from the author's frame of reference. If the analyser of the autobiography is oblivious to the motives operating, he or she is treading on precarious interpretative ground (Annis, 1967).

It can also be argued that the selected themes of which the autobiography is composed, as well as the structure and content of the accounts, and the audience to whom it is explicitly or implicitly addressed, provide direct access to the author's cognitive matrix, which is the organized system for social knowledge and belief on which he or she draws in acting and accounting for action, and his or her system of prevailing motives. Thus, the autobiography is an important source of information and is distinct from other sources such as diaries and biographies.

The extent to which responses are accurate or consistent could affect the utility and validity of any biodata study. Perhaps the most common objection to using any self-report measure is that because people can lie or fake good on self-report measures, the measures must be invalid because they do not yield true scores, especially on the assessment of undesirable traits or behaviour patterns. One of three related objections is frequently made: people deliberately sabotage results by random responses; there is motivation distortion or faking to achieve a particular profile (positive, desirable); and there is sheer ignorance whereby the respondent (through lack of self-insight) cannot, rather than will not, accurately report on his or her attitude, beliefs or behaviours. Academic discussion on these issues has revolved around the controversy concerning whether the term 'faking' implies conscious versus unconscious efforts to distort response patterns. For most lay people the term 'fake' would imply a conscious effort at distortion, which would not necessarily be related to unconscious efforts at test distortion.

Shaffer, Saunders and Owens (1986) found that objective and moderately subjective biodata items were accurately reported. When respondents are instructed to do so, it is apparent that they are capable of distorting their answers both to empirical keys and rationally developed scales (Klein and Owens, 1965; Goldstein, 1971; Thornton and Gierasch, 1980; Lautenschlager and Atwater, 1986).

Researchers have been concerned about the possibility of socially desirable responding and faking in self-report biodata measures (Crowne and Marlowe, 1960; Shaffer, Saunders and Owens, 1986; Hough, Eaton, Dunnette, Kamp and McCloy, 1990). Various important conclusions were drawn in a review of the literature (Furnham, 1986a, 1986b). The first was that no matter who the subjects were (students, policemen, army recruits, employed people), they showed a similar pattern of faking (Burbeck and Furnham, 1984). Second, most studies have simply got people to fake good or bad. Some studies have got people to fake according to other instructions (that is, fake a librarian or fake a mental patient), although the results have usually been predictable (Furnham and Henderson, 1982; Archer, Gordon and Kirchner, 1987; Furnham and Craig, 1987). Third, studies done in 'real life' as opposed to 'experimental' settings have yielded comparable results. Fourth, testing occasions can be shown to be differentially prone to dissimulation and this proneness can be measured from the test results (Michaelis and Eysenck, 1971). This suggests that experimental work using any population group, and using fake good and bad instructions, would yield comparatively robust results and replicable faking templates.

What is the evidence for faking in biodata research? Several studies have compared self-reported biodata with information checked from other sources. Keating, Paterson and Stones (1950) investigated the accuracy of three work history items (wages, length of previous employment, and duties) obtained by interviewing 385 unemployed clients of the US federal employment service. The lowest correlation between self-reported and previous employers data was 0.90, suggesting high accuracy. Of course, it may be that individuals are less likely to fake in face-to-face encounters than on paper, and that these results overestimate the accuracy of written accounts. Mosel and Cozan (1952) compared the application blanks of 126 sales and office staff with work histories supplied by their previous employers. Correlations of 0.93 and 0.99 between applicants and employers' accounts of previous earnings and duration of job were obtained.

Klein and Owens (1965) conducted a study to investigate the role of the criterion in determining the transparency of a scoring key. When college students (n=55) were instructed to fake a life history questionnaire, they were able to do so, but a scoring key empirically derived from a subjective criterion of creativity was more transparent than one based on an objective criterion (patent disclosure). It also seemed that prior exposure to the questionnaire facilitated faking on the former key more than on the latter. Also investigated was the possibility that the difference in transparency was attributable to the subjective key having been biased by a fallacious stereotype. To evaluate this possibility, recruiting interviewers (n=79) filled out the questionnaire as they thought a creative scientist would. As expected, they selected a greater proportion of the items thought to be associated with creativity than of those actually shown to be correlated with creative output. Klein and Owens concluded that:

- non-verifiable items probably are not answered with the veracity classically attributed to responses on the application blank;
- selecting and/or weighting items in such inventories on the basis of their relationship to a subjective criterion may cause them to be relatively transparent;
- interviewers should distrust their unaided abilities to distinguish occupational stereotypes from characteristics actually relevant to job performance.

Doll (1971) found that individuals told to fake looking good but to be aware of the presence of a lie scale distorted their responses less than did individuals who were instructed to fake looking good without such a strong warning regarding possible detection. Subsequently, Cascio (1976) obtained a similar correlation of 0.94 between reported and verified responses to 17 'historical and verifiable' application blank items (from Glennon, Albright and Owens, 1966). All this seems to suggest that self-reported biodata can be reliable, but this has been challenged by Goldstein (1971), who also contrasted self-reports (the application forms of 94 nursing aides) with previous employers' data, but found marked discrepancies between the two sources. The sources were less discrepant for 'previous position held' (95% agreement) and 'reason for leaving' (75% agreement) than for 'size of previous salary' and 'duration of previous employment' (57% disagreement). It is noticeable that a greater percentage disagreement was obtained for the last two items, measured on a continuum of response options, than for the former two, which were presumably categorical in nature. Since Goldstein did not report the size of the difference that constituted a disagreement for the continuous items, it is hard to judge the practical significance of these results.

Many methods of scoring biodata require continuous items to be reduced to a number of broad response categories. Small disagreements may not be particularly important. Moreover, the extent of faking reported seems to be a function of the index of agreement used. One could imagine a situation in which all respondents exaggerated by exactly 10%. Here, there would be no *agreement* whatsoever between applicants' reports and employers' records, but there would be perfect *correlation* between the two. Although this hypothetical situation would be highly unlikely, in Goldstein's study: 'the average overestimation was not raised substantially by a few applicants but, rather, occurred across most of the applicants' (Goldstein, 1971: 491). Response distortion might thus be largely absorbed by most objective methods of scoring biodata.

Some support for this view has been provided by Kluger, Reilly and Russell (1991). They contrasted an item-keying (IK) strategy, which assumed a linear monotonic relationship between item scores and the criterion, with an option-keying (OK) strategy in which each item response alternative was analysed separately. In an experimental study involving 85 graduate students in a US university, they found that IK scores were susceptible to inflation because of socially desirable responding and knowledge of the job in question, whereas OK scores were not. This perhaps explains some of the inconsistencies in the literature noted above, but is also reassuring for users of England's (1971) WAB approach as this is probably the most popular OK method. Kluger, Reilly and Russell (1991) concluded that biodata scoring keys should always be developed in applicant samples if impression management is to be minimized. In this way, the 'motivational set' or tendency to respond in a socially desirable way would presumably be the same in the research sample and in samples of real applicants, and hence would cancel out. Nevertheless, the scrupulously honest applicant could be penalized unless further attempts are made to control response distortion, assuming of course that biodata scores can be distorted to fake good.

Student volunteers, indeed anybody, can fake high scores on empirically keyed biodata blanks (Klein and Owens, 1965; Schrader and Osburn, 1977). Walker (1985) administered a 112-item questionnaire to 1,788 US army enlistees who were instructed to 'play a role while completing the questionnaire: the role of a civilian applying for military service'. The subjects were then divided into four groups. The control group was given no further instructions, whereas the remaining three were instructed to either fake unrestrainedly good, fake discreetly good, or fake discreetly bad. All three faking conditions produced response distributions that were significantly different from that of the control group, although the effect was only large and consistent in the fake discreetly bad conditions. This suggests that these recruits knew the characteristics of bad applicants better than they knew those of good ones; a problem shared by the selectors (Webster, 1964). Rejection, it seems, is easier to define than acceptance.

To accept that applicants can fake does not help to show when and why they do fake their biodata. Means and Laurence (1986) compared the biographical blank responses of 855 US army enlistees with the responses they had previously made to the same blank as applicants. They argued that the former responses were more accurate because the recruits knew the questionnaire was being administered for research purposes and would not affect their careers in the army. The mean percentage agreement for the 121 multiple-choice items was 85%. The percentage agreement rate was higher for items that were rated as particularly sensitive (for example, questions about drug misuse) and for items rated highly on 'verification expectancy'. This suggests that the recruits were either more careful about their responses to sensitive items or, perhaps, that they remembered the responses they had given previously, precisely because the items were sensitive. Atwater, Abrahams, Wiskoff and Sands (1984) found that response distortion was reduced when experimental subjects were warned that their responses would be verified and that negative consequences would result if fake information was detected. An important implication of this is the idea that a simple warning does diminish faking.

Limiting biodata to objective or verifiable items poses a problem for advocates of rational approaches to building such instruments. Objective actions tend to be heterogeneous and therefore difficult to attribute to unitary constructs. The homogeneous and subjective items preferred by the rational approach would therefore be excluded. Mael and Hirsch (1993) noted that this presents a dilemma for the construction of effective biodata instruments. Verifiable items tend to be purely descriptive and hold least promise for theoretical advancement in this area.

Mael and Hirsch explored two approaches to objective biodata that were designed to yield a stable instrument with low fakeability. The first approach was a quasi-rational attempt to derive biodata analogues from an existing temperament measure and then use them as rational scales. The second was a theory-based variant of criterion-referenced keying, termed 'rainforest' empiricism. This was not an entirely new approach. Biodata items were monitored for their predictive abilities in relation to a range of performance criteria. This research was conducted among 2,565 US Military Academy cadets to predict leadership performance over four rating periods.

Biodata items were selected if they addressed behaviours or events hypothesized to be related to: (a) the criteria of interest, with leadership performance at various stages as the primary criterion and attrition as a secondary one; (b) the temperament measure's scales, especially dominance; or (c) other aspects of military adaptability seen by subject-matter experts as potentially relevant to success during and after the cadets' tenure at the academy. The last item included such things as membership of sports teams and preference for rugged pastimes. Using the 'rainforest' approach, biodata scales were created that were empirically related to each of the four performance criteria. However, using this approach, empirical test results were considered in a rational context in which biodata items shown empirically to have correlations with key competencies were included only if they were judged to provide logical connections to those competencies. Thus, the usual dry 'dustbowl empiricism' was replaced by a more theoretically tinged ('rainforest') approach. This quasi-rational approach was found not only to yield effective competency predictors, but also to present a procedure that was labour-saving. Although biodata items were empirically verified, their ultimate selection and use depended also on more rational considerations of the logicality of their relevance to the competency prediction context.

Stokes, Hogan and Snell (1993) developed an index of Socially Desirable Responding (SDR) to measure the extent of impression management shown in applicant and incumbent samples when responding to a biodata form. The sample consisted of 2,262 incumbent sales representatives and 2,726 applicants for sales positions. Greater applicant than incumbent SDR was observed, but differences varied across a priori item content areas. Impression management was minimal in item categories such as previous work experience and economic motivation, but it was more prevalent in categories such as work style and preferences and self-evaluations of prior sales success. Using a smaller sample of 810 incumbents and 555 applicants, largely equated for experience, an item-keyed biodata inventory was developed for selection purposes. When regression procedures were used to develop final keys, no comparable items existed across the keys from the two samples. SDR was more strongly related to the applicant key than to the incumbent key. Applicants showed greater social desirability in their biodata responding than did job incumbents.

In another test case, Kluger and Colella (1993) randomly warned a subsample of a job applicant sample against faking. Although the advance warning mitigated the propensity to fake, the specific warning effects depended on item transparency. For transparent items, warning reduced faking, whereas for less transparent items, the warning had no effect on the way applicants responded.

As Drakeley (1988) noted, the problem that response distortion presents to the psychometrician should be minimized if biodata devices are developed with the following points in mind:

1. Where possible, historical and verifiable biodata should be used.
2. Instructions for biodata blanks should imply that attempts will be made to verify factual information and that responses distortion carries a penalty.
3. Biodata scoring keys should be developed on job applicants rather than current employees (that is, predictive designs are preferable to concurrent ones).
4. Originally continuous items should be reduced to a small number of broad response categories.
5. Sensitive items may suffer less distortion, but it may still be necessary to control for socially desirable responses.

Whether or not response distortion reduces or enhances validity is also an open question. Pannone (1984) found that his biodata form was significantly more valid for his sample of 'non-fakers' than for the sample of 'fakers'. Crosby (1990) showed that responses to a measure of social desirability were unrelated to total biodata scores as well as to most of the biodata items taken individually. However, she also found that social desirability was a significant predictor of her criterion measures, increasing validity beyond that obtained from the biodata key alone for males in her sample.

On a final point, faking on a biodata instrument can itself prove to be an effective and relevant predictor of performance in certain job contexts. Knowing how to fake effectively to create a better impression was found to be the best predictor of performance for salesmen (Ruch and Ruch, 1967). Good salespeople need to be able to present a positive image regardless of their real personality or true feelings about whatever it is they are trying to sell. Similarly, Crosby (1990) found that responses to the Marlowe–Crowne social desirability scale (Crowne and Marlowe, 1964) were related to sales success, but that low scores were related to high performance levels. Variations in the findings of these studies are likely to reflect the various definitions of social desirability being used. Ruch and Ruch (1967) used the K of the lie scale of the MMPI (Minnesota Multiphasic Personality Inventory), which is more a measure of impression management (Paulhus, 1984, 1986). The Marlowe–Crowne scale has been considered more a measure of need for approval. Salespeople must handle rejection regularly and so a high need for approval might be detrimental to sales success (Crosby, 1990).

Generalizability of Biodata

There is considerable evidence to show that mental ability tests can effectively be used across different jobs and different organizations (Hunter and Hunter, 1984). The evidence for the generalizability of biodata, however, is not so compelling. Whether used in application forms or in longer questionnaire formats, biodata invariably do not travel well (Reilly and Chao, 1982). They tend to be specific to the criterion they were developed against: a weighted application form that predicts tenure, for instance, may not necessarily predict some other, quite distinct, measures of work performance. Biodata items empirically developed in one organization may not work in another organization. This is because effective biodata predictors are sensitive to idiosyncratic situational elements of the organization in which they were developed, which may have no relevance elsewhere.

Biodata also seem to be specific to the criterion used in their development. Drakeley, Herriott and Jones (1988) found that items which predicted voluntary turnover were different from those which predicted training performance in the same sample. Moreover, the same responses were a 'good' sign for one criterion and a 'bad' sign for another (Drakeley, 1988).

This lack of generality reflects the largely atheoretical approach that is traditionally associated with biodata. Where items are chosen rationally and inductive methods of combination are used, the resulting personal history constructs do seem to generalize to different groups and organizations (Owens and Schoenfeldt, 1979). The lesson for practitioners is that the validity of a key developed in one setting cannot be *assumed* in another, and it may be necessary to develop new keys whenever the job, the criteria or the applicant group change from those used in the development process.

Pioneers of biodata research believed in the generalizability of biodata forms (Owens, 1968, 1976; Campbell, Dunnette, Lawler and Weick, 1970). A strong emphasis of the well-known Standard Oil New Jersey's (SONJ) Early Identification of Management Potential (EIMP) study was on the common core of all management activities rather than on narrow functional specialities. The biodata instrument that resulted from this study had validities that were generalizable across varied functions in SONJ and the five affiliate companies (Campbell, Dunnette, Lawler and Weick, 1970). A later study (Laurent, 1970) showed that the variables generalized to different (non-English-speaking) countries as well. Similarly, the Aptitude Index Battery (AIB), a biodata inventory used by the North American insurance industry, showed a degree of transportability. It was developed by a central research group (LIMRA) for use in different life assurance companies (Thayer, 1977). Brown (1981) analysed AIB data for 12 453 insurance salespeople from 12 large US life assurance companies. A validity generalization analysis showed the AIB's mean true validity coefficient was $r = 0.26$, and that 62% of the variation in validity in the 12 companies could be accounted for by sources of error differences in range restriction, sample size and criterion reliability. This means that: (a) the AIB was valid for all 12 insurance companies, and also (b) that it is genuinely more valid for some than for others. Brown divided the companies into group A, which recruited through press advertisements and agencies, and group B, which recruited by personal contacts. Group B had higher average production levels, and selected more people with higher AIB scores. Brown compared AIB validities in the two groups, and found that it was higher for group B companies.

The most complete theory of biodata validity discussed so far, that proposed by Owens (Owens, 1968, 1976; Owens and Schoenfeldt, 1979), also emphasizes the potential generalizability of the method. Owens' assessment-classification model assigns people to membership in relatively homogeneous life-history subgroups, determined by one's pattern of scores on 13 biodata factors. Because membership in these groups has been found to be differentially related to performance and satisfaction in various kinds of work, it would seem that general life experience factors are related (differentially) to performance in a variety of different jobs. Indeed, an unpublished study by Kirkpatrick in the USA (Owens, 1976) retested Chamber of Commerce managers after five years using different criterion variables, and found that the keys held up surprisingly well.

According to Rothstein, Schmidt, Erwin, Owens and Sparks (1990), the organizational specificity of biodata validities is traceable to the methods used to select and key items for the final scale (that is, the method of scale construction) rather than to any inherent inability of biodata scores to yield generalizable validities. Items are typically selected and keyed on the basis of samples from a single organization; as a result, items whose validity does not generalize across organizations may not be detected and eliminated.

Rothstein, Schmidt, Erwin, Owens and Sparks (1990) describe biodata research in which a different approach was taken to constructing and keying biodata items. Item selection and keying were based on samples from multiple organizations; only items that performed adequately across organizations were retained in the final scale. Cross-validation of the final key was performed on a sample of about 11,000 first-line supervisors working in 79 different organizations. The resulting validities were subjected to meta-analysis to determine the generalizability of the validities of the biodata scale. The instrument investigated was the empirically keyed autobiographical component of the Supervisory

Profile Record (SPR) (Richardson, Bellows, Henry & Co., Inc., 1981). The complete SPR consists of a judgement questionnaire in addition to the biodata-questionnaire. The prototype SPR contained 99 judgements and 128 autobiographical items.

The performance rating criteria were: (a) developed on the basis of a thorough job analysis conducted in all organizations used in the first stage of development; and (b) rechecked using the same job analysis methods in all organizations in both developmental and validation consortia. Job analysis and instrument development were aimed at identifying and measuring the broad common core of supervisory tasks, and capacities to perform those tasks, shared across first-line supervisory jobs in all settings. The job analysis results indicated that the basic duties and required capacities were similar across organizations.

The resulting criterion instrument had two parts. Part I consisted of 28 statements about the individual's performance of specific job duties and an overall rating of performance across all duties. Ratings were made on nine-point scales in terms of the 'extent to which the individual meets job requirements'. Anchors were 'well below', 'somewhat below', 'meets', 'somewhat above' and 'well above' normality.

Part II contained 21 statements about the individual's specific supervisory abilities (for example, ability to plan work for unit supervised) and a statement about overall ability to do the job. Ratings were made on the nine-point scale, similar to that for duty ratings, but in terms of 'extent to which individual resembles other first-line supervisors'. Anchors were identical to those for duty ratings, except the mid-point of the scale was anchored by *average* rather than *means*. Because supervisory jobs are similar but not identical in their duty and ability requirements, and some raters may not have had full opportunity to observe performance on some elements, raters were given the option on each statement to indicate that an element was not part of the job or that they could not evaluate the individual on that element.

Rothstein, Schmidt, Erwin, Owens and Sparks (1990) presented results that ran against the prevailing belief that biodata validities are intrinsically specific to particular organizations. (They also present strong counter-evidence to the hypothesis that biodata validities are necessarily moderated by age, sex, race, education, tenure or previous experience.)

These results do not, of course, indicate that the level of generalizability shown here can always be expected from biodata; given conventional methods of biodata instrument construction and validation, these may represent the exception rather than the rule. The point is that biodata instruments can be constructed and validated in a way that will lead to validity generalizability. The findings in this study show that large sample sizes, multiple organizations and cross-organizational keying of the biodata scale can yield generalizable validities. Thus, the findings also point up the advantages of consortium-based multiple organization biodata research. Rothstein, Schmidt, Erwin, Owens and Sparks (1990) concluded that, from a psychological point of view, their findings indicate that biodata questionnaires are capable of capturing general characteristics of people that are conducive to success or failure on the job in a wide variety of settings, organizational climates, technologies and so on.

Differential Item Functioning

Another aspect of generalizability concerns whether biodata items elicit the same kinds of responses from different demographic, ethnic or cultural subgroups. Evidence has emerged, for example, that ethnic subgroups do not respond consistently to particular kinds of biodata items. This differential responding is not necessarily indicative of variations in job-relevant qualifications, experience or views of the world. Differential item functioning (DIF) occurs when subgroups responding to particular items are attracted to distinct response options. For example, DIF could occur if black respondents tended to choose option A for a particular item and most white respondents tended to choose item C.

Schmitt and Pulakos (1998) investigated potential explanations for findings of differential validity for a biodata instrument given to blacks, whites and Hispanics in a large US federal government agency. In this analysis, about one in three items on the biodata instrument were found to show ethnicity-related differential item functioning. Whitney and Schmitt (1997) provided a further examination of whether differences in cultural values could lead to differential item functioning on biodata employment tests. In this study, white and black college students completed a cognitive ability test, an intercultural values questionnaire and a biodata instrument. The cultural values instrument asked respondents to endorse the degree to which they would live their lives or raise their children by the values expressed in the questionnaire items. The biodata test was also scanned for items reflecting particular cultural values. The students completed this battery of tests as if they were applying for a job as a police officer.

Black and white respondents were found to show different cultural values responses relating to their perceptions of basic human nature and other perceptions of the world. Further analysis provided evidence that the cultural values of respondents influenced their selection of responses to certain biodata items. In fact, 16% of items on the biodata instrument used in this study were affected in this way. One in four biodata items showed differences in responding between blacks and whites, quite apart from any effects related to cultural values on the choice of answer to biodata options. These results provided a clear indication that biodata items that enquire about respondents' basic world views or perceptions of human nature could produce differential item functioning among job applicants from different ethnic groups or who adhere to different cultural values. Black respondents in the study, for example, consistently displayed a more cynical view of human nature than did white respondents. Whites, for instance, were less likely than blacks to believe that people would put professional goals ahead of personal friendships.

Stability Over Time

As with other types of predictor, it is important to run checks that predictive relationships (biodata items predicting job performance) remain stable over time. In respect of biodata, the critical question is, how likely is it that weighted items or scoring keys, developed at one point in time, are successfully going to predict aspects of job-related behaviour at some later time? As we shall see, the evidence on the stability over time of biodata keys is mixed, but indicates that certain items last better than others. Many biodata items do not retain their initial levels of predictability indefinitely, and the validity of some biodata may 'shrink' in use (Drakeley, 1989). Indeed, some studies have showed that validity shrinks so fast that sets of biodata can cease to have any predictive validity within a few years and have to be rewritten, with new scoring weights.

Research has investigated the stability of biodata items by testing respondents once and then retesting them some years later using the same questions on the form. A second method has involved checking the accuracy and validity of respondents' biodata responses against the corroborative evidence of independent judges who are in a position to verify the information given.

Buel (1964) found that 13 out of an original 16 valid items retained their predictive efficiency 'in use', even though a substantial change had taken place in the population of job applicants (the company had actually relocated its clerical offices). Hughes, Dunn and Baxter (1956) reported the validity of a rating form developed in 1951 and follow-up validities in 1952, 1953 and 1954. Despite good cross-validated results in 1951, by 1954 the scoring key was no longer differentiating to any significant degree. This drop in validity was attributed both to the 'in-use' phenomenon and to the fact that the managers responsible for testing candidates may have 'abused' the process.

The managers who scored the forms were supposed to use them to reject 'unsuitable applicants'. Instead, they 'guided' favoured applicants into giving the 'right' answers. In 1954 far more applicants reported that they owned $7000 life insurance, $7000 'just happening' to be the border between one and two points. Clearly, the scoring system for biodata must be kept secret, but if application forms lose their predictive power as soon as people become familiar with them, they could never be used on a really large scale.

Studies that specifically examined the stability of an application blank scoring key were those of Wernimont (1962) and of Dunnette, Kirchner, Erickson and Banas (1960). Both of these studies examined the change in predictive validity of the valid items found in the earlier Kirchner and Dunnette (1957) study. The Dunnette, Kirchner, Erickson and Banas (1960) study reported the follow-up data on the key developed in 1954 as shown in Table 4.1. The decrement in validity over time is quite apparent.

Wernimont (1962), in a final study, found that the correlation between scores on the 1954 key and job tenure had dropped by 0.07 by 1959. He then

Table 4.1: Numbers of long-term and short-term 3M employees scoring above and below a score of 15 on the weighted application blank

	Women hired during 1954		Women hired during 1955		Women hired during 1956	
	Short-term	Long-term	Short-term	Long-term	Short-term	Long-term
Score of 15 or above	5	76	12	32	27	45
Score of 14 or below	28	29	28	13	18	12
Tetrachoric correlation (r_t)	0.74		0.61		0.38	

Source: Adapted from M.D. Dunnette et al. (1960).

developed a new key which, when cross-validated on a hold-out sample, gave a correlation with job tenure of 0.39. The only items that retained their prediction efficiency from 1954 to 1959 were: (1) high proficiency at shorthand, (2) did not leave last job because of pregnancy, marriage, sickness or home problems, and (3) will begin work on the new job one week or more from now.

Wernimont strongly recommended that scoring keys be revalidated at least every three to five years – a caution that applies to all other selection devices as well. However, Roach (1971) reported shrinkage for a similar key of 0.46 to 0.29 within two years, and suggested that the loss could have been a consequence of changes in the company hiring policies and labour market conditions. Similarly, changes in attitudes, the opportunity structure of society, and the education system could all contribute to this shrinkage in validity over time. These latter are all long-term changes, yet Brown (1978) investigated the long-term validity of a personal history item scoring key over a 38-year period. The key was originally developed on a 1933 sample of 10,111 life assurance agents, subsequently re-evaluated on a 1939 sample of 857 agents and finally cross-checked on a 1969–71 sample of 14,738 agents. The results indicated that over both the 6-year and 38-year cross-validation periods, little, if any, validity was lost. This was true despite drastic labour market and economic changes, as well as dramatic changes in the job itself. The apparent conflict of these results with those reported in other long-term validity studies was attributed to the impact of scoring key confidentiality, test maintenance and adequate developmental sample sizes.

Loss of scoring key confidentiality was an explanation given for loss of validity in the Hughes, Dunn and Baxter (1956) study. Brown got round this problem by having all scoring completed at a centralized, 'unbiased' location. Scoring keys were kept strictly confidential. Brown added, however, that not every aspect of the instrument and scoring key remained stable over the 38 years for which he examined data. Specific scale values for individual items do change over time. A biodata instrument needs to be properly maintained by reweighting and revalidating individual items at regular intervals. If these conditions are met, biodata instruments can be usefully employed over many years.

One study distinguished between three types of item. These were objective, moderately subjective and subjective. Responses were examined for individual items as well as for item clusters. On determining biodata accuracy, test–retest reliability was best for objective and moderately subjective items and somewhat less reliable for subjective items. The same pattern occurred in respect of level of agreement between information supplied by respondents and verification by independent judges. These scores throughout were generally better when assessments were made on clusters of items than on individual items. The results indicated that respondents provided quite accurate responses to very objective factors and to moderately subjective factors. There were larger shifts over time in responses given on some factors than on others.

Niener and Owens (1982) examined relationships between two sets of behaviourally based biodata. They found that biodata collected from female and male college freshers accounted for 17% and 12% respectively of the variance in independently derived biodata from the same individuals seven years later. Although ostensibly an analysis in prediction, when measures are taken on the same individuals at two or more points in time, it may seem more appropriate to regard it as a test of stability than one of prediction. The two biodata instruments used in this study were developed independently of one another and did not contain exactly the same factors. There was some continuity between the two inventories, nevertheless, in that three of the nine dimensions on one instrument had counterparts on the other.

Thus, it is not simply individual biodata items that may lose their predictive validity over time; clusters or groups of items deriving from statistical factor analyses may also do so. This phenomenon has been further corroborated by Eberhardt and Muchinsky (1982a) who investigated the factor structure stability of Owens' Biographical Questionnaire (BQ). They administered the BQ to 816 people (437 women and 379 men). They computed the main underlying factors and compared these with those reported by Owens. Although the factor structure was consistent for men, it was not entirely the same for women. Several previously observed factors failed to emerge. An explanation for this lack of congruence involves the recognition of the changing life experience of women.

The results pointed to the fact that researchers using standardized biodata forms need to be aware of any changing societal trends that may cause a change in the experiences of a particular group of people. To keep abreast of such changes, periodic analyses of subjects' responses to biodata items should be conducted to examine the combined stability of the factor structure.

What, then, can be concluded about the validity of biodata over time? The extent to which an item is historical and verifiable has a bearing on this question. Objective factors such as socioeconomic class, academic achievement, religious activity, family background and so on, can be fairly readily verified. Moderately subjective items such as relationship with parents, interest in various subjects or knowledge, attitudes towards work and certain personality attributes can be verified to some extent also through consultations with other sources or standardized tests. Subjective items that deal with personal opinion on issues, feelings of social inadequacy, self-esteem and wanting to do the socially desired thing, may often prove more difficult to verify.

Thus, individual items, if carefully selected, can prove to be stable over time and hence reliable measures of individual character. Others may fluctuate wildly, however. Research that has examined the content of less stable biodata items has revealed that many of them deal with individuals' feelings and perceptions rather than their behaviour or past experience.

More objective items based on actual events seem to be less likely to be distorted. Subjective items are influenced more by the desire to say the right thing. When asking about past events, however, it is important to get the time frame right in order to generate useful responses. Items that ask about an occurrence during a very specific time period cannot be expected to be stable over the long term.

One solution to the stability problem may be to develop biodata items that are related to specific attributes of the person rather than more global measures of job performance (Wilkinson, 1993). This requires identifying criteria based on attributes of individuals that may be relevant to performance across a variety of work situations. This approach could be particularly valuable in the context of developing biodata instruments to assist in the selection of managers. In this case, general person attributes associated with good management could be isolated (for example, Hirsch and Bevan, 1988) and used as a foundation on which to build a biodata inventory. The latter would be validated against those management attributes (Wilkinson, 1994). In an exploratory study to test the potential of biodata as predictors of cognitive and personality attributes, Wilkinson (1994) found that biodata items performed well.

Wilkinson (1994, 1995) showed that a biodata inventory is capable of predicting the scores of a range of adult respondents on psychometric tests of a cognitive attribute (Walson-Glaser Critical Thinking Appraisal – overall score), a personality trait (Eysenck Personality Inventory – Extroversion-Introversion Scale) and occupational interest (Holland Self-Directed Search – Enterprising Scale).

Users therefore need always to be cognizant of the shrinkage of longer-term validity of empirically developed biodata items. Although background data items may have been stable, predictive implications, the empirical keying strategy's efficiency may shift over time. Consequently, biodata instruments derived through empirical procedures may require periodic updating (Mumford and Owens, 1987). In general, the evidence suggests that the 'shelf-life' of biodata is between three and five years. It should be noted, however, that most of the studies that have reported large amounts of shrinkage have used turnover as the criterion. Turnover is more readily affected by labour-market conditions than performance measures and where the latter are used the outlook may not be as bleak.

Fairness and Legality

It is impossible to answer with complete certainty whether biodata are fair and legal without recourse to concrete and specific examples. Certainly, if WAB/biodata items are linked to race, religion, sex or age, they must exclude these protected minorities or majorities disproportionately, and give rise to claims of *adverse impact*.

As far as race is concerned, there has been little evidence reported in the literature of differential validity for members of different racial groups. Biodata studies reviewed by Reilly and Chao (1982) did not create adverse impact for ethnic minorities. No adverse impact was found in studies of bus drivers, clerical staff, army recruits or supervisors. Owens (1976) found that biodata inventories of creativity were completely uncorrelated with race. Cascio (1976) found that a WAB predicted turnover in white and non-white female clerical workers equally accurately. This generally positive finding has been confirmed in a number of situations, most recently by Rothstein, Schmidt, Erwin, Owens and Sparks (1990).

Although biodata inventories seem more or less colour-blind, they do sometimes distinguish between men and women. Biodata for US navy recruits need different predictors for men and women (Sands, 1978). Nevo (1976) found that different predictors were needed for male and female promotion in the Israeli army. The US insurance industry's AIB can be used for men and women, but has to be scored differently. On the other hand, Ritchie and Boehm (1977) developed a biodata inventory for US telegraph and telephone managers, which achieved equally good cross-validity for women and men. Ritchie and Boehm conclude: 'the same kinds of experiences and interests that characterise successful managers of one sex are also predictive of success for the other' (1977: 365). Certainly, all researchers in this area should at least check that there are no systematic sex differences.

The evidence concerning sex differences is therefore equivocal. As we noted in the previous section, Eberhardt and Muchinsky (1982a) concluded that factor structures in the biographical questionnaire were not especially stable across sex. In contrast, Stokes, Lautenschlager and Blakley (1987), examining sex differences in the same questionnaire, concluded that the factors were very similar, and that only the mean factor scores of men versus women were different. Certainly, all researchers in this area should at least check their own results and see whether any sex differences exist.

Robertson and Smith (1987) found that applicants greatly disliked biodata inventories, and thought them both inaccurate and unfair, which suggests strongly that biodata measures are much more likely to be challenged than, for example, interviews. WAB/biodata inventories as a principle do not seem to create too much adverse impact, but many of their component items are likely to prove inherently objectionable to 'fair employment' agencies: age (if over 40), arrest record, convictions, height and weight, marital status, home ownership and so on. The Equal Opportunities Commission in the UK does not approve of any requirement that 'inhibits applicants from one sex or from married persons'. Mitchell and Klimoski (1982) note:

> Items such as age, sex and marital status may in fact be challenged by the courts if such items are included in inventories for the purpose of personnel selection. In that event whatever gains in predictive power to be derived through the inclusion of these items must be weighed against the possible expense of legal defence.

In the UK, discrimination in employment is not confined to race, sex and other characteristics covered by law. 'Old school tie' policies still operate in many organizations, both public and private. Social class pervades certain kinds of biodata items:

- owns own car;
- owns own home;
- lives in suburbs;
- finished secondary school;
- person/room ratio at home;
- father's occupation;
- mother's occupation;
- father's education, and so on.

'Parental occupation', which appears in most WABs, is often used by researchers to *define* a person's social class. It is not against the law to discriminate on grounds of social class, but it is potentially risky, for two reasons:

1. On both sides of the Atlantic being non-white tends to mean being poor, so indices of class are often also indices of race.
2. On both sides of the Atlantic an enterprising journalist or politician could make considerable capital attacking a selection process that looks both capriciously arbitrary, and blatantly biased in favour of middle-class applicants.

Practitioners of biodata would do well to think through possible legal implications of their work, particularly if major biographical predictors are related to factors on which it is simply illegal to discriminate. Moreover, in the future, actual discrimination may not be the only issue. There is much current debate about citizens' rights, not the least of which is the right to privacy. Questions currently regarded as innocuous – items concerning leisure pursuits and use of spare time, for example – might well be regarded as objectionable by certain applicants. At the moment, the most severe potential consequences for organizations of asking such questions is that some candidates might simply tear up their application forms. This suggests strongly that biodata measures are much more likely to be challenged than, for example, interviews if invasion of privacy becomes an issue governed by legislation.

Although frowned on as a practice, and in some countries outlawed, some organizations continue to request information from job applicants that may result in discriminatory selection. Miller (1980) examined the application forms of 151 Fortune 500 companies in the USA and found that 98.7% included one or more application blank items that were considered to be inappropriate, in that they did not seem to be job-related, were potentially discriminatory and were not a business necessity.

Burrington (1982) reviewed the application forms of state personnel offices in 50 states across the USA and found that every form had at least one inappropriate information request. Other similar studies found that many organizations sought inappropriate or irrelevant information from job applicants (Lowell and De Loach, 1982; Saunders, Leck and Vitins, 1989; Saunders, Leck and Marcil, 1992) across the United States and Canada.

Asking questions about what seem to be unnecessary or irrelevant matters can create a bad impression with job applicants (Macan and Dipboye, 1990). Candidates are much more likely to form a favourable impression of the selection procedure when it focuses on asking about strengths and weaknesses relating to job-relevant aptitudes, skills and experiences (Alderfer and McCord, 1970; Taylor and Sniezek, 1984). Job applicants may become especially irritated when faced with having to complete long batteries of selection test items of dubious relevance to the job for which they have applied (Lumsden, 1967).

Presenting job applicants with application forms that contain discriminatory questions can result not only in applicants reacting badly to the selection procedure, but also in their forming a negative impression of the recruiting organization (Saks, Leck and Saunders, 1995). Even when the application form contains an employment equity statement (equal opportunities employer), this may not be enough to alleviate candidates' negative reactions if discriminatory questions are included as part of the application process. The perception of an employment equity programme per se, however, could lead applicants to react more positively towards an organization – and increase the likelihood of their recommending it to friends. Discriminatory questions, in contrast, could reduce applicants' motivation to continue to pursue employment with the organization (Saks, Leck and Saunders, 1995).

Perception of organization attractiveness can influence how many candidates respond to job advertisements and how many candidates will accept job offers (Smither, Reilly, Millsap, Pearlman and Stoffey, 1993). Furthermore, discriminatory questions could have a negative effect on an organziation's public relations and result in 'spillover' effects. These might include applicants' decisions about doing business with the organization in the future. Prejudicial practices in an organization's job application and recruitment procedures can seriously affect its reputation and image (Rynes and Barber, 1990). Application forms with discriminatory questions may also have an effect on the validity of selection procedures (Mael, 1991; Smither, Reilly, Millsap, Pearlman and Stoffey, 1993). Inappropriate questions may lower applicants' motivation to perform well during selection and result in biased or inaccurate test scores (Rynes, 1993). They may also lead to an increased likelihood of distortion or falsification of application forms. They may cause resentment in some applicants and encourage them to fake information or respond at random, hence spoiling the form (Mael, 1991).

Conclusion

This chapter posed the obvious question: why use biodata as opposed to, say, traditional interviews, personality questionnaires or aptitude tests. Fierce debates over the usefulness of personality to predict performance continue to rage and the evidence is highly equivocal, both because of the great unevenness of the tests used, and also because of the unreliability of the work performance measures.

It was argued that there are good theoretical, practical and organizational (political) reasons for using biodata. Biodata are strictly empirical, accurate, cheap and free of various sources of systematic bias. They have been proved, time and again, to be valid in the sense that scored biographical inventory items relate significantly to objectively measured work behaviour. The size of the correlations are modest but important, and are certainly as good as, if not better than, any other methods of assessment in predicting various aspects of work.

Nearly 10 common objections were recorded, some of which were considered more serious than others. A few more serious problems were, however, examined in detail: the fakeability and accuracy of biodata, the generalizability of biodata findings across companies and worker groups, and the stability of findings over time. Research on the stability of biodata suggests that biodata validation needs to be redone every few years.

By their very nature biodata are frequently caught in time. Organizations' products and services change, as do the human factors that relate to them. Various issues concerning structure and group process mean that some organizations or sections encourage, and others suppress, certain individual differences. Furthermore, because biodata are not theoretically driven, it becomes more difficult to predict which and how much predictors change over groups or time, let alone why this occurs.

If biodata are to be used as part of a recruitment, selection or evaluation process, it is vitally important that their relevance to the employment situation is clearly established. The significance of this point stems not just from the need to ensure that the data obtained are predictive of future performance, but also that they do not unfairly discriminate against respondents or create a bad impression among job applicants. A poorly conceived biodata instrument that asks questions that respondents regard as having dubious relevance to the job context could seriously damage not only the validity of the selection procedure but more importantly the reputation of the organization.

Chapter 5
How to Use Biodata

Introduction

The construction of a biodata questionnaire is not particularly complicated. But those who believe it takes no more skill than common sense and a command of the salient language frequently find their amateur efforts unsuccessful. The essential features of the task involve, first, a sensitive job analysis in order to decide what abilities, competencies, skills and traits are required to perform the job well. Second, some thought is required to derive sensible, testable hypotheses about the biographical determinants of the skills derived from the job analysis. For instance, if the job requires the ability to do detailed, highly concentrated work (such as proof-reading) or the ability to sell insurance, what earlier biographical factors are the best predictors of those skills? Clearly, the more accurate one is in choosing correct biographical data, the less expensive in time and cost will be the whole exercise in validating the questionnaire.

Once it has been decided which biographical correlates are predictive, the question remains as to how to select, write and organize appropriate items. Although there are good examples of many of these, some have to be adapted or written afresh. Writing clear, unambiguous questions with appropriate answer codes is not as easy as it first seems. At this stage, it is important to determine how the questionnaire is to be scored.

Perhaps the most important feature of the questionnaire concerns how to test its validity. Although concurrent validity studies are more common, it is important to do predictive validation as well. This lets the test constructors know which items or groups of items (constructs) are the best predictors. Finally, for all sorts of reasons, biographical predictors of occupational success go out of date, primarily because jobs change and so, too, do the skills that are required to them, and hence, the validation process needs to be updated.

Job Analysis

Job analysis refers to one or more procedures designed to collect information about the skills people need to do jobs effectively. Among the kinds of information sought during job analysis, McCormick (1976) listed the following:

- work activities, including both individual behaviours and job outcomes;
- machines, tools, equipment and work aids used;
- job-related tangibles and intangibles, such as materials processed and knowledge applied;
- standards of work performance;
- job context;
- personnel requirements, such as education, experience, aptitudes and so forth.

Ideally, every job in any organization should exist because that job makes a meaningful contribution to the organization's overall goals, whether those goals entail producing a product, providing a service, or 'maintaining the organization'. Job-analysis procedures are designed to assess these intended outcomes or job results, as well as the conditions under which those results are obtained.

Products and/or services are the *output* of an organization. They are the end result of the thousands of *tasks* that are performed by members of the organization. Some of these tasks relate directly to the production of the product or the delivery of the service. Others relate to the management of the organization. Still other tasks, such as those performed in the personnel department, are support tasks for those who produce the organization's product or service and/or for those who manage the organization.

The tasks that are performed by any individual define his or her specific *position* in the organization. All of the identical or similar positions in an organization make up one *job* in that organization. Groups of jobs that are similar in terms of the demands they make on employees are called *job families*. Positions, jobs and job families are the basic building blocks of an organization's structure, which can be described in an organizational chart organogram.

Because job analysis is an activity that requires examining the work people do, it can be confused with other organizational activities that also focus on this work. Job analysis is a process for describing *what is done* in any job – not the best way to do it, how well it is being done, or what it is worth to have the job done.

The end product of job analysis is often a *job description*, which is a factual statement of the tasks, responsibilities and working conditions of a particular job. There also may be a *job specification*, which is a statement of the human characteristics needed for the job to be done. For our purpose, a job analysis is performed to specify the skills and competencies that arise from biographical experience.

Blum and Naylor (1968) listed nine different techniques for gathering information on job analysis:

- questionnaires, where workers answer written questions about their jobs;
- checklists, where workers simply indicate whether or not their jobs include any or all of a list of possible tasks;
- individual interviews, where workers are presented with oral questions about their jobs;
- group interviews, where several workers are questioned simultaneously;
- diaries, where workers are asked to record their daily work activities;
- technical conferences, where 'experts' (usually those who supervise the job in question) meet in order to identify all the aspects of the job;
- critical incidents, where workers and/or 'experts' are asked to describe aspects of the job in question that are crucial either to success or failure;
- observation interviews, where workers are interviewed at their work-stations by the job analyst, who also observes them going about their daily activities;
- work participation, where the job analyst actually performs the job in question.

This list is by no means exclusive or exhaustive. These methods can be categorized under one or more of the following headings: (1) asking, (2) observing or (3) doing. Usually, the more different sources of information one collects, the more complete and accurate the job analysis, in the sense that sources of systematic bias are ruled out or compensated for. In most cases, job analysts restrict themselves to asking or observing, or a combination of the two.

There are other ways of categorizing techniques of job analysis. All can be categorized into one of three groups, depending on the primary source of information: techniques based on obtaining information (a) from one or more job incumbents, (b) from supervisors or outside experts, or (c) from records made by others. Methods of job analysis that rely on information obtained from a job incumbent include interview methods, observational methods, structured questionnaires and checklists, and worker logs and diaries.

Observation is probably the best way for those concerned to discover what is done on a job (Markowitz, 1981). Interview methods of job analysis are the most frequently used of all procedures for collecting information about jobs. Worker logs and/or diaries have been used for job analysis, but this method is the least common of all procedures.

In most instances, there is little difference between the way job analysts interview supervisors and outside experts and the way they interview job incumbents. Questionnaires and checklists are also used in a similar fashion. The critical incident technique (Flanagan, 1954) approach to job analysis requires supervisors or managers to record incidents of worker behaviour that show especially good or especially poor performance for the job in question.

Various job records can be valuable aids to the process of job evaluation. Among these sources of information are company records (such as those relating to the initial design of the job), filmed records of the job being performed, blue-prints of work layout, equipment and so on, and existing job descriptions or job specification (from another source or organization).

Choosing a Method of Job Analysis

The many available methods for job analysis are not strictly comparable, even though they have the same purpose. They differ in several ways, including (a) type of information yielded, (b) time and expense involved and (c) level of skill required of the job analyst. For practical purposes, the method chosen will depend to a considerable extent on the resources available and the purpose for which the information is obtained. Two popular methods will be briefly described.

A technique of job analysis that has been widely used and studied is the Position Analysis Questionnaire (PAQ) developed by McCormick, Jeanneret and Mecham (1972). Basically a worker-oriented approach, the PAQ consists of 194 different job elements or statements describing human behaviours that could be demanded by any given job. These job elements are organized into six different categories or divisions: (1) information input, (2) mental processes, (3) work output, (4) relationships with other persons, (5) job context and (6) other job characteristics. A central question that underlies each category, and the major subheadings included in each category, are presented in Table 5.1.

Table 5.1: Summary of Position Analysis Questionnaire

1. *Information input:* Where and how does a worker get the information to be used in performing the job?
    1.1. Sources of job information.
        1.1.1. Visual sources of job information.
        1.1.2. Non-visual sources of job information.
    1.2. Sensory and perceptual processes.
    1.3. Estimation activities.

2. *Mental processes:* What reasoning, decision-making, planning and information-processing activities does the job involve?
    2.1. Decision-making, reasoning and planning/scheduling.
    2.2. Information-processing activities.
    2.3. Use of learned information.

3. *Work output:* What physical activity does the worker perform, and what tools or other devices are used?
    3.1. Use of devices and equipment.
        3.1.1. Hand-held tools or instruments.
        3.1.2. Other hand-held devices.
        3.1.3. Stationary devices.
        3.1.4. Control devices (on equipment).
        3.1.5. Transportation and mobile equipment.

(contd)

Table 5.1: (contd)

3.2. Manual activities.
3.3. Activities of the entire body.
3.4. Level of physical exertion.
3.5. Body positions/postures.
3.6. Manipulation/co-ordination activities.

4. *Relationships with other people:* What relationships with other people are required to perform the job?
    4.1. Communications.
        4.1.1. Oral (speaking).
        4.1.2. Written.
        4.1.3. Other communications.
    4.2. Miscellaneous interpersonal relationships.
    4.3. Amount of job-required personal contact.
    4.4. Types of job-required personal contact.
    4.5. Supervision and co-ordination.
        4.5.1. Supervision/direction given.
        4.5.2. Other organizational activities.
        4.5.3. Supervision received.

5. *Job context:* What are the physical and social contexts in which the work is performed?
    5.1. Physical working conditions.
        5.1.1. Outdoor environment.
        5.1.2. Indoor temperatures.
        5.1.3. Other physical working conditions.
    5.2. Physical hazards.
    5.3. Personal and social aspects.

6. *Other job characteristics:* What activities, conditions or characteristics, other than those already described are relevant to the job?
    6.1. Apparel worn.
    6.2. Licensing.
    6.3. Work schedule.
        6.3.1. Continuity of work.
        6.3.2. Regularity of working hours.
        6.3.3. Day–night schedule.
    6.4. Job demands.
    6.5. Responsibility.
    6.6. Job structure.
    6.7. Criticality of position.
    6.8. Pay/income.

Source: E.J. McCormick, P.R. Jeanneret and R.C. Mecham (1969) *Position Analysis Questionnaire* Purdue Research Foundation, West Lafayette, Indiana 47907, USA.

The PAQ is intended to be used as a guide for a highly structured oral interview. That is, the job analyst reads each of the 194 items to the job incumbent, listens carefully to the worker's responses, asks any clarifying questions deemed necessary, and then mentally integrates the information obtained and chooses the appropriate response on the rating scale that applies to each particular item or job element. Depending on the item or question, rating scales may address: (1) *extent of use*, with responses ranging from 'nominal' or 'very infrequently' to 'very substantial'; (2) *importance* to the job, ranging from 'very minor' to 'extreme'; (3) *amount of time*, ranging from 'less than one-tenth of the time' to 'almost continually'; and (4) *possibility of occurrence*, ranging from 'no possibility' to 'high'. In addition, there are a limited number of statements that require special rating scales or response codes.

The end result of rating a job on the PAQ questions is considerable information about the pieces, or *elements*, of the job. Recent research using a data analysis procedure called factor analysis suggests that all of this information represents 12 relatively distinct basic job dimensions (Mecham, 1977):

- having decision-making/communicating/general responsibilities;
- operating machines/equipment;
- performing clerical/related activities;
- performing technical/related activities;
- performing service/related activities;
- working regular day/versus other work schedules;
- performing routine/repetitive activities;
- being aware of work environment;
- engaging in physical activity;
- supervising/co-ordinating other personnel;
- public/customer-related contacts;
- working in an unpleasant/hazardous/demanding environment.

Perhaps the PAQ's greatest strength is its applicability to many different kinds of jobs. This is especially important if one of the job analyst's goals is to meaningfully compare, contrast or discriminate between several dissimilar jobs. Of course, the price one pays for this luxury of being able to 'compare chalk and cheese' is a possible reduction in the specificity with which any particular job can be described.

The *critical-incidents technique*, which focuses on specific behaviours deemed critical or crucial to successful (or unsuccessful) job performance (Flanagan, 1954), is a second approach to job analysis. 'Job experts' (usually the job holders or their supervisors) are asked, either individually or in groups, to provide anecdotes or examples of things that they have either done or neglected to do (or witnessed, in the case of supervisors) that had a profound impact on the quality of the work. That is, they are asked to supply critical, work-related incidents from their own experience. After collecting as many of these as possible, the job analyst typically eliminates redundancies and, usually with the assistance of the job experts, organizes the remaining incidents into meaningful categories or job dimensions. These categories and their associated critical incidents, both good and bad, reflect composites of the essential elements of the job being analysed.

Robinson (1981) listed the following steps:

1. Convene a panel of experts.
2. Ask the panel to identify the broad, all-encompassing objectives that an ideal job incumbent should meet.
3. Ask the panel to list all of the specific behaviours necessary for meeting each of the broad objectives.
4. From among these, ask the panel to identify 'critical tasks' – tasks that are crucial to the job because of their frequency, their importance or the cost associated with making an error.
5. Determine the extent to which the experts agree on the relative importance of the major dimensions of the job.

Other methods involve filling out structured questionnaires. Banks, Jackson, Stafford and Warr (1983) recommend the Job Components Inventory (JCI) for analysing jobs that require only a limited amount of skill. They reported significant agreement between supervisors and job holders who used the JCI, and support for the contention that the JCI is capable of differentiating among different jobs. The JCI (a British instrument) assesses five different kinds of requirements: (1) tools and equipment, (2) perceptual and physical requirements, (3) mathematical requirements, (4) communication requirements and (5) decision-making and responsibility.

The Occupational Analysis Inventory (OAI, a US instrument) is a structured job analysis questionnaire that contains 617 'work elements' (descriptions of work activities and conditions) for rating jobs and occupations. These work elements are also organized into five major divisions: (1) information received, (2) mental activities, (3) work behaviour, (4) work goals and (5) work context. According to these authors, who described the OAI as more 'job-oriented' than the PAQ, each of the 617 work elements is rated by the job analyst on one of four scales: significance, extent, applicability or a special scale designed specifically for a particular element. Based on their study of OAI ratings obtained from 12 job analysts and 21 psychology graduate students for 1,414 different jobs, they concluded that OAI job-related factors 'would seem the logical choice for describing concrete activities and conditions as they exist in jobs' (Banks, Jackson, Stafford and Warr, 1983: 247).

There are various sources of error in job analysis. The number of uses to which job analysis information may be put suggests that it is important for this process to be carried out as carefully as possible. The specific kind of error to which job analysis is subject depends somewhat on the method used, but all such error stems from three sources – the database, the interpretation of the information collected, and the environment in which the job analysis is carried out.

The term *database* refers to the number and representativeness of the positions (that is, jobs) examined during a job analysis. As a general rule, the smaller the database, the more likely there is to be error in the final job description. A major reason that a small database can lead to error is that the information collected may be biased or incomplete. For example, if only one job incumbent is interviewed, he or she (a) may not perform the full range of duties actually encompassed by the job being analysed and/or (b) may be unwilling or unable to report accurately on job duties. The best protection against such risks is multiple sources of different types of information. In short, the bigger and more representative the sample of jobs evaluated (and thus the cost of the exercise), the more certain one can be about the accuracy of the data.

Incomplete or distorted information, whether deliberate or not, is not the exclusive province of job incumbents or other interviewees involved in the process. Interviewers and researchers can also misinterpret the data for a variety of reasons. In addition to making mistakes, there is some evidence that the biases and values of job analysts may creep unnoticed into their work. One study, for example, found a tendency for female job analysts using the PAQ to rate jobs somewhat lower than male analysts describing the same jobs with the same instruments (Arvey, Passino and Lansbury, 1977).

The physical and social environments in which the process takes place are the sources of a number of possible errors in job analysis. Among these sources are:

- *time pressures* that restrict the database or rush the analyst through the information collecting and/or interpretation;
- *lack of interest and commitment* (or even obstruction of job analysis efforts) on the parts of managers and/or supervisors;
- *distracting physical environmental conditions*, such as extreme heat, cold or noise;
- *rapidly changing job technology* that can make a job description out of date in a very short time.

A general strategy for dealing with all the potential sources of error in job analysis is: (a) use multiple sources of information about the job, (b) use more than one analyst if possible, and (c) check and recheck information and results. This is an expensive undertaking and many organizations will lack the resources or the commitment to follow it.

Towards a Better Job Analysis

Klinger (1979) has pointed out that traditional job analytic procedures do not specify the *conditions* under which job tasks are performed and the *standards* by which employees doing the job will be evaluated. He suggests an alternative to traditional job description, which he calls the Results-Oriented Description (ROD). The major advantage of RODs seems to lie in the explicit link they make between the *task domain* (duties involved) and the *performance domain* (actual work) of the job. For example, it is one thing for a prospective employee to know that he or she must be able to type 40 words a minute, but another for the employee to know that this typing will be done on a particular machine in a particular style to an error-free standard in a given time.

RODs give employees clearer statements of expectations and explicitly set out the standards by which their performance will be evaluated. Their most obvious practical drawback seems to lie in this very specificity, because an ROD must be written for every job position. In addition, RODs would be difficult or impossible to write in situations where groups of employees work co-operatively to accomplish some task, which is frequently the case.

A second inadequacy of traditional job analysis that many have noticed relates to the use of the resulting information for selection and placement. It has been recognized for some time that a successful individual/job/organization match is more than a matter of skills, knowledge and abilities. It also involves a fit between the needs of, or rewards desired by, the individual and those things that the organization and job offer (Wanous, 1977). From a matching perspective, conventional job descriptions and specifications give those involved in selection and placement only half of the information they need. They know what an employee must be able to do for the job, but not what the job can do for the employee.

Job rewards are individually valued outcomes of doing certain work and/or being in a particular work environment. The reward potential of work often has been examined from a motivational perspective. The relatively simpler systematic *description* of the rewards offered by a job and an organization as an addition to traditional job descriptions is a newer idea.

It remains crucially important to do a good job analysis. This not only provides useful hypotheses as to which biodata items predict occupational behaviour, but, perhaps equally importantly, indicates which work-related criteria measures to use as the dependent, predicted variable. It is extremely important in any validational work to have salient, robust, important work-related performance measures.

Deriving Hypotheses about Biographical Correlates of Performance

Most people, particularly those in managerial roles in business and those who are professionally involved in selection, have fairly elaborate and extensive ideas about what characteristics, abilities, traits and biographical characteristics are associated with success in certain occupations. Thus, some believe:

- evidence of enthusiastic participation in team sports is associated with managerial skills;

- evidence of parental divorce is associated with poor interpersonal skills;
- having attended public/private schools is a sign of intelligence and confidence;
- the age at which one first left one's country of birth is associated with the ability to adapt well in a foreign country;
- the class or grade of degree is (possibly negatively) associated with speed of adaptation in the business world;
- having strong religious beliefs (independent of what the actual religion is) is associated with organizational commitment;
- 'cognitive' hobbies such as computers, chess and bridge are associated with numerical ability and preference;
- occupation of mother (and father) is strongly associated with entrepreneurial behaviour;
- the fact that a candidate has had various illnesses like glandular fever is frequently associated with high rates of absenteeism.

The list is potentially endless. Once pressed, people will come out with an amazingly rich set of 'theories' about biographical correlates, or indicators of occupational success in certain areas. One of the great advantages of biodata is that they allow these often implicit and somewhat vague theories to be stated as clear, unambiguous hypotheses and then tested.

To a large extent, the sort of information that is collected in any biodata questionnaire depends on the hypotheses derived for testing. Thus, if it is supposed that school career or hobbies/pastimes are largely predictive of some particular occupational activity, it is important to systematically gather all the salient information from the candidate on his or her primary and secondary school career and the range of hobbies he or she has, as well as when, why and with whom he or she indulges in them.

It is important to be imaginative, wide-ranging, but specific in drawing up these hypotheses, as many can be tested simultaneously. All too often, practitioners using biodata do not spend enough time thinking through, after the job analysis, the sort of biographical correlates of occupational success. Usually, the more time spent analysing the job and the nature of successful and less successful job holders in the past, the more subtle, sensitive and accurate are the hypotheses generated.

The Development of Biodata Items

Many researchers who use biodata fail to provide any information on how their items were derived when they publish their results. Methods of item generation that have been reported implicitly involve two sets of constraints. The *target* constructs make up the criteria domain and typically consist of job-related knowledge skills and abilities, job performance measures, or job or career choices. The antecedent developmental constructs reflect the processes that precede performance on the targeted criterion constructs. Examples of the developmental constructs domain include cognitions, affective responses, attitudes, behaviour and demographic characteristics that result from previous life experiences.

Owens and Schoenfeldt (1979) generated elements of developmental processes in their evaluation of the Developmental/Integrative (DI) model (Owens, 1968, 1971, 1976). The DI model, which we discussed in Chapter 3, is a general descriptive and predictive approach to human development that can be used to distinguish people with homogeneous life histories (including career choice).

According to Owens and Schoenfeldt (1979), 'fifty-two pages of topics for potential outcomes were developed in flushing out the outlines implied under input variables and prior behaviours. Two thousand items were constructed from or adapted to this outline' (1979: 574). In other words, their research team used the DI model as an outline of the developmental construct domain in hopes of creating construct-valid items. The actual items were created from investigators' best judgements (that is, 'fleshing out') regarding the substance of the developmental construct domain. Subsequent research indicates that this approach does yield items with consistent and meaningful underlying factor structures (Mumford and Owens, 1984, 1987).

Like the predictor-based efforts of Owens and his colleagues, criterion-driven methods for item generation have resulted in biodata scales that predict performance criteria in organizational settings. Investigators construct hypotheses about what kinds of developmental episodes are related to subsequent criterion performance.

As noted by Mumford and Owens (1987: 5), 'this process requires substantial judgement' on the part of investigators. Mumford and Owens suggested six sources of information for investigators to use in making these judgements:

- the developmental literature;
- life history interviews with incumbents;
- known life history correlates of various characteristics in a specific population;
- typical factor loadings of background data items;
- known predictive characteristics of various background data items;
- hypotheses formulated on the basis of general psychological knowledge.

Recent qualitative and theoretical efforts are just beginning to provide guidance for the identification of life history events in the developmental construct domain that affect the subsequent performance of managers and leaders (Kuhnert and Lewis, 1987; Lindsey, Homes and McCall, 1987; Kuhnert and Russell, 1990).

Identifying life history events that predict performance criteria is made easier when there is a great deal of overlap between the criterion construct domain and the developmental construct domain (that is, it is presumably easier to identify developmental life episodes if candidates have had opportunities to show what they can do in previous positions).

Criterion-content sampling procedures will not work when (a) no previous opportunities existed (for example, for entry-level jobs or for economically disadvantaged subgroups) or (b) entry-level personnel are selected with an ultimate criterion of performance in much higher-level, non-overlapping jobs (for example, selection of 'fast-track' entry-level managers to be groomed for top-level positions).

External versus Internal Approaches

Brown (1994) distinguished between two broad alternative strategies for developing biodata scales: (1) *externally based* approaches and (2) *internally based* approaches. External strategies deploy empirical test procedures to investigate the strength or relationships between specific biodata items and individual criterion variables. Those items yielding the strongest relationships as such receive the greatest weights. Externally based strategies were further divided into two subcategories: additive keying methods and configural keying methods. Additive keying methods focus on relationships between individual biodata items and criterion variables, and select or weight most heavily those items that are the best predictors. Configural keying methods cast the net wider and examine how items relate to criterion variables across a sample of individuals. Individuals are placed in a particular biodata category only when their responses to key items match those of everyone else in that class.

Internally based approaches examine the internal relationships among biodata items with a view to grouping items that belong together, either on the basis of some a priori scheme of categorization or through empirical testing by examining similarities in the way people respond to sets of items. Three subtypes of internally based approach have been differentiated. A priori dimension methods produce items designed to measure predefined behavioural constructs using expert judgements or tests of internal consistency among items. Dimension discovery methods produce biographical dimensions through factor, component or cluster analysis. Such dimensions may have a psychological basis. Finally, subgrouping methods profile individuals on scores derived from clustered measures. Groups of biodata items rather than individual items are used as predictor variables.

External-based Approaches

Additive methods: The Weighted Application Blank identifies individual item responses that differentiate between desirable and undesirable criterion groups. By determining the predictive power of each item response, it is possible to assign weights to each possible item response. This procedure requires a sample for which criterion data exist in order to develop a weighting scheme. The groups on whom these scales are developed must be as similar as possible to the groups to which the developed scale will be applied. The WAB is easy to apply and can yield high validity estimates when the instrument has been properly constructed. Sadly, the WAB yields little understanding of the predictor-criterion relationship.

Among additive methods, a number of different approaches can be distinguished. With the *horizontal percentile* technique, for each item response alternative the total number of high criterion group responders is divided by the total number who responded to the alternative regardless of criterion group membership. This technique is not used often and has yielded mixed results (Telenson, Alexander and Barrett, 1983). The *item/criterion regression* technique derives item weights directly from item-criterion correlation coefficients or other applicable measures of covariation. Items are retained that meet some level of statistical significance (Gandy, Outerbridge, Sharf and Dye, 1989). *Deviate keying* uses criterion groups defined by the distance above or below the regression line between the existing predictor and the criterion. Criterion scores for developing item weights are the differences between actual and predicted criterion scores. Item weights are derived by any of the additive approaches. Again, this technique does not always produce stable results (Malloy, 1955; Webb, 1960).

Configural methods: These methods assume that predictive information is contained in the pattern of responses to a set of items, whereas responses taken singly contain no useful information (Meehl, 1950). As with additive approaches, a number of subcategories of configural approaches can be differentiated. *Reductive approaches* begin with an individual's response pattern across all items. Analytical procedures reduce the total response pattern to one or more patterns of less than all the items. In so doing, these approaches isolated the major response patterns that are unique to each criterion group of subjects. There has been limited research on this technique, but what research has been done suggests that results can compare favourably with other empirical item-scaling approaches.

Dual-pattern approaches are another configural method in which individuals are classified into groups on the basis of scores on multiple criteria. Each criterion pattern of scores is represented by a class of subjects. Next, the technique determines the pattern of responses to predictor items that characterize each criterion class of subjects. Thus, a predictor item response pattern is associated with each criterion pattern. The predictor response patterns are then cross-validated as predictors of criterion patterns in a holdout sample (McQuitty, 1957). Thus, the dual-pattern analytic technique yields core types – empirically derived types of individuals.

Internal-based Approaches

Some internally based approaches to biodata scaling begin with an a priori determination by the test developer that particular psychological constructs are to be measured. Typically, the constructs chosen are those believed to underlie job performance or other criteria of relevance. Biodata items are then written or chosen from existing item pools based on the belief that they tap one of the constructs of interest. Such approaches can yield understanding of the relationships between predictor and criterion variables, although this understanding can depend also on how well the items are written to reflect key constructs. Using *dimension discovery* techniques, biodata test developers use some kind of factoring or clustering analysis to identify how groups of biodata items cluster together to represent biographical dimensions.

Other internally based approaches use *subgrouping methods* in the belief that people can be grouped on the basis of patterns in their prior experiences. Individuals who have shared common past experiences may therefore be expected to behave similarly in the future. The Developmental/Integrative model, which was introduced earlier, proposes the subgrouping of people based on similarities in patterns of prior experiences. Groups of people who have behaved in a similar way in the past are expected to behave similarly in the future. The general procedure begins with the development of an item pool of biodata experiences covering a broad spectrum of situations. Items are administered to a large sample of individuals and principal components analysis is carried out. This analysis yields dimensions that are then used to profile individuals. Next, the profiles are entered into a cluster analysis procedure to identify subgroups of individuals with similar profiles (Owens, 1968, 1971, 1976; Owens and Schoenfeldt, 1979).

Many scaling strategies and techniques can be applied to the development of biodata tools. Each has particular strengths and weaknesses. Moreover, many of the various approaches can easily be combined. One general approach might be to develop the tool using an additive externally based approach and to follow that up with a dimension discovery approach. The latter step will aid in understanding the dimensionality of the predictive items as keyed to the specific criterion. This approach has been successfully applied by Crosby, Dalessio and McManus (1990). An alternative route would be to begin with a more theoretical a priori dimension approach and subsequently develop scaling through an externally based strategy. Predictions developed through an additive externally based approach could be used in conjunction with those developed configurally. Then, according to Brown (1994): 'Dimension scores, whether developed through a priori techniques or discovery techniques, might also be combined configurally or through subgrouping' (1994: 226).

The Importance of Theory

As we noted in Chapter 3, there has been growing recognition of the importance of developing a theory-based system of biodata analysis. It is worth including a reminder of the significance of this approach in this discussion of instrument development. Biodata instruments generally work more effectively when the items they comprise were selected on the basis of hypotheses about the key dimensions underlying job performance (Quaintance, 1981; Mumford and Owens, 1987). Thus, basing an instrument purely on empirical evidence concerning correlations between scores on its items and criterion measures of job performance may produce limited results that lack long-term predictive robustness. Biodata items should be selected according to a primarily well-defined model of job-related behaviours and how they link to past experiences in theoretical and explanatory terms (Himmelstein and Blaskovicks, 1960; Mumford and Owens, 1987).

One study of the prediction of combat effectiveness and other aspects of job performance among military personnel hypothesized that risk-taking was an important construct in the context of the key criterion variables. The analysis of predictor variables in this theoretical frame of reference led the researchers to develop items that were appropriate for testing propensity to take risks in different situations. Such measures were found to be strongly linked to the criterion behaviours that characterized the type of employment into which respondents were being recruited (Himmelstein and Blaskovicks, 1960).

Later research, again in a military context, began by identifying major dimensions believed to underlie job performance before specific items were developed. Initial qualitative data were generated by respondents, in the form of narrative essays, in which they described their past experiences and performance in different situations. A content analysis of these essays was used to generate biodata items (Russell, Mattson, Devlin and Atwater, 1988).

According to Nickels (1994),

> Biodata items capture differential patterns of antecedent behaviours and experiences must exist in the content of these items. This is true regardless of whether any particular set of antecedents may look as though it should be a good predictor of criterion performance. It is inappropriately restrictive to exclude from measurement a given antecedent behaviour because it may not appear to be job related. To do this would be to maintain that predictors that lack face validity must also lack predictive power. (Nickels, 1994: 10)

The development of biodata items is a crucial aspect of biodata deployment in employee selection and recruitment. The development of biodata instruments has tended to be a highly empirical exercise in which large pools of items are reduced to smaller, more manageable batteries through statistical techniques that explore cluster patterns among the items or external relationships between items and job performance criteria. Some attempts have been made to develop more sophisticated approaches to the creation of biodata instruments grounded in theoretical models. Such approaches require detailed job analysis procedures that unveil the competency and skill attributes associated with specific jobs and an understanding of the factors that underpin the development of these attributes.

Methods of Obtaining Biodata Items

Employers' references can provide a good source of work history-related items and educational biodata can often be obtained from school and university reports. There is no reason why biodata cannot be obtained from a suitably structured interview as long as candidates' responses can be recorded without too much interpretation by the interviewer. Interviews are, of course, time consuming and expensive, and employers do not usually take up references until the later stages of recruitment. The aforementioned methods are probably suitable only when biodata are used as a part of a longer selection procedure. For preselection, there is really no substitute for a purpose-designed self-report questionnaire.

A number of distinct forms of constructing biodata instruments can be distinguished. Schneider and Schneider (1994) outlined three approaches: the *individual*, the *cluster* and the *career* methods. With the *individual* method, biographical information is collected from individuals and weights for the information are derived against individually based criteria. The eventual biodata measure is a scored composite of valid items in which both the predictor and the criterion are expressed in terms of individual differences. In a classic biodata procedure, applicants for a job complete a biographical information blank (BIB) and one year later turnover is assessed. Weights for valid items – those items that correlate strongly with turnover – are determined, and the score for future applicants on the BIB is a composite of the valid (weighted) items.

The *cluster* method has been pioneered by Owens and his colleagues (Owens, 1976; Owens and Schoenfeldt, 1979). In this technique, BIBs have been completed by college students and, on the basis of similarity in response patterns, students are placed into biodata clusters. These clusters comprise individuals who share common life history experiences and, as such, they are called life history subgroups. Owens and his co-workers have shown that predictions of an individual's future behaviour based on that individual's cluster membership is at least as accurate as predictions based on that individual's own biodata factor scores. In fact, membership in a biodata cluster can validly predict such diverse criteria as college major, grade point average, participation in extracurricular activities and future vocational choice (Mumford and Owens, 1987).

The *career* method is typified by studies showing that individuals who enter particular occupations or careers share common life experiences (for example, Eberhardt and Muchinsky, 1982b; Niener and Owens, 1985). In these studies, the emphasis is on biographical information associated with people in a career, and the goal is to find similarities between persons within a career and differences between persons in different careers. The method begins with the career and predicts similarity in life history experiences. This differs from the cluster method in which individuals are first clustered based on their life history experiences.

Each of these approaches has value and effectiveness under different circumstances. Schneider and Schneider (1994) suggested that the three approaches could be conceptually organized along a continuum. The choice of which approach to use would depend on the nature of the criterion variables – that is, whatever it is one wishes to predict or explain. The individual method would be appropriate under circumstances in which one wished to predict employee performance in a specific job or their development in an organization. Individual characteristics of that person would be related to job performance criteria. The cluster method would be more appropriately applied under circumstances in which the objective was to find out whether individuals can be clustered into groups according to past life experiences. Then, in turn, further analysis would consider whether individuals in a cluster or group follow a similar career track and experience similar degrees of success. The career method traces back whether individuals in the same vocation have certain biographical characteristics in common in the hope of discovering the magic ingredients that predict entry to and success in that vocation.

Selecting or Generating Items

Items can be selected from catalogues, questionnaires and previous studies and slightly adapted to each study. For instance, Russell, Devlin, Mattson and Atwater (1990) studied US Naval Academy students. They derived criteria for success from a performance appraisal instrument for officers. A pool of life experiences that were thought potentially to be related to performance dimensions were generated from biographical essays the students were asked to write. The essay topics were chosen so that antecedent developmental elements of the five key dimensions of officer fitness were likely to be reported. Essays were analysed by content to produce biodata items. Biodata items were developed from each life experience extracted from the essays.

Two items were generated for each incident – the first asked how frequently this type of situation occurred; the second asked how often this type of situation was handled effectively. Separate biodata scales were constructed for each criterion. Separate predictor scales were developed by contrasting all biodata responses of individuals in the top third of their respective criterion distributions with responses of those in the bottom third.

Weights of +1 were applied to scored item responses that the high criterion group endorsed more than the low criterion group, and weights of -1 were assigned to item responses for which the reverse was true. These scales were then cross-validated on the remaining third of students and another sample. Items scored on one or more of the cross-validated biodata scales were factor analysed to identify any underlying developmental constraints.

These empirically derived biodata scales predicted peer ratings of leadership as well as ratings of military and academic performance. Furthermore, the biodata scales significantly contributed to the prediction of military and academic performance beyond validities generated by the current predictor set. Thus, biodata items developed by using the retrospective life experience method have potential.

Contraindicated Items

Harrell (1960) has suggested that people with experience in specific positions have useful theories about biographical attributes that signal unsuccessful performance. These attributes were called 'knock-out' factors – such as too-frequent change of address, excessive personal indebtedness, unexplained gaps in the employment record and frequent change of jobs. Thus, biodata items can be used to 'select out' people just as much as they can be used to 'select in' possible employees.

Harrell found that no successful salesmen in his study had more than one 'knock-out' factor whereas eight of 52 non-successful salesmen had two or more. The implication is that the 'knock-out' strategy reduced the selection of unsatisfactory applicants by 15% without simultaneously excluding any who would be satisfactory salesmen.

Self-descriptive Items

Most items used in biodata are simple self-descriptive, self-report items. Walther (1961) attempted to predict performance and turnover criteria of foreign service clerical applicants. The predictor was multiple choice items related to grades, interest in school, job likes and dislikes, relationship with parents, social activities, steadiness of employment and hobbies. Sample items were:

Were your parents:
a. Always very strict with you?
b. Usually very strict with you?
c. Seldom very strict with you?
d. Never very strict with you?

Which of the following characteristics of a job is *least* important to you:
a. Opportunity to ask questions and consult about difficulties.
b. Opportunity to understand just how one's superior expects work to be done.
c. Certainty one's work will be judged by fair standards.
d. Freedom in working out one's own method of doing the work.
e. Co-workers – congenial, competent and adequate in number.

These items may be classified as 'soft' in contrast with 'hard' items usually included on an application blank. These self-descriptive items are 'soft' because (a) they cannot be verified and (b) the options are expressed in abstract value judgements rather than realistic behaviour. Nevertheless, validity coefficients were remarkably high in cross-validation, with some positions predicted with correlations of 0.49 and 0.60. Other positions of mail clerk, code clerks and record clerks were in the range of 0.28 to 0.38.

Multiple-choice Items

Biodata items in a multiple-choice format are attractive because they are easy to score, and because the retrieval of information from the respondent's memory may be enhanced if his or her task is merely to recognize a printed alternative.

The risk is that ready-made options may increase the tendency for leniency error or even fictionalization, especially for biodata items that cannot be verified. A fill-in type of biodata item, by contrast, may provide fewer cues to indicate the item's transparency. Furthermore, a biodata item that needs to be filled in can be classified in several different ways so that one fill-in can generate a number of independent items. These two formats, the fill-in versus the multiple-choice, should be contrasted in further research with biodata items.

Characteristics of Good Items: Reliability

Owens, Glennon and Albright (1966) administered 200 life history items to 43 subjects and then two months later readministered the same items. Eight rules of thumb differentiated the consistent from the inconsistent items. These rules could be valuable as heuristic aids in developing biographical items. The rules are:

1. Brevity.
2. Options should be expressed in numbers, for example, How old are you now?
   20 to 29
   30 to 39
   40 to 49
   50 to 59
   60 or over
3. Options should contain *all* alternatives or, if this is not possible, then an 'escape' option should be provided.
4. Items should convey a neutral or pleasant connotation.
5. An item should not try to retrieve information beyond the memory of the respondent.
6. Extremes on the continuum of choices may be more consistent than those in the middle position.
7. Statements should be positively worded.
8. A response continuum should not be defined in qualitative terms, as, for instance, 'seldom', 'occasionally' and 'frequently'.

This is a useful checklist to determine item reliability in response.

Accuracy

Accountability may be a powerful determinant of an item's accuracy. Operationally, accountability would be present if the respondent was asked to grant permission for verification of information by contacting former employers, teachers and other referees cited on the form. This is rarely done, however, and it may not need to be done as long as the employee believes that it might be done. Clearly, this is possible only with 'hard' rather than 'soft' data.

Realism

Biodata questionnaire/application forms can be expanded beyond verifiable factual items – and some experts have argued that this can be useful. Questions can be asked about the applicant's/respondent's perception of work experiences, attitudes towards relevant issues and so on. The important thing is that such items should be clearly worded and empirically tested against performance criteria. Selecting and writing your biodata items looks simple, but it takes skill and experience because there are so many potential traps for people to fall into.

Predictive versus Concurrent Designs

There are essentially two ways to test the validity of biodata items. In a predictive design biodata are obtained from all job applicants *before* hiring. Selection decisions are then made on the basis of the *existing* selection procedure. After an extended time period (up to five years), criterion data are collected on the successful applicants (that is, those who are now employees of the organization), the biodata are combined using one of several methods and the validity of the total score is determined. Much depends on the sensitivity, robustness and reflectiveness of these 'criteria' (see Chapter 5).

The advantage of the predictive design is that it is practical and specific; the questionnaire is intended to be used for applicants, hence it is developed by using data *from* actual applicants. The main disadvantage is that it is a time-consuming and hence expensive process. It might, for example, take at least 24 months to obtain reliable, meaningful criterion data on new employees. If an organization does not have a regular intake of new staff, there could be a two-year or three-year delay between sending the draft biodata form to applicants and obtaining a large enough sample of employees to warrant further development work. Hence, big organizations, those that are growing, or those with a reasonably high throughput tend to be able to do predictive testing, but small organizations, with relatively little turnover, find it difficult and expensive.

Thus, concurrent designs are often used in practice. Here the biodata are collected from existing employees and criterion data are collected *at the same time*. The biodata are then combined and validated as for predictive designs. Although this approach cuts down drastically on development time, it has major disadvantages.

For instance, the participating employees are usually asked to complete the biodata form as if they were applying to the organization for the first time, and to recall their own situation immediately before hiring. This may cause memorial distortion unless the tester of the device chooses recent employees;

then there is a trade-off against obtaining reliable criterion data. More importantly, the responses of typical applicants (even those who go on to be selected) may be different from those of 'typical' employees. This may be because of applicants' natural desire to present themselves in a favourable light, although a potentially more serious problem is criterion contamination, whereby the biodata responses of current employees become perhaps unconsciously distorted through contact with the organization. If an assertive, competitive work style is part of the culture of an organization, for example, employees' responses to items that seem to measure these characteristics might be biased towards the cultural norm. The use of relatively hard biodata can reduce this problem, but there is ultimately no substitute for a final check of a concurrent scoring key using actual job applicants. In this way a compromise can be reached between obtaining a usable biodata device quickly and a truly predictive design.

Scoring, Interpretation and Cross-validation

Strebler (1991) has noted that because biodata ultimately rely on a single score similar to a test, the method for developing the procedure is not dissimilar to developing any psychometric test. The method to arrive at this single score represents the most fundamental difference between biodata and other less systematic paper sifts, and probably causes most of the technical complexity of biodata. The stage of weighting and combining items objectively requires the most technical expertise. It is paradoxically the least well documented and the most inaccessible. It is also the one stage when there is the least consensus as to the best approach. Often, the information has to be inferred, or guessed, from the method section of published research.

To use a biographical data blank, it is first necessary to ascribe values or 'weights' to the individual items and combine these to produce a total score analogous to that produced from a test. Weights can be determined empirically (preferably), intuitively (occasionally) or by a combination of the two. The solely 'intuitive' method relies on expert judgements concerning hypothesized predictor–criterion relationships. Essentially, this means that 'experts' with specialist previous knowledge or expertise in the field decide on the 'correct', 'ideal' or 'optimal' answer to each question as well as the less desirable answers, and apportion scores or 'weights' appropriately. The choice of items and the magnitude and direction of the weights are thus based purely on theoretical/past experience considerations. The validity of these intuitions can be tested, and this feedback information used to modify the original weights. This 'iterative' approach characterized some of the early work in the area (Goldsmith, 1922), although it was historically superseded by more objective empirical methods. There has, however, been a resurgence of interest in the theoretical underpinnings of biodata–criterion links. Although this approach is undoubtedly simple, it does not seem to be particularly effective (Mitchell and Klimoski, 1986).

There are two distinct objective approaches to combining biodata. In the first, items are weighted with respect to their ability to predict an external job-specific criterion: the 'empirical' approach. Most external methods use a dichotomous criterion, and it becomes necessary to identify 'good' versus 'bad' employees – hence the preponderance of studies on turnover (see Schwab and Oliver, 1974). The stages of the typical external method are illustrated in Figure 5.1 (Drakeley, 1988).

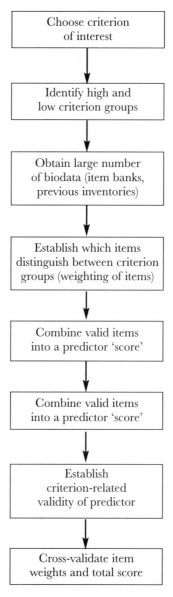

Figure 5.1: External (empirical) model

Items can be weighted in several ways, although the 'percentage' method (Guion, 1965) is probably the most popular. The *horizontal* per cent method weights a response by the likelihood of success that is associated with it. To take a purely hypothetical example to illustrate the method: suppose that an oil company wished to determine weights for the biodata item 'higher education (HE) qualifications' for predicting success as a research scientist. Further suppose that the company employs 267 such scientists and that it chooses 172 of them as good and 95 as bad. Having obtained details of the scientists' qualifications from their personnel records, the distribution of types of qualification might look like the first two columns of Table 5.2.

It seems that 146 scientists possess PhDs or master's degrees and that 110 of these are 'good' – that is, the *probability of success* associated with a postgraduate degree is 0.75 (110 divided by 146). In the horizontal per cent method, this probability is simply converted into a raw weight by moving the decimal place and rounding to a whole number; the raw weight for 'postgraduate degree' is thus 8. For 'bachelor's degree' it is 6 (41 divided by 69 = 0.59 = 6) and so on.

Note that the raw weights for the horizontal per cent method are always positive; it is possible to have a 'zero' probability of success but not a negative one. These raw weights are sometimes converted into unit ascribed weights (Guion, 1965) which take the base rate of success into account. Weights $(1, 0, -1)$ are ascribed to responses only where the associated probability of success either substantially exceeds or falls below the current base rate – say, by 20%. In Table 5.2 the base rate is 0.64 (172 of the 267 scientists are classed as 'good' – that is, are successful). The ascribed weight for 'postgraduate degree' is actually zero in

Table 5.2: Horizontal weighting of one biodata item

HE qualifications	Frequency good	Frequency bad	Total	Probability of good	Raw weight	Ascribed weight*
Postgraduate (e.g., PhD/MSc)	110	36	146	0.75	8	0
Bachelor's degree (e.g., BSc/BA)	41	28	69	0.59	6	0
Other HE qualifications (e.g. Diplomas)	18	15	33	0.55	5	0
No HE qualifications obtained	3	16	19	0.16	2	-1
Total	172	95	267	0.64		

Note: * Taking into account base rate of success of 0.64.

this example because its associated probability of success does not exceed the base rate by 20%. The weights for the remaining categories are also zero except for 'no HE qualifications obtained' where it is -1. In this case the probability of success is more than 20% below the base rate. Ascribed weights may be more desirable than raw weights for two reasons. First, the weights more accurately reflect the 'value' of a response. In this example the raw weight makes it seem as though a PhD or MSc would be a good thing for a research scientist to have, whereas it would be more true to say that not having a HE qualification would be bad – a subtle difference but one that, if not understood, could affect the organization's entire recruitment strategy and lead it to impose a 'PhDs only' rule. Second, ascribed weights are more 'conservative' and less likely to be susceptible to chance effects, particularly in small samples. Thus, on balance, and particularly where the biodata inventory contains a large number of items, ascribed weights are preferable.

The *vertical* per cent method weights on item proportional to the discriminating power of the response. Table 5.3 shows calculations for this method using data from the previous example. Of the good scientists, 64% (110 divided by 172) from Table 5.2 possess PhDs or MScs whereas only 38% (36 divided by 95) of the bad scientists do. The vertical difference in per cent is +26%. This difference in per cent has been transformed into a weight for PhD/MSc by reference to tables attributed to Stead and Shartle (1940), although these were published as Strong's 'Tables of Net Weights' (see England, 1971: 27). Vertical per cent weights can be either positive of negative depending on the direction of the difference, but a constant can be added to help eliminate errors in

Table 5.3: Vertical weighting of one biodata item

HE Qualification	Percentage good*	Percentage Bad*	Difference in %	Weight**
Postgraduate (e.g., PhD/MSc)	64	38	+26	+6
Bachelor's degree (e.g., BSc/BA)	24	29	–5	–1
Other HE qualifications (e.g., Diplomas)	10	16	–6	–1
No HE qualifications obtained	2	17	–15	–5
Total	100	100		

Notes: * Groups of high and low performers; ** Derived from Strong's Tables of Weights (see England, 1971).

coding (similarly, horizontal unit weights can be adjusted to 2, 1 or 0). The distinction between the vertical and horizontal methods may seem to be rather fine. If conservatism is important, the vertical per cent method can be regarded as less cautious. In the example, the difference between having a postgraduate degree and having no HE qualification at all would add 11 points to the total score on the biodata. As long as both the item and its weights are *reliable*, this is not a problem. However, most practitioners would be unhappy to allow a difference of 11 points to result from candidates choosing one option over another, if the item were 'soft' (for example, how often do you go out with a group of friends?: seldom or often) or if the weights were developed in a small sample.

With either method, researchers should take care when weighting response alternatives that are *contingent* on the answers to other questions. In our example, 'no HE qualifications' is the opt-out response to the question. If the oil company went on to weight 'type of subject studied for HE qualifications', this opt-out option should not be scored again. Weights should be ascribed to legitimate answers to contingent items only, otherwise candidates would be penalized (or rewarded) for the same piece of evidence twice. The same argument can be seen to apply to any *highly correlated* items, and researchers sometimes discard some of these before weighting the remaining biodata items.

The per cent methods are two ways of weighting biodata, but they both assume a dichotomous good/bad criterion. Many of the other methods permit the researcher to retain a contingent criterion. It is possible, for example, to use the mean criterion score of respondents in a particular category (for example, those with postgraduate degrees) as an index of success for that category. These indices of success can be treated as independent variables in a regression analysis (Bittner, 1945) or simply treated as weights (Nevo, 1976).

Drakeley (1989) quotes a 'marital status' example: if 50% of the married employees were 'good', then this percentage would be converted to a basic weight by simply moving the decimal point. The weight for 'married' would thus be 5. If 70% of the single employees were good, the weight for 'single' would be 7 – and so on for divorced, widowed, etc. The basic weight can, if desired, be converted to an ascribed weight which takes into account the base rate of successes in the organization (Guion, 1965).

According to Drakeley (1989), the vertical percent method weights an item proportional to the discriminating power of the response. In his marital status example, if 60% of the good group were single, whereas only 40% of the bad group were, the vertical difference in percentage would be 60% –40%=20%. This difference in percentages can then be transformed into a weight for 'single' by reference to published tables. Where there is a desire to retain a continuous criterion, it is possible to use the mean criterion score of respondents in a particular category (for example, married employees) as an index of success for that category. These indices of success can be treated as independent variables in a regression analysis (Bittner, 1945), or simply treated as weights (Nevo, 1976).

Strebler (1991) noted that the vertical per cent weighting method is popular. The method is mostly associated with the Weighted Application Blank (WAB) described in detail by England (1971). It allocates weights to items according to the discriminating power of response. In the above example (loosely based on England's WAB method) the percentages of item responses on degree subjects for high and low performers are computed and subtracted. Weights are given which are a function of the significance of the difference between two criterion groups. These weights can be extracted from tables or calculated separately and they can include negative as well as positive weights. Although weights can be calculated manually, actual decisions on the most appropriate weighting methods and calculations would usually involve some research. A total biodata score can then be obtained by adding items showing a statistically significant relationship with the criterion. At this stage, it may be possible for a few non-significant items to be included to ensure a better balance between the different categories of item (for example, education, work, leisure and so on). Provided

Table 5.4: Items that could be included in a biodata scoring key*

Items	Weights*
• degree items (× 2)** (subject, class ...)	Max 10
• school achievements O levels or equivalent (× 3) A levels or equivalent (× 3)	 10 10
• positions of responsibility (× 3) (school, university, community)	6
• vacation work (× 2) (number, type)	4
• other work experience (× 2) (number type)	4
• leisure activities	4
• project work (school, university/voluntary work)	2
• career choice	2
• work planning	2
• reason for application	2
Total biodata score	56

Notes: * Weights can also be given a negative score; ** Numbers of items for each category given in brackets.
Source: Strebler, 1991.

these are job related and fair, they can be monitored for subsequent years as they may become significant and replace items that have lost their validity.

> The process of weighting predictive items such as these is also known as empirically keying, since it enables a *biodata scoring key* to be developed with normally about 20/30 items. A biodata scoring key is, therefore, a document setting out the items in detail including a guide to the rating system and the weights for scoring each item to derive the biodata total score for each candidate. (Strebler, 1991: 6)

We have seen that the most frequently cited criticism of the external method is its very dust-bowl empiricism – the calculation of valid biodata items is based purely on how they statistically predict future behaviour and their meaning does not derive from any theory about human behaviour (Pace and Schoenfeldt, 1977; Matteson, 1978; Mitchell and Klimoski, 1982). The 'shotgun' approach in testing out large numbers of items with little recourse to theory can reveal spurious relationships between non-job-relevant items and work performance. These in turn may lead to discriminatory selection procedures (Pace and Schoenfeldt, 1977); items should thus be selected with great care.

Strebler (1991) noted:

> The external has been said to amount to 'raw empiricism in the extreme' (Guion, 1965) and to capitalise massively on chance that individual items will be related to the criterion (Hunter & Hunter, 1984). Although establishing the relationship between item results in a better structured instrument, the internal approach presents difficulties since it relies on individual items that may, or may not, be related to the criterion in the first instance. Research on comparing both methods is scarce. The evidence available so far has tended to err towards the internal method as the best to maximise prediction (Mitchell & Klimoski, 1982; Drakeley, 1988). Since it is also easier to calculate, as it does not need complex factor analyses, it has tended to be used quite frequently with a very good prediction rate. More recently, attempts have been made to combine the two methods by conducting a factor analysis of the keyed items to better understand and structure the content of the scoring key which would enable items to be grouped into meaningful background scales (McDaniel, 1989). In practice, the choice of method would depend on the researcher or developer's own methodological preferences and on the purpose for which biodata are to be used. When the purpose is to maximise prediction of a criterion, the external method would appear to result in a slightly higher predictive validity than the internal (Drakeley, 1989). (Strebler, 1991: 18/99)

The desire to unravel biodata scores and determine what underlying constructs they measure prompted researchers to develop keys based on the relationships between items. This second objective method of combining questionnaire items has been called the *inductive* or 'internal' approach (Hornick, James and Jones, 1977).

The internal approach aims to use techniques that maximize the homogeneity of a set of items. An example is known as 'keying patterns of response' (Levine and Zachert, 1951). Levine and Zachert grouped biodata items into subjectively judged sets (for example, all items concerned with hobbies). With these groupings, their ability to predict future behaviour exceeded chance. In consequence, the items continued to be used in groups rather than singly as performance predictors.

The rationale underlying this procedure is that if enough items concerning, say, school career, are related to success, then *all* relevant school activities should be predictive; deviations from this rule are attributed to chance. This is true only if the 'item sets' are homogeneous to begin with, but similar looking items may measure different constructs – for example, the quantity of work experience versus the quality of it.

More recently, the different categories of biodata have been arrived at by multivariate statistical procedures which reduce biodata items to a limited number of clusters or 'factors'. For example, Mitchell and Klimoski (1982) found that their 'educational background' factor included biodata items related to academic success, social activities in school years, participation in extracurricular activities, early leadership and so on. In this case, factor score coefficients derived by the statistical analysis act as weights and are used to score the biodata into composites. The validity of these composites against the criterion is then determined through multiple regression. Drakeley (1989) provided a model for this method (Figure 5.2).

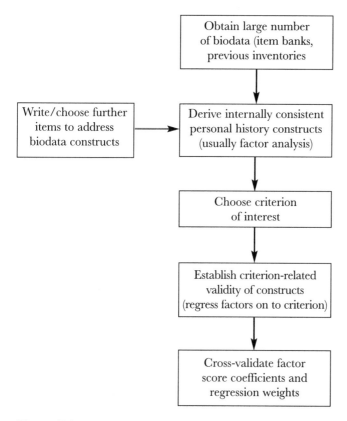

Figure 5.2: Internal (inductive) model

A criticism of the internal approach is that the composite factor scores, so derived, can assume an importance out of proportion to the usefulness of the technique that is used. The interpretability of factors can lead researchers to suggest that they have discovered something 'real' rather than a more parsimonious way of describing their data. Factor analysis is often preferred to external methods because the latter are said to capitalize on chance relationships (Schwab and Oliver, 1974; Childs and Klimoski, 1986). Yet, regression weights and factor scores may also be dependent on the effects of chance (Gorsuch, 1974).

It has been suggested that factor solutions are relatively stable (Owens and Schoenfeldt, 1979), that their criterion validity may shrink less over time and that they are more rational than external devices (Baehr and Williams, 1967, 1968; Childs and Klimoski, 1986). Yet, the evidence for factor stability from population to population is equivocal (Eberhardt and Muchinsky, 1984; Lautenschlager and Shaffer, 1987), even though similar populations have been used. The decay of, or change in, factor structures over time, particularly for soft biodata, has been mentioned (Davis, 1984; Shaffer, Saunders and Owens, 1986) and this instability is usually attributed to changes in the life experiences of individuals as a consequence of changes in their jobs. The short-term reliability of biodata devices may largely depend on the size of the sample and the theory and hypotheses guiding item selection. Factor analytic studies should use large samples and items should be chosen with care, so that this may account for their claimed superiority in this respect (for example, Baehr and Williams, 1967; Owens and Schoenfeldt, 1979).

The suggestion that factor analysis is necessarily more 'rational', empirically valid or clear than external methods depends on how the term is defined. Many writers have discussed the virtues of the hypothesis testing approach to the development of selection instruments (Guion, 1965; Cascio, 1976; Heneman, Schwab, Fossum and Dyer, 1983). Finally, Drakeley (1989) provides a third model for biodata (see Figure 5.3).

Any method of combining items is acceptable by the model. However, some approaches do not lend themselves well to obtaining evidence with which to confirm, or reject and modify, the original hypotheses. Hypothesis testing using these methods must proceed at the item level. The complexity and sheer number of inter-item and item-criterion relationships increases the appeal of methods that reduce the dimensionality of the data. This can be achieved by using more sophisticated multivariate techniques, such as factor or cluster analysis or multidimensional scales.

Setting Cut-off Scores

Irrespective of the collecting method chosen, a last step is to establish a *cut-off score* that will secure enough candidates for the selection stage of the process. Strebler (1991) has provided the following example: suppose that a financial

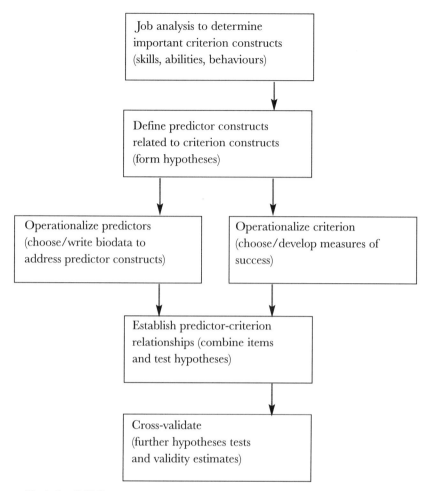

Source: Drakeley (1989)

Figure 5.3: Rational (deductive) model

services company recruits a small number of graduates each year for its fast-track management development programme. Based on previous years, the organization expects to receive about 1,000 applications but has had to reduce its intake to 20. Assessment is by means of a costly assessment centre so the number of candidates needs to be reduced to a maximum of five per vacancy. From the biodata scoring key shown in Figure 5.2, we know that the biodata scores of candidates can be distributed between 0 and 56. A way to calculate an approximate cut-off score would be to examine the distribution of the first 100 applications as shown in Figure 5.4. On this basis, this organization is likely to decide to call the five candidates scoring between 40 to 56 and to reject the 70 candidates scoring between 0 and 27.

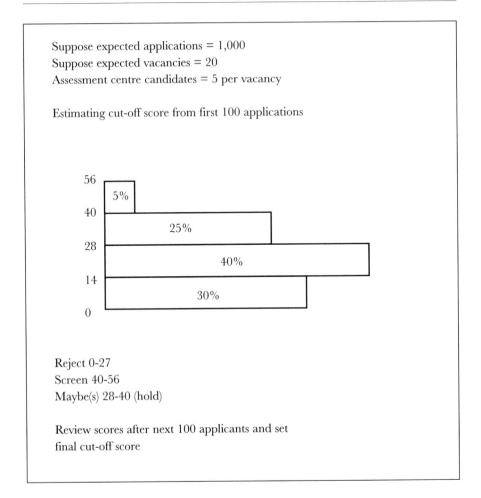

Suppose expected applications = 1,000
Suppose expected vacancies = 20
Assessment centre candidates = 5 per vacancy

Estimating cut-off score from first 100 applications

Reject 0-27
Screen 40-56
Maybe(s) 28-40 (hold)

Review scores after next 100 applicants and set
final cut-off score

Figure 5.4: Calculating a cut-off score

Updating and Replicating Findings

As technology, markets and products change, so do jobs. The same abilities, traits and skills that characterized, say, a bank manager 20 years ago are rather different from what they are today. Furthermore, as other changes occur in society, the same biographical experiences are not possible. One example of such changes is that young people travel extensively far more today than did previous generations. The availability of transportation, special package deals and greater affluence have facilitated this development. Thirty years ago, overseas travel was far less commonplace.

Similar new biographical experiences may now be possible that are in themselves largely predictive. For instance, women are being 'let into', even encouraged into, various institutions that they were previously barred from, and these may be highly predictive of occupational success. For the above reasons it is wise to update biodata analyses every so often – at least every five years. The job analyses and biographical items need to be rechecked, as things might have changed.

Conclusion

This chapter concentrated on how to use biodata. The first step is job analysis, which provides important clues as to what biographical items to select and, perhaps more importantly, finds what dependent criteria to measure in each job. There are various methods of job analysis available, each with its own strengths and weaknesses. Some techniques break jobs down into their constituent components and then formulate statements about these particular job elements. Job interviewees can then be tested for their level of experience in relation to these specific job aspects. Another technique is to formulate descriptions of incidents that are deemed to be 'critical' elements in relation to a particular job. This method represents an attempt to analyse a job into its basic behavioural components, which can then be used to assess the capabilities of job applicants to cope with different job-relevant situations.

Some management researchers have argued for improvements in job analysis techniques. One suggestion has been that such techniques should include an analysis of the rewards associated with jobs and the expectations of applicants associated with the particular job for which they have applied. Effective job analysis is vital to the development of biodata instruments that will yield accurate predictive assessments of job applicants. However, an analysis of the current job alone is not sufficient to guarantee a good biodata instrument. Careful conceptualization of the job itself is one element, but systematic empirical assessment of the relationships between particular biographical details about job applicants and on-the-job performance is equally important. Once again, a variety of strategies are available to organizations that wish to develop biodata instruments as part of their employee selection process. Some techniques opt to examine individuals in isolation, whereas others prefer to develop categories or groupings of individuals based on job-relevant criteria, and against which individuals can be compared.

In selecting items for biodata instruments, one approach is to establish items that predict good job performance. In contrast, biodata instruments have been developed in which items are included that predict poor or inadequate job performance. In the latter case, any job applicants who score above a threshold are automatically excluded. Biodata items must be relevant to the job at hand, be tested regularly for their continuing reliability as job performance predictors, and be phrased in such a way that respondents are able to reply meaningfully. These responses must then be weighted appropriately so that the data they yield can be statistically checked against performance indicators that can be scored. In weighting biodata items, scoring techniques may focus on the distribution of responses across applicant populations or be based on absolute scores or scales on which a minimum score is required. The decision that then needs to be made is whether to depend on raw empiricism or whether to try to develop meaningful explanations as to why certain biodata items work, whereas others do not. Each approach has its own supporters and detractors. In the end, a little bit of each approach may be best. It is essential to show, through proper and effective empirical tests, the strength of relationship between certain biographical measures and job-related performance measures. Equally, blind empiricism does not explain why such relationships exist. Through understanding why certain kinds of background result in the presence of more strongly developed job-relevant skills and mental attitudes, management researchers may be able to develop even better biodata instruments.

Chapter 6:
What Do Biodata Predict?

Introduction

The real power and usefulness of biodata stem not simply from providing interesting profiles of job candidates or employees, but from the ability of biodata keys to predict future job performance. Research into the life history antecedents of worker behaviour has attempted to find out whether future job success can be effectively predicted from information about background and past experience. This kind of research has examined an extensive array of different life history items to determine how they are related to one another and to aspects of job performance.

As with any test, the effectiveness of biodata can be confidently assumed only once appropriate validation procedures have been carried out. These procedures take the form of cross-validation to find out whether and which biodata items can predict performance across more than one sample: criterion-related validity over time and validity generalization over more than one type of performance variable.

One of the problems in assessing the real effectiveness of biodata has been the lack of consistency in the use of appropriate validation procedures. It is vital, in particular, to distinguish between the *original* sample on which the biodata items were constructed and any other samples on which those same items may be used. Validity can be calculated only from a cross-validation sample. A WAB or biodata inventory that has not been cross-validated should not automatically be used for selection, although this has been known to happen. Indeed, Cureton (1950) called coefficients based on any tests that had not been cross-validated 'baloney coefficients'. WABs and other such biodata inventories are particularly likely to 'shrink' on cross-validation because they are purely empirical and are sensitive to chance differences between samples. Most of the studies reviewed in this chapter have reported cross-validation statistics – but it is not always clear from published accounts whether this is universally the case. Hence, we have attempted to make it clear whether development or cross-validation coefficients were used throughout the following sections.

Standard Oil of Indiana

The single group most active in the area of personal history research has been at Standard Oil of Indiana, where a series of studies was done in the early 1960s which examined various aspects of biographical data as predictors. In the first study in the series (Smith, Albright, Glennon and Owens, 1961), a personal history questionnaire was given to a group of petroleum research scientists. The questions were both validated and cross-validated against three different criteria: (1) overall performance ratings, (2) creativity ratings and (3) number of patents. The concurrent cross-validation indices for these three criteria were 0.61, 0.52 and 0.52 respectively – a rather impressive set of validities.

A second study (Albright and Glennon, 1961) based on the same data found 43 different personal history items (out of an original 484) which differentiated significantly the petroleum scientists who 'desired to advance in to laboratory supervision' from those who desired only increased salary but who preferred to remain scientists. Thus, the degree to which a scientist has supervisory aspirations is apparently related to biographical history of that scientist.

The third study in the series (Morrison, Owens, Glennon and Albright, 1962) was designed to determine the underlying 'dimensions' of life history experience by using the technique of factor analysis to group together similar life history item 'types'. The researchers factor-analysed 75 different items that had been found to discriminate on at least one of the three criterion measures used in their first study (performance ratings, creativity ratings and patents).

Five different factors or groupings of items were obtained:

1. *Favourable self-perception*
The items which grouped together to define this factor were:
   a. In the top 5% of performance in their occupation.
   b. Could be highly successful supervisors if given the opportunity.
   c. Work at faster pace than most people.
   d. Desire to work entirely autonomously selecting both a method and a goal.
   e. Like a lot of responsibility.
   f. In an unpleasant situation, try to react and formulate a decision immediately.
   g. Are friendly and easy-going and have many friends.

All of these items are highly favourable or flattering towards the respondent. Thus people scoring high on this factor (that is, checking agreement with these statements) are those having a highly favourable self-impression. The remaining factors were:

2. *Inquisitive professional orientation*
   a. Completed their PhD.
   b. Belong to one or more professional organizations.
   c. Do not limit themselves to undergraduate work as an educational goal for their sons.
   d. Have some close friends and a number of acquaintances.
   e. Devote much time to reading of many kinds, preferring current and political topics among non-professional areas.
   f. Desire to work entirely autonomously.
   g. Have high salary aspirations.

3. *Utilitarian drive*
   a. Desire extrinsic rewards – that is, from business and society.
   b. Prefer urban dwelling.
   c. Started dating before age 20.
   d. Feel free to express their views and perceive themselves as influencing others in group and individual situations, do not want to work with just one other person.
   e. Do not desire to work entirely autonomously; want to choose their own method, but not necessarily the goal towards which they are to strive.
   f. Feel dissatisfied with themselves at times.

4. *Tolerance for ambiguity*
   a. Desire to have many work projects going simultaneously.
   b. Are not single.
   c. Have solicited funds for charity and made speeches.
   d. Have high salary aspirations.
   e. Have friends with similar and dissimilar political views.

5. *General adjustment*
   a. Feel that school material was adequately presented.
   b. Came from happy homes where they were well treated.
   c. Express their opinions readily and feel that they are effective in doing so.
   d. Have high salary aspirations.
   e. Can tolerate inefficiency in a job better than less controllable problems.
   f. Prefer verbal to laboratory course work.

The next question concerned the relationship of the three criterion measures to these five different life history dimensions. What was interesting was that the two criteria involving ratings showed similar patterns. Thus, petroleum scientists who received high ratings on performance and on creativity tended also to get high scores on the factors of self-perception, utilitarian drive and general adjustment. It is notable that the pattern for patent disclosures was exactly opposite to the pattern for the ratings. Those scientists with many patent disclosures scored low on self-perception, utilitarian drive and self-adjustment, but very high on inquisitive professional orientation and tolerance for ambiguity.

It is clear that studies such as this go far beyond the practical questions of selection and provide a good deal of insight and understanding as to why one particular group of individuals is more likely to be successful (as defined by a particular criterion) than some other group. A subsequent study was reported by Chaney and Owens (1964). This study differed from the earlier ones in that it attempted to predict interests of college freshmen in the area of sales, research and engineering using life history items. Responses to a 170-item, multiple-choice life history questionnaire were analysed.

A sample of 388 university freshmen in engineering was used for the sales and research portions of the analysis, and 700 freshmen were used in appraising general engineering interest. The significant items were used to develop scoring keys for each interest criterion. When these keys were cross-validated on completely independent samples, correlations of 0.57, 0.42 and 0.51 were obtained for sales, research and general engineering respectively.

Early Reviews: Narrative Studies

Although knowing that biodata seem to work for Standard Oil of Indiana might bring some comfort (not least to other US oil companies), a far more extensive body of knowledge has been assembled by earlier reviewers of the area. These 'narrative studies' have attempted to bring together results of research across different organizations to determine whether there are any trends in the criterion-related validity of biodata.

A great many analyses of the research literature have focused on the predictive validity of biodata compared with other tests. The result of these analyses has largely been positive for biodata. However, biodata have not been effective predictors of all kinds of performance variables to which they have been related.

Reviews by Owens (1976), Asher (1972), Schuh (1967) and Henry (1966) strongly supported the validity of biodata. Asher's review compared the predictive power of biodata with that of other predictors, such as tests of intelligence and aptitude. In all cases, and at all arbitrary validity coefficient cut-off points, biodata were clearly seen as the most valid predictors. The superiority of biodata was found to hold for criteria of trainability and for job proficiency. Other reviews were less supportive.

One of the problems in assessing the real effectiveness of biodata has been the lack of consistency in the use of appropriate validation procedures. It is vital, in particular, to distinguish between the *original* sample on which the biodata items were constructed and any other samples on which those same items may be used. Validity can be calculated only from a cross-validation sample. A WAB or biodata inventory that hasn't been cross-validated should not be used for selection, although this has happened.

Schwab and Oliver (1974) questioned the optimism of Schuh's (1967) findings by pointing out that only 14 of the studies reviewed were cross-validated. Caplan and Schmidt (1977) reviewed the literature for two specific biographical items: education and experience. Their review found zero or near-zero validities for both types of data. In Korman's 1968 review, the validity of biodata for predicting managerial performance was generally lower than validity for other measures, such as peer ratings. In addition, personal history data had less predictive power for higher-level managers. These latter reviews offered only minor demurrals to what was otherwise strong positive research evidence for the predictive validity of biodata.

Reilly and Chao (1982) reviewed 58 studies using biographical information as a predictor. They did not discuss individual biodata studies in detail. Instead they presented results for various types of criteria within broad occupational categories, for occupational categories pooled across criteria and for criteria pooled across occupational categories.

Only cross-validated coefficients were used in computing the averages. Nine coefficients were reviewed for military personnel, including correlations (average r=0.39) and ratings (average r=0.25). For clerical personnel six coefficients with only one criterion, tenure, yielded an average r of 0.52. The average validity for rating criteria for managers was r=0.40 (over four coefficients). The only other management criterion for which coefficients were available was salary. Only two coefficients were located for non-management jobs other than clerical, yielding an average validity of 0.14.

Schmitt, Gooding, Noe and Kirsch (1984) reviewed research published between 1964 and 1982. The weighted average of 99 validity coefficients was r=0.24, which was poorer than assessment centres, work samples and peer ratings, but better than personality inventories. Biodata were used to predict:

performance ratings	r=0.32
turnover	r=0.21
achievement/grades	r=0.23
status change	r=0.33
wages	r=0.53
productivity	r=0.20

The high correlation with wages, based on seven samples and 1,544 subjects, is unexplained.

Earlier Reviews: Meta-analysis

Narrative reviews provide one important insight into the criterion-related validity of biodata, but they are severely limited in one sense – they may be insensitive to some of the statistical artefacts that can cause differences between studies, such as the effects of 'differential range restriction'.

Range restriction refers to the attenuation in the obtained validity of a test (interview or whatever) caused by using the test or anything correlated with it for selection purposes. Typically, only those individuals who 'pass' the test are selected, the validity of the test is calculated in the selected group and a lower validity is obtained than if everyone had been allowed to join the organization (because of the assumed monotonic relationship between the test and job performance, individuals who fail the test should do badly in the job, hence increasing the range of data points used to calculate the validity coefficient). 'Meta-analysis' is a set of techniques for accumulating the results of several studies (or independent results within a single study) that account statistically for these kinds of artefacts; usually sampling error, restriction of range in the predictor and the criterion attenuation (for example, Hunter, Schmidt and Jackson, 1982). Early US meta-analysts were primarily concerned to show that cognitive ability tests were valid for virtually all jobs where training is required after entry and thereby reverse the trend away from the use of tests that was apparent in the USA at the time.

Such is the weight of evidence that meta-analyses have accumulated that Hunter and Hunter were moved to write:

> The results are clear: most of the variance in results across studies is due to sampling error. Most of the residual variance is probably due to error in typing, computation, or transcription. Thus, for a given test–job combination, there is essentially no variation in validity across settings or time. (Hunter and Hunter, 1984)

Emphatic statements such as these have not endeared Hunter, Schmidt and their co-workers to certain of their US colleagues. Nevertheless, they have developed a powerful set of techniques and their contribution has been widely recognized.

More recently, the need to consider alternative selection procedures where tests cause adverse impact has led meta-analysts to turn their attention elsewhere; hence the availability of meta-analyses of biodata. Hunter and Hunter (1984) reanalysed Reilly and Chao's narrative review and confirmed the relative superiority of biodata among alternatives to tests (a mean validity of 0.38 versus the next best alternative reanalysed, the interview, at 0.23), but they questioned whether *any* alternative was the equal of tests of cognitive ability. They reported that the three best predictors of entry-level job performance (as assessed by supervisors' ratings) were ability tests (average validity 0.53), job try-outs (0.44) and biodata (0.37). However, since empirical data on restriction of range were available only for measures of cognitive ability, correlations for this artefact were made to the validities of the tests, but not the validities for the other predictors. Moreover, Hunter and Hunter argued that the alternatives they had considered were largely uncorrelated with cognitive ability and that any *indirect* restriction of range would be negligible. This assumed that ability tests were usually used for selection. Although this may be true in some countries, the use of a test as the main selection device in Britain is not especially widespread (Anderson and Shackleton, 1986). Where biodata are used for pre-selection, or application forms are read before the selection interview (the more usual case in Britain), both direct and indirect restriction of range in biodata scores can occur.

Schmitt, Gooding, Noe and Kirsch (1984) did not attempt to correct for range restriction or any other artefact except sampling error. They argued that such corrections had little effect on conclusions concerning the *variability* of validity coefficients. This probably accounts for the difference between their results and those of Hunter and Hunter. Schmitt et al.'s best predictors of performance ratings were assessment centres (0.43) and work samples and biodata (both 0.32). The validity of general mental ability tests for predicting performance ratings was only 0.22.

The mean validity of the biodata was 0.24 from a total of 99 studies (total sample size 58,107). This estimate was lower than that obtained by Hunter and Hunter from the reanalysis of Reilly and Chao's data, and, of the other seven predictors considered, only personality tests yielded a lower average validity. However, biodata were used to predict turnover more frequently than any other predictor and validities for this outcome were generally low. When the mean validities for different combinations of predictors and criteria were calculated, biodata were nevertheless the best predictors of turnover (0.21) and of wages (0.53). They were also the second-best predictor of performance ratings (as noted above) and the only predictor with more than three published validities against productivity (0.20). Only in the case of more objective measures of achievement (for example, examination grades) was the superiority of ability tests apparent. Here the mean validity for tests of general mental ability was 0.44, whereas for biodata it was 0.23; again, only personality tests had lower validities.

The Validity of Different Kinds of Biodata

The different types of biodata and different methods of combining items were described in Chapters 2 and 4. On the basis of Schmitt et al.'s (1984) results, it might be reasonable to suggest that soft biodata reminiscent of personality items would have lower validity than hard biodata. Few authors list the items they have used, however, and even when variable names are given it is often impossible to tell whether hard or soft biodata are implied. 'Educational attainment', for example, could be measured by examination grades or by a question such as 'compared with your classmates, how well did you do in school?'

Thus, soft and hard biodata can sometimes be compared only indirectly. There is certainly evidence that biographical questionnaires containing a majority of soft items can be predictive (Walther, 1961). However, Shaffer, Saunders and Owens (1986), in one of the few studies that directly compared 'objective, verifiable' items with those that were 'subjective and unvariable', obtained results that tend to confirm a more pessimistic view of soft biodata; hard biodata were more reliable and stable over a five-year period suggesting that they may hold their validity over time rather better.

Although there is little evidence with which to compare soft and hard biodata, different methods of combining items have been compared. However, only the Mitchell and Klimoski (1982, 1986) study reported in Chapter 2 is easily accessible.

In reviewing earlier studies, Mitchell and Klimoski (1982) noted that Berkeley (1953) failed to find any difference in the effectiveness of internal and external methods of combining biodata. Hornick, James and Jones (1977) came to a similar conclusion on comparing different methods of scoring a psychological climate questionnaire. They failed to note, however, that the empirical method yielded the same validity as the internal (factor analytic) method, whereas the empirical device contained only one-third as many items.

Mitchell and Klimoski (1982) also compared empirical and factor-analytic methods. They found the cross-validity of an empirically keyed biodata device was superior to that for a regression of component scores (0.46 versus 0.36, n=359) and they later extended this analysis to include intuitive methods (Mitchell and Klimoski, 1986). In their later study, cross-validities for vertical per cent keying (empirical), a simultaneous regression of component scores (inductive or internal) and wholly intuitive methods were 0.21, 0.13 and 0.03 respectively. There is thus some evidence that the method of combining items potentially moderates the validity of biodata (a 'moderator' is said to affect the strength of the relationship between two other variables, although other definitions have been used – Zedeck, 1971). Moderator effects are best investigated through the meta-analysis technique described earlier. If sampling error or other artefacts account for most of the variability between studies, then the presence of a moderator is doubtful. If, however, a substantial amount of variability remains after the necessary corrections have been made, that 'something' is differentially affecting the validity of biodata is a distinct possibility.

Drakeley (1988) addressed this issue in a meta-analysis of largely unpublished military technical reports. The potential moderators of the validity of biodata investigated were 'occupational group' – officers or enlisted personnel; 'criterion measure' – achievement, turnover, ratings of potential, ratings of performance and flying training success; and 'biodata scoring method' – empirical, inductive or intuitive.

From the 15 studies reviewed, a total of 63 conceptually or statistically independent cross-validation coefficients were obtained, representing a total sample size of 70,914. The mean validity of biodata across all of these studies was 0.21 with a corrected standard deviation of 0.12. However, sampling error accounted for only 6% of the variability between studies, suggesting that some between-study variability might be a result of a moderator effect. Further analysis revealed the most likely moderator to be the method by which the biodata were combined into a total score. The mean validities for different types of biodata were:

Empirical keying 0.26 (n=50,387)
Inductive composite 0.16 (n=6,287)
Wholly intuitive 0.04 (n=14,240)

In each case, the between-study variability within each type of biodata was less than the *total* between-study variability – a prerequisite for showing a moderator effect.

Drakeley's results are very similar to those of Mitchell and Klimoski (1986), obtained within a single organization. It would thus seem that the validity of wholly intuitive methods is less than impressive (0.04 – Drakeley, 1988; 0.03 – Mitchell and Klimoski, 1986).

Bliesner (1992) again used meta-analysis to investigate different study characteristics and the validity of different approaches to biodata. His design parameters were: type of experimental design, method of combining items and the extent of item reduction from development to cross-validation tables. The mean validity of biodata across all of the studies accumulated by Bliesner was 0.33 (SD 0.18). From this analysis it was apparent that both the method of combining items and the extent to which items are retained or dropped during development could affect the validity of biodata.

Bliesner's results reinforced arguments that empirically keyed biodata yield better predictions (see Mitchell and Klimoski, 1986; Drakeley, 1988) – although the results for 'non-empirical' (presumably inductive plus intuitive) methods of combining biodata are not *substantially* different – and that cross-validation is necessary. 'Double cross-validation' (developing scoring keys in two samples and checking out only the consistent results in a third sample) and similar procedures would seem to be a particularly effective strategy to avoid shrinkage. Drakeley (1988), for example, noted average shrinkage of 25% for empirically keyed biodata after conventional cross-validation.

Before leaving meta-analysis and biodata we should perhaps make one caveat concerning the indiscriminate use of the technique: it may not be appropriate in certain circumstances. Hunter and Hunter (1984), for example, comment that biodata keys seem to be specific to the criterion measure used to develop the key. Reilly and Chao (1982) note that biodata devices seem not to 'transport' from one organizational setting to another. Meta-analysis of test validities could be said to show that general mental ability underlies performance in most jobs because this is what tests measure. This is useful to know, but what is measured by biodata when different studies are all lumped together?

Meta-analysis would not usually wish to accumulate validities for essentially different kinds of predictor. The studies reviewed above suggest that accumulating validities for empirically keyed hard biodata and intuitively keyed soft biodata, for example, would be as misleading as accumulating those from job sample and personality tests. And yet this is what some meta-analysts have done. In the next section, we want to 'unpick' some of these meta-analysts' findings and return to the subject of 'what do biodata predict?' in greater detail.

Validity of Specific Cues

Certain biographical pointers seem to have fairly general predictive validity, yet early WAB research occasionally gave some very contradictory results. Owning one's own home is generally a 'good' sign, but was not for one firm's shop sales-women where the most efficient performers lived in boarding houses. Are there any biographical pointers that have fairly general predictive validity?

Experience

This has moderate predictive validity for supervisor ratings, but zero validity for training grades (Hunter and Hunter, 1984). There is little evidence that experi-ence predicts productivity. *General* experience in supervising people or selling has no predictive validity. Research on air traffic controllers found that experience was used only when it was *directly and specifically* relevant; having used a radio or flown an aircraft did not predict efficiency as an air traffic controller, but expe-rience of instrument flying does.

Seniority

Seniority, or how long a person has been working in the job, is often used to decide who gets promoted. Unions in Britain and the USA often insist that it should be the sole criterion for promotion, irrespective of performance or aptitude. Seniority almost always plays a big part in deciding who is 'released' when the workforce has to be reduced ('last in, first out'). There is no reason to expect seniority to be related to efficiency and not much research on the link; indeed a good case could be made for the opposite being true. In one study, however, Gordon and Fitzgibbons (1982) found that seniority was quite unre-lated to efficiency in female sewing machine operators.

Age

Hunter and Hunter (1984) reviewed more than 500 validity coefficients and found that age alone had zero validity as a predictor, whether the criterion was supervisor rating or training grade. Age did, however, predict turnover, as younger employees were more likely to leave (Muchinsky and Tuttle, 1979). Age was found to distort biodata scoring – older men tended to have more depend-ants, higher living expenses and to belong to more organizations than did younger men (Thayer, 1977), so a biodata instrument using age-related items for respondents with a diverse age range could give misleading results.

Referral Source

Although not usually regarded as a biodata item, the question 'how did you find out about this vacancy?' is included on many application forms and could be scored. Moreover, there is an extensive literature on the effectiveness of referral sources, showing that, for example, employee referrals produce new workers who stay with the organization longer than those recruited by other means (Decker and Cornelius, 1979; Breaugh, 1981) and who receive higher appraisals from their superiors and have better attendance records (Taylor and Schmidt, 1983). One explanation for this phenomenon is that applicants who find out about the job informally through close friends, relatives or other contacts gain a more realistic view of the job than those who find out through more formal channels such as advertisements. This 'realistic job-preview' seems to realign applicants' expectations and so heighten commitment (Popovich and Wanous, 1982).

The use of existing employees to refer on possible new hires can, however, be a dubious practice: 'word of mouth' recruitment has been challenged in the courts on both sides of the Atlantic. Nevertheless, other kinds of formal versus informal referral sources could be included as biodata items and keyed empirically against turnover or job success – for example, responding to a press advertisement versus attending a recruitment fair to talk to actual employees of the organization.

Different Criteria Predicted by Biodata

We have already seen that biodata compare favourably with many other kinds of test data in the assessment of job applicants and employees (Asher, 1972; Owens, 1976). The predictive validity of biodata can, however, vary from one criterion variable to another (Reilly and Chao, 1982). The validity of biodata also varies between occupational groups (Drakeley, 1988). Even so, biodata generally fare well against other tests.

In assessing the predictive validity of any biodata item, construct or inventory, the criterion variable specificity of the predictor items needs to be borne in mind and so does the occupational group with which it has been tested. Criterion variables tested against biodata include success in gaining employment, early performance in employment, longer-term success, leadership potential, productivity, absenteeism, loyalty and turnover.

Career Choice

What relation is there between biodata and actual vocational choice? Studies have varied in the level of analysis used in classifying vocations. Some have classified jobs broadly in terms of Holland's six vocational environmental categories: realistic, investigative, artistic, social, enterprising and conventional.

Different environments place distinct demands on the individual. Some individuals will often show a preference for one situation or environment over others and how they perform in this preferred setting may reveal a great deal about their personality. Others have classified jobs into occupational or job families. A number of studies have used life-history data to research vocational behaviour and job choices. A group of studies has relied on large-scale surveys of the life histories of engineers, lawyers, doctors and other professionals to investigate typical life experiences of the members of such occupations (Laurent, 1951; Kulberg and Owens, 1960; Nachman, 1960; Albright and Glennon, 1961; Chaney and Owens, 1964). For example, Kulberg and Owens (1960) correlated responses to a 100-item life-history form with the scores of freshers in mechanical engineering on the engineering scale of the Strong Vocational Interest Blank.

The results suggest that the typical engineer has a history of painful or somewhat unsuccessful personal-social relationships. Also, the engineer has a history of superior performance in science along with more enjoyment of quantitative and practical courses rather than courses in linguistics and social studies. Finally, the prospective engineer 'had a history of long career planning, of liking to work with things and ideas as opposed to people, and of enjoying creative work and disliking routine' (Kulberg and Owens, 1960: 29). Laurent's (1951) study of engineers yielded similar results and provides some oral histories of other occupations that are also consistent with some of traits attributed to those professions. For instance, Laurent found that lawyers have often come from families characterized by high social activity. These types of studies, which examine the past experiences of members of particular occupations, provide a preliminary basis for understanding the origins of vocational preference. It would not be practical to investigate the life histories of the members of hundreds of different occupations, however. A more rational approach would be to examine the past experiences of individuals who belong to a limited number of vocational classifications.

Albright and Glennon (1961) studied supervisory and research-oriented scientists. Employees completed a personal history questionnaire, along with a questionnaire assessing their desire to advance in research or supervisory functions. Forty-three personal history items effectively differentiated the research group from the supervisory group.

Eberhardt and Muchinsky (1982a) conducted a study to investigate the nature of the relationship between life history experiences and vocational preferences. Holland's Vocational Preference Inventory (Holland, 1975) and Owens' Biographical Questionnaire (Owens and Schoenfeldt, 1979) were administered to 816 people (437 women and 379 men). Multivariate statistical analyses were computed to reveal a complex set of relationships between scores on the two questionnaires.

The Vocational Preference Inventory (VPI) is a personality inventory entirely composed of occupational titles. A person completes the inventory by indicating the occupations that he or she likes or dislikes. There is evidence that indicates that the VPI is useful for assessing the nature and strength of vocational preferences. The Biographical Questionnaire (BQ), in its original form, was a 659-item instrument based on 2000 item specifications that covered a broad spectrum of prior experiences. The biographical information covered such areas as family life, school-related activities, religious activities, interests and attitudes derived from life experiences, sports participation, and extra-familial relationships. The final version of the BQ was reduced to 118 items through the application of factor-analytic techniques. Independent factor analyses of the items by sex resulted in the identification of 15 interpretable factors in the women's data and 13 in the men's data (Owens and Schoenfeldt, 1979).

Eberhardt and Muchinsky (1982a) found the same number of biodata factors for men and women, which accounted for more than half of the variance in BQ responses in each case. On relating respondents' scores on these factors to vocational preferences, evidence emerged that a person's vocational type seems to be shaped by his or her past life experiences. Indeed, life history experiences would seem to account for a substantial amount of the variance in vocational interests and preferences, being at least as important, if not more so, than other predictors noted in the research literature.

Biodata and Vocational Choice Distinctions

Brush and Owens (1979) studied more than 2000 employees occupying 19 job groups (verified through job analysis) in a large oil company. Participants completed an inventory of life history experiences, as well as interest and personality variables. The researchers found a significant relationship between subgroup membership (characterized by individuals with similar patterns of life experiences, personality and interests) and job family membership.

Baehr and Williams (1967) examined personal history items and their ability to discriminate between widely different occupational groups. Participants consisted of employees in 10 occupations (chemists, middle and upper management, salespersons, line managers and school administrators). Virtually all biographical factors discriminated between the occupational groups.

Biodata and Vocational Stability

Holland (1973) argued that people tend to remain in vocations compatible with their personality structure. People with personality types that are incongruent with their vocational environment will eventually leave their job in search of a more congruent one. Some evidence suggests that personality–vocational environment congruence is related to vocational stability (Villwock, Schnitzan and Carbonari, 1976; Weiner and Vactenas, 1977; Rose and Elton, 1982). Some evidence has also emerged to suggest that certain kinds of biodata may be indicative of degree of vocational stability.

Rose and Elton (1982) examined the vocational stability of a sample of college students over a four-year period. First-year students completed a vocational interest inventory (to assess their personality) and provided information about their intended college major (to be used as evidence for their vocational choice). Intended majors were classified into one of Holland's six vocational environments. They found that students whose vocational interests were congruent with their expressed college major tended to remain in that major four years later, whereas students whose vocational interests were incongruent with their expressed college major tended to switch majors by the end of four years.

Weiner and Vactenas (1977) found that people who expressed intent to remain in enterprising occupations could be distinguished from people who expressed intent to leave enterprising occupations by personality characteristics such as dominance, endurance, order, responsibility, ascendancy and sociability.

The literature on biodata and vocational choice suggests that people's life history experiences strongly influence their vocational preference and subsequent choice of a vocation. Thus, vocations are composed of similar types of people. People's life history experiences are likely to determine which type of vocation they are attracted to initially. The fit between individual and vocational characteristics is likely to determine whether individuals remain in a vocation.

In a more recent conceptual development in the study of biodata as predictors of career choice, Wrzesniewski, McComisky, Rozin and Schwartz (1997) distinguished between individuals showing varying degrees of commitment to their job. Bellak, Madsen, Sullivan, Swidler and Tipton (1985) had argued that there are three distinct relations people can have to their work – as jobs, careers or callings. People who have jobs are interested only in the material benefits from work and do not seek or receive any other type of reward from it. The work is not an end in itself. The major interests and ambitions of job holders are not expressed through their work.

People who have careers have a deeper personal investment in their work and mark their achievements not only through monetary gain, but also through achievements in the occupational structure. This achievement often brings higher social standing, increased power within the scope of one's occupation and higher self-esteem. A person with a calling works not for financial gain or career advancement, but instead for the fulfilment that doing the work brings for the individual. Another related analysis is that which contrasts intrinsic and extrinsic motivation to work. Amabile, Hill, Hennessey and Tighe (1994) analysed the extrinsic orientation into two subfactors: compensation and outward orientation. Correspondingly, intrinsic motivation was analysed into challenge and enjoyment. Callings can be regarded as intrinsically motivated occupations, jobs as purely extrinsically motivated, and careers as a mixture of intrinsically and extrinsically motivated. Establishing a biodata predictor of occupational selection needs to incorporate into the selection model the degree of extrinsic and intrinsic motivation underlying job choices.

Choosing an Organization

Research into career choice has been extended into the realm of choosing an employer. Once a choice has been made about the type of occupation or job one wishes to pursue, a further choice then has to be made about the type of organization in which employment will be sought. Is biographical information indicative of the type of organization to which an individual will be best suited?

Schneider and Schneider (1994) outlined a framework in which it is assumed that people in a particular occupational grouping or career tend to share life history experiences. This framework is built on ideas concerning the attraction-selection-attrition (ASA) cycle. The ASA cycle proposes that people are attracted to, are selected by, and stay with organizations that are in keeping with their own attributes. The ASA model predicts that people in an organization will be more similar to each other than they are to people in other organizations.

Literature on this subject has derived from diverse areas of psychology, such as theoretical tests of expectancy theory (Vroom, 1966), conceptualization of careers and career environments (Holland, 1985), interpersonal attraction (Byrne, 1971) and biodata predictions of academic major and participation in extracurricular activities (Owens and Schoenfeldt, 1979). The root conceptualization of behaviour on which the ASA process is based is interactional psychology. Interactional psychology is a subfield of personality theory that is based on the idea that situations and people are inseparable (Bowers, 1973; Endler and Magnussen, 1976) and that situations are what people construe them to be (Weick, 1979).

Much of the research in industrial and organizational psychology and organizational behaviour that may be viewed as interactional in its basic impetus has followed the person-environment (P-E) fit model. The basis of the P-E fit approach to understanding behaviour is the idea that particular individuals are more likely to be productive and/or satisfied in particular environments because they fit that environment.

In Schneider and Schneider's ASA model, the nature of settings is a consequence of fit that is achieved through three mechanisms: attraction, selection and attrition. They proposed that these three mechanisms yield increasingly homogeneous environments and that this homogeneity in people comprising environments determines the way organizations look and feel to participants and observers (Schneider, 1987). Schneider has suggested that the ASA process has important effects on the climate and culture of organizations. It is thus proposed that the climate and culture of a setting are actually a product of the people in the setting, rather than an outcome of the structure or technology of the setting.

There are various potential moderators of the ASA process, including poor economic performance, low morale and restricted opportunities. Another important factor in this context is the quality of organizational information and the effectiveness with which it is communicated to job applicants during the recruitment and selection process. People who do not receive complete and accurate information during the organizational choice process may join an organization only to discover eventually that they do not fit the organization. On the other hand, applicants who are given realistic and complete information about an organization may be better equipped to select organizations into which they will fit. Thus, homogeneity in life history experiences should be greater in organizations that advocate information dissemination, such as realistic job previews, than in organizations that do not – at least during the attraction and selection phases of the ASA cycle.

The ASA model was developed to explore the ways by which the choices that people make – whether implicitly or explicitly – about the vocations and organizations in which they work might shed light on the nature of organizations. According to Schneider (1987), people choose to seek employment in organizations that attract them and choose to leave organizations in which they do not fit. These choices may well be shaped in important ways by life history experiences (Niener and Owens, 1985). People tend to choose to enter organizations where they might expect to find people similar to themselves in certain biographical details (Schneider and Schneider, 1994).

Job Success

In the field of graduate recruitment, there have been relatively few studies of the relationship between candidate attributes and decisions taken by graduate recruiters. Campion (1978) in the USA and Wingrove, Glendinning and Herriott (1984) in the UK have investigated preselection decisions based on application form data. Campion found that, out of nine predictors, only grade point average and fraternity or sorority membership successfully discriminated between accepted and rejected forms. Wingrove et al. (1984) used a much larger number of variables and, although predictors varied both with the individual and the type of organization, educational achievement, work experience and leisure activities generally predicted success in preselection. Carroll (1966) investigated the job-seeking success of business studies graduates. Out of 19 predictors investigated, only appearance (relative handsomeness) and having had experience of office work were associated with success.

Keenan and Scott (1985) reported a study that attempted to identify predictors of success in obtaining employment in a cross-section of graduates. Previous work had indicated that biographical information (such as academic success and leisure activities) ought to be included as predictors. As well as background information, the ways in which candidates prepared for interviews and interview style were also included as factors that could have an important bearing on the outcome of a job application.

Two measures of success in gaining employment were used. First, the ratio of the number of follow-up interviews obtained to the number of initial interviews taken was calculated (*follow-up success*). Second, the ratio of number of jobs offered compared with the number of initial interviews taken was computed (*job success*). A number of variables emerged as predictors of job application success. Estimates of how much time respondents said they spent reading employer's literature was significantly correlated with *follow-up success* and *job success*. Class of degree was the only academic performance variable to be significantly associated with success. Relevance of vacation work was another significant predictor.

The finding that academic performance measured by class of degree was associated with job-seeking success was to some extent consistent with the evidence that interviewers say they place high value on a graduate's academic record (Keenan, 1976). Although a number of candidate attributes were identified as significant predictors of success in seeking employment, the results are undermined to some extent by the fact that only about one-quarter of the variance was explained by the predictors. Thus, it seems that there are other relevant variables not identified by this study which also have important effects on job selection success.

Dyer (1987) investigated factors associated with university success and first-year job performance among healthcare trainees and workers. A 145-item biographical inventory was compared with the Strong-Campbell Interest Inventory and the California Psychological Inventory. Grades and achievement scores were also obtained from university records. One year after their graduation, participants' supervisors described their job performance. Inventories were used together and separately as predictors of grade point average and job performance.

Results showed that students' self-reports of high-school academic performance derived from the biographical inventory accounted for 15–20% of the 30–35% of variance explained in achieving nursing and university performance scores. Personality variables added 3–5%, and interest variables just 1%.

Staff Turnover

Can an application form containing weighted biographical items or a more extensive biographical inventory be used effectively to predict likelihood of staff turnover among new recruits and job applicants? A number of researchers have investigated this issue and provided positive evidence.

Many models of turnover acknowledge that the interaction between individual and job or organizational characteristics influences the turnover process (Mobley, 1982; Sheridan, 1992). Just as individuals who do not fit certain vocations are likely to leave that vocation, individuals who do not fit certain organizations are likely to leave for another. The rationale for using background data, whether obtained through an application blank or questionnaire, is that an applicant's personal history, such as his or her previous experience and interests, is predictive of future success in the job. It does indeed seem reasonable to assume that such data as previous employment history, specific skills, education, financial status and so on reflect a person's motives, abilities, skills, level of aspiration and adjustment to working situations.

A number of assumptions can be made from such information. For example, the fact that applicants have held a similar job indicates the likelihood of their transferring some of their training to the new job. Similarly, what they have done successfully before is likely to reflect their basic abilities in that area, as well as their interest in and satisfaction derived from these activities. Such personal-history items as age, number of dependants, years of education, previous earnings and amount of insurance have also been found to correlate with later proficiency on the job, earnings, length of tenure or other criteria of job success. In this section, we shall focus on length of tenure. The efficacy of biodata in predicting job performance will be examined in a later section.

For more than 30 years, research has consistently shown a relationship between biodata and turnover (Fleishman and Berniger, 1967; Cascio, 1976; Brown, 1978; Muchinsky and Tuttle, 1979; Owens and Schoenfeldt, 1979; Reilly and Chao, 1982). Fleishman and Berniger (1967) outlined one method for ascertaining the predictive validity of a Weighted Application Blank in connection with staff turnover. They explored a scoring technique for a form designed for use in the selection of clerical and secretarial employees, with a view to obtaining information to reduce turnover.

The first step in their study was to find out which items in the application blank differentiated between short-tenure and long-tenure employees who had been hired at the same time. Long-tenure employees were those women whose tenure was from two to four years and who were still in the job at the time of the study. The short-tenure group comprised those women who had been recruited at around the same time but whose employment had terminated within two years. Of the latter group 20% had terminated within six months and 67% in the first year. All those included had originally been hired as permanent employees. The application form took up four pages and included about 40 items that dealt with personal data, work history, education, interests, office skills and so on. The original application forms of the employees in both the short- and long-tenure groups were examined and responses to individual items were compared to determine which, if any, differentiated between these two groups.

Some items were found to be better discriminators than others, and hence, by implication, better predictors of tenure. It was decided that these items should be assigned more weight in the hiring procedure. Thus, items that did not discriminate were weighted zero (that is, they were not counted). Others were weighted negatively (they counted against the applicant), and still others positively (in favour of the applicant).

Next the size of the weight was determined. Items that showed the biggest percentage differences between long- and short-tenure groups were given a higher weight. Fleishman and Berniger found that even a simple weighting procedure can work quite well here. Thus, an applicant under 20 years of age got −3 points toward her total score, an applicant living within the city limits got +2 points towards her score, and so on. Biodata scores as used in this study are illustrated in Table 6.1.

Table 6.1: Biodata discriminators of short-tenure and long-tenure employees

Items on Application Blank	Short-tenure Group %	Long-tenure Group %	Weights assigned to response
Local address			
Within city	39	62	+2
Outlying suburbs	50	36	−2
Age			
Under 20	35	8	−3
21–25	38	32	−1
26–30	8	2	−1
31–35	7	10	0
35 and over	11	48	+3
Previous salary			
Under £2000	31	30	0
£2000–3000	41	38	0
£3000–4000	13	12	0
Over £4000	4	4	0
Age of children			
Nursery school	12	4	−3
Public school	53	33	−3
Secondary school	35	63	+3

Source: Fleishman and Berniger, (1967).

An applicant's total score was calculated by adding or subtracting the weights scored on each item on the application form. In the first sample Fleishman and Berniger analysed, they found that total scores ranged from −17 to 27, the average score for the short-tenure group being −2.3, whereas that for the long-tenure group was 8.9 – a difference of 11.2, which was highly significant statistically. This result was somewhat misleading and spuriously high because it had been calculated from the very sample from which the weights for the individual items had been determined at the outset. It was necessary, therefore, to find out whether the scoring procedure had predictive validity among a different sample of office workers.

A second sample was thus analysed in the same way, with the scoring system developed from the first sample applied to application blank response of the second sample. The range of scores was not quite as wide for the second sample as for the first, and the correlation between weighted application score and length of tenure was 0.57, a statistically significant result. The average score for the short-tenure group was −0.7, while that of the long-tenure group was 6.3. Again this was a statistically significant difference.

Having established the instrument's ability to differentiate between employees on the basis of length of tenure, the question of how to use it in reaching the actual hiring decision needed to be addressed. Although realizing that other factors such as the relative importance of turnover in the organization, the number of available applicants during a hiring period, and other selection procedures in use had to be taken into account, it was nevertheless necessary to see a score on the application form that did the best job of differentiating between probable short- and long-tenure risks at the time of employment. Fleishman and Berniger therefore set about devising a cut-off score that would maximize correct hiring decisions. This would be a score that would minimize both the number of people hired who would eventually turn out to be short-tenure employees and the number rejected who would have remained in the job.

To establish the cut-off score, they used a method called 'maximum differentiation'. This involved tabulating the percentage of employees reaching or exceeding each score point in the range −10 to 21. They then calculated the differences between the percentages obtained in the two groups at each score point to find the point of greatest differentiation. This analysis identified the point at which the difference between the two groups reached its maximum and this represented a cut-off score for selection purposes. Candidates who scored above this point were the most likely to stay in the job for two years or more, whereas those scoring below could be considered potential short-tenure employees.

Earlier, Kirchner and Dunnette (1957) used *job tenure* as the criterion, with short tenure being under 10 months and long tenure being over 18 months. They examined 40 items on the blank and found 15 to differentiate between tenure groups. Using a key based on these items, they obtained the validity results on their original validation group, as shown in Table 6.2

Table 6.2: Biodata and Job Tenure

	Original Group				**Cross-Validation Group**			
	Median	Mean	SD	n	Median	Mean	SD	n
Short-tenure group	10	10.79	4.51	33	12	12.32	3.95	40
Long-tenure group	18	17.59	4.78	105	18	17.69	4.89	45

Source: Kirchner and Dunnette (1957)

The long-term group received a mean score of over 17 using the key, while the mean score for the short-tenure people was 10.79. The key was then applied to a new sample of employees for the purpose of cross-validation. The key retained its ability to discriminate between the two criterion groups. Thus, the organization could feel confident in using the WAB scoring method to select future staff.

Dunnette and Maetzold (1955) devised a WAB to reduce turnover in a pea-canning factory. After inspecting the workforce, they found that the typically stable production worker lives locally, has a telephone, is married and has no children, is not an ex-serviceman, is either young (under 25) or old (over 55), weighs more than 150 pounds but less than 175, has obtained more than 10 years of education, has worked for the company, will be available for work until the end of summer, and prefers field work to inside work. The WAB was used only for male applicants; female employees didn't present a turnover problem. This profile retained its predictive validity over three successive years, and in three other canning factories, but it didn't work for non-seasonal cannery workers. Scott and Johnson (1967) found that turnover of permanent workers was predicted by the regression equation:

Tenure = 0.30 (age) + 8.82 (sex) – (miles from plant) + 5.29 (type of residence) + 2.66 (children) + 1.08 (years on last job) – 1.99.

(where female = 1; male = 0; lives with parents or in a room (bedsit) = 0; lives in own home = 1)

Further research has shown the predictive validity of biodata in relation to length of tenure. Buel (1964) used a similar research design to that of Fleishman and Berniger (1967). The personnel records of female clerical and secretarial employees of a major petroleum company were examined, focusing on those individuals who had joined the company three years earlier. From among these individuals were isolated those who were still with the company and those who had left within nine months of joining.

The initial sample was converted into two subsamples. The first of these was used to establish those biodata items that best differentiated the short- from the long-tenure employees. The second subsample was used for cross-validation purposes. Thirty-five items of information were selected for analysis, on which simple frequencies of category response were computed. On the basis of differences in percentages between short-tenure and long-tenure groups, 16 items were chosen for differential weighting. These items and their weights were then amalgamated into a single overlay scoring key.

The weighted items represented typical bits of application blank information – distance from home to the office, work best qualified for, acquaintances in the company, who referred the applicant to the company, marital status, length of time married, schooling, participation in school-sponsored sports, participation in class organizations, participation in other related activities, how the applicant spent summer vacations, references, type of residence, how long applicant had lived in city, and age.

During the course of this study the organization moved its general office about 25 miles into the suburbs of the city in which it was located. This had a knock-on effect, reducing the value of some the scoring key items. Indeed, although the correlation between WAB biodata score and length of tenure was statistically significant, at 0.33 it was less than that reported by Fleishman and Berniger (1967).

Scott and Johnson (1967) did a similar study which compared short-tenure (6 months or less) and long-tenure (one year or more) unskilled employees at a small canning factory in western Massachusetts. To compare these two groups on 19 biodata items obtained from their application forms, 12 items were assigned differential weights. The authors reported that the WAB proved to be an effective technique in selecting long-term unskilled workers. The higher the individual's score on the WAB, the greater the likelihood of his staying with the company a reasonable length of time.

Two characteristics of biodata-turnover research contribute to the lack of clarity regarding the type of turnover that is associated with biodata. First, many studies use demographic variables (for example, age, marital status, tenure, educational level, number of children) to predict turnover (Cascio, 1976; Federico, Federico and Lundquist, 1976; Jackson, Brett, Sessa, Cooper, Julan and Peyronnin, 1991). Many demographic variables found on a typical application blank may predict the types of individuals likely to leave any organization or job. These items are not useful in identifying the types of people likely to fit or not fit in particular organizations.

Most extensive research on biodata and turnover has been conducted by the Life Insurance Marketing and Research Association (LIMRA) in the USA. LIMRA developed a life history measure called the Aptitude Index using a large sample of life insurance agents hired in the 1930s. Initial research on the validity of the Aptitude Index indicated that a weighted combination of 10 life history items yielded the best prediction of life insurance agents remaining in a company.

Since the 1930s, the Aptitude Index has undergone numerous revisions – it is now called the Aptitude Index Battery. Brown (1978) investigated the long-term validity of the instrument. He found that the same biodata key that predicted life assurance agents remaining in a company in 1933 also predicted the same characteristic for agents 38 years later.

The relationship between biodata and turnover has also been investigated using biographical information blanks. Brush and Owens (1979) used a large sample of employees in a wide variety of jobs in an oil company to investigate the relationship between biodata and turnover. Based on participants' responses to such biographical information blank items as educational and work experiences, leadership activities, interests, perceived self-confidence and introversion, 18 biodata subgroups were formed. They found that cluster membership significantly predicted turnover from the oil company. Different life history clusters also predicted turnover in different job categories.

Biodata have also been used to predict military attrition (Laurence and Means, 1985). Drakeley, Herriott and Jones (1988) conducted a study to determine whether biodata could predict voluntary turnover from a naval training programme. These researchers obtained a set of biographical data for a sample of 420 Royal Navy officers in training. Different scoring keys were developed for four training criteria by using England's (1971) WAB technique, and these were cross-validated on a further sample of 282 officers. Biodata predictors were compared with four psychometric tests of aptitude and an overall assessment rating derived from a lengthy assessment centre procedure.

The biodata succeeded in predicting voluntary withdrawal from training at a low level whereas none of the other predictors was successful in this respect. However, different measures of future performance and commitment to the organization were available and not all of these were equally well predicted by specific items. Thus, the research showed that biodata can provide good predictors of professional training success, but that some aspects of biodata are more relevant to the prediction of withdrawal whereas others are more relevant to leadership training success.

Organizational Identification

Mael and Ashforth (1995) explored the use of biodata in combination with measures of organizational identification as predictors of staff turnover. They used social identity theory (SIT) in explaining the efficacy of biodata in this context. According to SIT, the self-concept comprises a personal identity that encompasses idiosyncratic attributes (for example, dispositions, abilities) and a social identity that encompasses salient group classifications (for example, nationality, political affiliation) (Turner, 1984; Tajfel and Turner, 1986). Individuals group themselves and others as a means of ordering the social environment and locating their place within it. Thus, social identification is the perception of belonging to a group. As individuals begin to identify with a group, they usually assume the perceived prototypical characteristics of the group as their own (Mael, 1988). Many individuals develop a sense of who they are, what their goals and attitudes are, and what they ought to do, from their group membership. Organizational identification is a special form of social identification in which people define themselves in terms of their memberships in a particular organization (Ashforth and Mael, 1989; Mael and Ashforth, 1992; Mael and Tetnik, 1992; Duttoon, Dukerich and Harquail, 1994). In identifying with an organization, people often internalize these attributes as their own.

It has been argued that SIT informs the use of biodata in that self-categorizations can shape behavioural patterns. Just as there are dispositional differences in the predilection to identify with an organization (Rotondi, 1975; Cox,

1985; Mael and Ashforth, 1992). Mael and Ashforth (1995) hypothesized that certain characteristics and life experiences captured in biodata may predispose one to identify with a given organization.

Organizational identification and biodata antecedents of it should predict attachment to a specific organization. In the military, for example, identification with the army or with one's branch or regiment, has been viewed as an especially crucial factor in motivated, effective, courageous and selfless behaviour by soldiers (Grinker and Spiegel, 1945; Segal, 1985; Manning, 1991). Mael and Ashforth (1995) used turnover as a negative indicator of attachment. They investigated the extent to which earlier behaviour and experiences, as embodied in biodata, predisposed new recruits to identify with the US Army and the extent to which these biodata and organizational identification measures in turn predicted subsequent attrition from the army.

Results indicated a significant association between biodata, organizational identification and attrition. Combining biodata and organizational identification items and entering them into a factor analysis produced four 'two-organizational' types: Rugged/Outdoors – activities that involve outdoor, hands-on work or pastimes; Solid Citizen – a non-delinquent and dependable pattern of behaviour at school and at work; Team Sports/Group Orientation – includes an interest and involvement in team-oriented sports and a preference for working in groups; Intellectual/Achievement Orientation – diligent involvement in intellectual pastimes and some supervisory experience.

The first factor was a major predictor of organizational identification, but was also the poorest predictor of attrition. The second factor was primarily related to early attrition, with delinquent tendencies rendering an individual unsuited to coping with the transition to the discipline of military life. The third factor had the strongest relationship to attrition and was related to the tendency to be willing to identify with the group. Team players were best suited to military life. The fourth factor was most strongly linked to short-term attrition, although it also showed a relationship to longer-term attrition as well. This factor may have reflected the perception that the army is a good place to achieve personal aspirations, either in an extended military career or subsequent civilian career.

Biodata and Job Satisfaction

Research showing that biodata predict job satisfaction provides indirect support for a relationship between biodata and turnover (Porter and Steers, 1973; Mobley, Griffith, Hand and Meglino, 1979). Sides, Field, Giles, Holley and Aronenakis (1984) conducted a study examining the relationship between biodata and job satisfaction. Supervisors at a large textile company completed a biodata instrument that assessed some of the following life history variables: perceived ability to communicate with others, athletic interests and abilities, school activities, and mechanical interests and abilities.

Mumford and Owens (1984) conducted a longitudinal study to determine whether biodata subgroup membership predicted various post-college behaviours, including job satisfaction. First-year college students completed Owens' Biographical Questionnaire and the College Experience Inventory. The latter measures behaviours and experiences from the college years, such as reading habits, academic experiences, academic achievement and religious involvement. They found that biodata cluster membership predicted job satisfaction six to eight years after college graduation, regardless of the type of job or organization the sample entered.

Childs and Klimoski (1986) conducted a study to determine whether biodata predicted career/occupational success. One component of career/occupational success studied was job satisfaction. Undergraduates completed a biodata instrument, and career/occupational success was assessed two years later. They found that life history variables significantly predicted job satisfaction. The most predictive variables were academic achievement, perceived self-confidence and self-reported sociability.

Biodata and Job Applicant Evaluations

Another aspect of the value of biodata as predictors of successful recruitment of candidates who will stick with the job and the organization is the way biodata may be used by recruiters alongside information gained from job applicants during selection interviews.

Carlson (1971) examined the value of combining biodata and job interview data. Managers in life assurance were presented with written profiles of candidates for the position of life assurance sales agent. Each manager in the study rated one of the applicant profiles representing one of a number of possible combinations of biodata test score and interview information for potential success as a sales agent. Significant main effects were obtained for both biodata test score and interview information, although the relationship was slightly stronger for the biodata test. But when the candidate either passed or did not take the biodata test, there were larger differences between candidates with favourable versus unfavourable interview information. Carlson concluded that when the applicant receives a passing score on the biodata test, the interviewer disregards the test and evaluates the applicant using other information, and when the applicant receives an unacceptable score on the biodata test, the interviewer disregards the candidate.

In another study, Heneman (1977) had university students evaluate written descriptions of candidates for the job of life assurance agent. Each participant received a booklet describing a mental ability and personality test that a large life assurance company had recently developed for selecting agents. Participants were asked to assume the role of a branch manager who was evaluating a candidate for the position of insurance agent. The three variables of applicant's sex, level of test score and level of test validity were manipulated on the written description. Heneman asked participants to evaluate the descriptions on three dependent variables related to suitability for the position. Significant main effects were obtained for the level of test score, indicating that the participants relied primarily on this information in making judgements about the candidates.

Dalessio and Silverhat (1994) examined how valid biodata test scores and interview information interact in the prediction of actual interviewer selection decisions and actual job performance. Respondents were a sample of 577 candidates for a position as life assurance sales agent evaluated by insurance agency managers from a single company. The results indicated interaction effects in predicting both the interviewers' decisions and the 12-month survival of newly recruited candidates. The interview information predicted the decision and candidate survival best for candidates with low passing scores on the biodata test and was poorest for candidates with high biodata pass scores. For candidates with low passing scores on the biodata test, the interviewer's evaluation of the candidate was related to the interviewer's decision to employ that individual. However, for candidates showing high passing scores on the biodata test, evaluations of candidates in the interview were not related to the interviewers' decisions. One interpretation of these findings is that interviewers may not be giving much weight to the candidate's performance in the interview when the candidate has obtained a high passing score on the biodata test, possibly because of the interviewers' faith in the biodata test and also because of recruiting pressures they face anyway.

Absenteeism

Several studies have attempted to use the application blank as a predictor of job *absenteeism*, which is universally recognized as an organizational problem. Naylor and Vincent (1959) carried out an extensive study of 220 women clerical workers, ranging in age from 18 to 58, who were employed in a large US manufacturing company. The variables that they obtained from the personal data sheet were marital status, age and number of dependants. The criterion of job success was lack of absenteeism from work over a six-month period. The three predictors and the criterion were dichotomized as follows:

Marital status	married, single/divorced, widow
Age	32 and above, 31 and below
Number of dependants	1 or more, none
Absenteeism	4 days or more, fewer than 4 days.

Half the subjects were put into a primary group, and the other half were set aside for purpose of cross-validation. The relationship between each of the predictors and the criterion was then determined and those predictors that were significant at the 0.01 level were then used with the second group to see whether the relationship would hold up in cross-validation.

Table 6.3 shows the frequency counts for each of the three predictors against the criterion. Only one of the three showed a significant relationship with absenteeism – number of dependants. This variable was then cross-validated on the other group. The resulting relationship was again significant, this time at the

Table 6.3: Biodata and absenteeism frequency counts and χ^2 for each variable (primary group).

	Married	Single	Old	Young	Dependants	No dependants
High absentee	36	16	24	28	25	27
Low absentee	31	27	29	29	13	45
	$\chi^2 = 2.87$		$\chi^2 = 0.16$		$\chi^2 = 7.99$	

(p 0.05)

Frequency count and χ^2 for dependants variables (hold-out group)

	Dependants	No dependants
High Absentee	34	29
Low Absentee	29	33
	$\chi^2 = 6.40$	

(p<0.05)

Source: Naylor and Vincent (1959)

0.05 level.

Although the number of dependants was the only variable to emerge as a predictor, Table 6.4 shows that marital status was correlated with absenteeism to some extent (r=0.21). The magnitude of this correlation suggested that the addition of the marital status variable, along with the age factor, might increase the overall accuracy of prediction beyond that which could be obtained by using the number of dependants alone. To test this, a multiple correlation of all three predictors against the criterion was computed. The multiple R exceeded by only 0.01 the r obtained using number of dependants alone. This was not significant. However, the ideas that a multiple regression should be used is an important one, because this analysis shows which factors best predict the criterion and by how much.

TABLE 6.4 Best prediction of absenteeism (variable intercorrelations)

	Age	Number of dependants	No dependants
Marital status	0.25	0.53	0.21
Age		0.49	0.06
Number of dependants			0.06

Source: Naylor and Vincent (1959)

Job Performance

Recent meta-analyses of different modes of selection (Hunter and Hunter, 1984; Schmitt, Gooding, Noe and Kirsch, 1984) have indicated that scored biographical data are highly valid predictors of job performance. Although all the research reviewed in these papers was from the USA, there were a number of important methodological and pragmatic lessons to be learned that have relevance to job markets elsewhere. Indeed, this has been borne out by the results of more recent research in the UK (Drakeley, Herriott and Jones, 1988).

Hunter and Hunter (1984) reported that for entry-level jobs there is no predictor of job performance as good as ability. In general, though, biodata predictors have emerged as second best after ability. The average validity of biodata measures reported by Hunter and Hunter was 0.37 in comparison with 0.53 for ability measures (with supervisor ratings as the job performance measure).

A number of studies have explored the validity of biodata in predicting job performance in a variety of different occupations. One early study by Mosel (1951) analysed the application forms of 170 women department store sales clerks to reveal that 12 personal data items significantly distinguished between high and low selling employees. When applied to 100 current employees, total weighted personal data scores showed a substantial relationship to selling performance.

The ideal saleswoman was 35–54 years old, had 13–16 years of formal education, had more than five years' selling experience, weighed more than 160 pounds, had worked on her next to last job for less than five years, lived in a boarding house, had worked on her last job for more than five years, had her principal previous experiences a 'minor executive', was between 4· 11·· and 5· 2·· high, had between one and three dependants, was widowed, and had lost no time from work during the past two years (in order of predictive validity). It is particularly difficult to explain why the ideal saleswoman stayed a long time in her last job but left her next to last job more quickly. Indeed, as we shall see, WAB and biodata techniques do not explain *why* some factors are predictors and others are not.

Goldsmith (1922) used application blank data to predict the success or failure of Guardian Life Assurance salesmen. Taking historical data on salesmen who had been working for the company, three classes of employee were identified: (1) those who were failures, (2) those who were borderline cases up to moderately successful, and (3) those who were successful. The criterion of success was the amount of insurance paid for during the first year after the man was licensed. The blanks for these three classes of men were studied and the essential or significant items that varied with the success of the agent were selected. Biodata items were then weighted and checked against the man's production record. A scoring system was created in which a cut-off point could be identified. Men scoring above that point were much more likely to be successful salesmen than those who scored below it.

In a completely different study, Laurent (1962) used a biographical survey to predict managerial success in an oil company in New Jersey. The survey was double-checked, and any item that reflected age or experience, rather than effectiveness, was eliminated. Successful executives were good in college, pursued leadership opportunities and saw themselves as forceful, dominant, assertive and strong. The US Navy also used a short WAB, combined with cognitive ability measures, to select recruits (Booth, McNally and Berry, 1978; Sands, 1978). The navy WAB covered only complete years of schooling, expulsions or suspensions from school, age at enlistment, and existence of 'primary dependants'. Using a huge sample (n=68,616), the researchers calculated an 'Odds for Effectiveness' (OFE) table, which allows recruiting office staff to read off 'survival' probability of applicants with particular combinations of age, dependants, education and ability.

Large sample size helped US Navy researchers find an apparently genuine interaction between age at enlistment and education. Men with 12 or more years of education were equally successful whether aged over or under 19, whereas less well educated men were more successful if age 19 or over, which implies that poorly educated 17- and 18-year-olds should be asked to come back when they're 19 (Hoiberg and Pugh, 1978).

Baehr and Williams (1968) assessed salesmen and sales managers on 15 personal background factors that had previously been identified by factor analysis. Three factors emerged as especially significant predictors of performance: financial responsibility (ability to manage a personal economy of defined proportions – to earn, invest, save and accumulate); early family responsibility (early marriage and establishment of a family, with the husband ordinarily being the sole provider, and demonstrated achievement in handling the family's financial affairs; outside the work situation, the greatest interest is in family activities); and stability (established security and stability in the work situation, resulting from a past history of good performance).

On the basis of their results, Baehr and Williams reported that the picture that emerges of the successful salesman or sales manager is one of a man with a background of competent handling of his personal economy, an early vocational start with prime or sole responsibility for managing family finances, and, particularly for the managers, a past history of sales achievement and present stability in the work and family situations.

Traditionally, two different research designs have been used by investigators in their use of biographical data. These are directly analogous to the present-employee and follow-up methods of test validation. Exemplifying the latter are the WAB studies, some of which have been reviewed already. In this approach, the pool of items for validation consists of those that appear on the employer's application form, filled out at the time of hiring by the criterion groups.

The second design is to use a more extensive questionnaire tracing personal history, which covers a range of background topics. This tends to be administered to presently employed individuals who have been segregated into different groups. Although the WAB method has probably been the one most frequently applied, there have been some interesting studies using the lengthier approach. Smith, Albright, Glennon and Owens (1961) conducted a validation study with an extensive personal history form with petroleum scientists, using three different criteria of success in research work. These criteria comprised a rating of the researchers by their supervisors, a questionnaire-based creativity rating and the number of patent disclosures filed by each man over a five-year work period.

Three biodata keys, totalling 59 items, were applied to a scoring sample of 100 randomly selected respondents. Good concurrent validity estimates were obtained in relation to overall performance ratings, creativity ratings and patent disclosures. The results indicated that biodata can provide a valuable predictive device in respect of job performance.

Career Success

Although life history data have been shown to be valid predictors of many occupationally specific criteria, they have rarely been used to predict career success over a wide range of occupations. In an effort to plug the gap, Childs and Klimoski (1986) obtained life history data from 555 participants in a larger study of the antecedents of success in the real estate business. After initial biodata collection, these individuals were contacted again two years later to provide data on 12 measures of general occupational success.

Success data were factor analysed to derive three occupational success criterion composites: job, personal and career success. The 72 items from the biographical inventory were further analysed separately. Multiple regression analysis was used to relate the resultant five biodata factors – social orientation, economic stability, work ethic orientation, educational achievement and interpersonal confidence – to the success composites. The biographical factors accounted for statistically significant proportions of variance in response, in respect of all three criterion factor variables.

Childs and Klimoski concluded that they would not expect the same factor patterns to emerge with another instrument and sample, because biodata factors are tied to initial item selection. Nevertheless, many were able to note some interesting commonalities between their own study in emergent biographical factor structure and ones produced in other published research.

Elsewhere, Tarnoiwski (1973) summarized a survey of businessmen who were asked to identify success in their own terms. The list of definitions he obtained showed a remarkable similarity to the factors reported by Childs and Klimoski. These included, for example, goal achievement, happiness, job satisfaction, job and financial security. Moreover, for an item defining success attitudes, respondents (49%) reported that, for most people, success represents greater job satisfaction and/or a desire for more meaningful employment; 34% chose realization of non-career-related goals, and 17% chose greater material and/or career advancement. These factors seemed to relate to the job, personal and career constructs uncovered by Childs and Klimoski.

Childs and Klimoski noted more particular similarities with Baehr and Williams (1968), whose study yielded five higher-order factors – namely, educational background and achievement, upward mobility and drive, personal/social leadership, financial achievements and background, and stability and status quo orientation. Klimoski (1973) found 10 factors using a sample of engineers. Several resembled the dimensions uncovered by Childs and Klimoski (1986) (for example, professional orientation and achievement – academic/personal). Some similarities were also found in the work of Owens and Schoenfeldt (1979) and Davis (1984) – for example, academic achievement, social introversion and socioeconomic status. All these similarities gave some credence to the notion that certain biodata factors could be somewhat general.

Management and Leader Selection

In ever more competitive business environments, it becomes increasingly important for companies to ensure they have capable top-level executives and leaders. Recently, management researchers have begun to explore the usefulness of biodata as predictors of management and leadership potential. If it is accurate to assume that prior life experiences reflect critical points of development necessary for performance as top-level managers, an objective and systematic assessment of these biographical experiences could provide an invaluable tool in selecting leaders for the future.

Meta-analyses of relevant research literature have indicated that systematically gathered and coded biographical information is one of the most powerful predictors of job performance in entry-level management, middle-level management and non-managerial positions (Hunter and Hunter, 1984). Furthermore, Owens (1976) described alternative interview and autobiographical procedures for systematically gathering life history information that might be used at top management levels. As we shall see, recent research indicates that anything that looks like a paper and pencil test is not likely to be viewed as acceptable to top-level managers.

Just a few studies have so far used these procedures. Lindsey, Homes and McCall (1987) used structured interview procedures to gather information about key learning experiences in 191 executives' lives (unfortunately no criterion performance data were available). Russell, Devlin, Mattson and Atwater (1990) described a method of coding biographical information from life history essays that predicted leadership and academic performance at the US Naval Academy.

Russell (1990) reported on a selection system that was designed and operated for three years to choose top-level managers for divisions of a *Fortune* 500 corporation. Candidates were those designated as 'first replacements' for division general manager positions in the corporate succession planning system. Unfortunately, a criterion of subsequent performance in top management positions could not be examined because of small sample size. Consequently, Russell focused on describing the method used for systematically gathering biographical information for predicting performance in top management positions and to determine whether this biographical information was related to candidates' current performance as members of top management *teams* in the divisions. Structured interviews and questionnaires were used to generate examples of prior life experiences in college, professional (non-managerial) positions and entry through middle-level management positions. The vast majority of biographical information came from the interviews. The major advantage of structured interviews over more traditional paper and pencil biodata questionnaires is the ability to ask customized follow-up questions after initial responses have been made to standard questions. The major disadvantage is that the resultant biographical information must be scored using subjective judgements of the interviewer(s). Regardless of this, various paper and pencil formats were considered and rejected by top-level management as unacceptable for this type of job – the uniform opinion was that no test could capture what was needed for top-level management. The biographical information was used to arrive at ratings on nine job dimensions and an overall recommendation. Then, relationships between these ratings, questionnaire responses by subordinates, peers, prior superiors, and three concurrent performance criteria for candidates in their positions as members of top-level management teams were assessed.

The procedure therefore comprised five parts. A *job analysis* was carried out using focus groups with top-performing general managers from the company. Each general manager in turn was discussed. Further discussions generated critical incidents consisting of outcome requirements (tasks and responsibilities) and process requirements (behaviours, procedures, tactics). The critical incidents were grouped into a final list of nine dimensions through consensus discussion, with about six critical incidents placed in each dimension.

Interviews were used to collect biographical information with the candidates and candidates' immediate boss. During these interviews, the candidates described the accomplishments, disappointments and what was learned from those experiences in college and all positions held since entering the workforce (excluding current position). The candidates were asked about any obstacles, assistance, conflicts or other aspects of the process that accompanied each accomplishment or disappointment. Then the same process was gone through in respect of the candidate's current position. Finally, the candidate was asked about career aspirations, prior formal developmental activities (training programmes attended and so on), self-perceptions and how he or she felt others (superiors, peers and subordinates) perceive him or her. The interview with the candidate's immediate superior followed the same format, except for asking about the candidate's former positions (unless the superior was present earlier in the candidate's career). Interviews with superiors lasted from two to three hours.

Questionnaires requesting respondents to assess candidates on the nine dimensions were anonymously completed by subordinates, peers and prior superiors whose names were provided by the candidate and his boss. The questionnaires contained three parts. Part I used open-ended questions to ask respondents to describe the candidate's major accomplishments and disappointments. In Part II, respondents were presented with clusters of critical incidents taken from focus group discussions, and arranged under nine dimension headings. Respondents were asked to rate the candidate on a total of 65 critical incidents in Part II. Part III contained open-ended questions about the 'functions mastered' by one candidate, the candidate's strengths and weaknesses, and any other comment that the respondent thought would be useful.

The *rating process* took place in two steps. In Step I, all information gathered on a candidate by the interviewer was distributed to the other four interviewers. Responses to the open-ended portions of the questionnaires were typed and distributed, as well as a numerical summary of the questionnaires (individual responses, means, standard deviations and so on, for superior, peer and subordinate responses). *No* information from the candidate's personnel records (for example, prior performance ratings or developmental action plans) was made available to the interviewers. This was to ensure that the evaluation was independent and uncontaminated by prior judgements. Each interviewer read all the material on each candidate.

Step II comprised the interviewers meeting at the corporate headquarters to agree an evaluation of each candidate. A narrative description was provided together with evaluative scale ratings of candidates. These data were combined and an overall recommendation regarding each candidate was recorded. These were made at three levels: 3='ready now – minimal (or no) weaknesses to be addressed in order to perform adequately'; 2='ready now – a small number of weaknesses that need to be taken into account in position placement'; or 1='needs development – numerous weaknesses need to be addressed before being considered for general manager position'.

The results of this investigation provided preliminary evidence of meaningful relationships between prior life experiences and the performance of individuals in higher-level management positions. Russell (1990) argues that this investigative framework allows for many different ingredients of top-level management skills and abilities to be explored in relation to the development experiences of the contenders for such posts. Systematically gathered biographical information can be used to investigate the supremacy of life events that interact with leadership components such as concern for people or for production, thus revealing individual profiles that can be assessed and classified in terms of their ability to select the type of leader needed for a particular senior management position.

This kind of procedure can provide an organization with an invaluable information base which can be used in its succession planning system. The need for organizations to engage in effective succession planning is of paramount importance to their long-term performance, competitiveness and growth. This is especially true of organizations whose business success has depended primarily on the efforts of one or two key individuals, very often the founders of the business, for whom retirement beckons.

Biodata and Management Selection

Since traditional biodata instruments are time-consuming to develop and require expertise and large samples (Strebler, 1991), it seems unlikely that they will become widely used for managerial selection in their current format. An alternative approach to the development of biodata models has been put forward by Wilkinson (1995). This approach is based on the premise that if biodata instruments are developed such that the criterion is a unidimensional person-specific attribute, this attribute is measured objectively, the biodata items used exclude job-specific items, and the developmental group is as diverse as possible, then biographical information models should be more generalizable across occupational groups. Moreover, if this approach is repeated over a number of individual attributes, then a biodata instrument with a range of scales will result. Since biodata questionnaires collect data on previous behaviours and experiences, it is possible that biodata measures will prove to be more predictive of job performance than the psychometric instruments from which they were derived.

Wilkinson (1997) noted that, despite having a good record as a predictor of job performance, biodata are seldom used for the selection of managers. Their infrequent use can be explained in part by noting that traditional biodata prediction models of job performance, developed in one context, do not readily transport into different contexts. Organizations wishing to use biodata must first develop and validate such an instrument. As this is feasible only for large organizations, an alternative approach is to develop biodata instruments to predict specific attributes of a person. Such instruments will be more generalizable than those developed to predict a person's job performance. This approach was tested by developing biodata models to predict vocational interest (as measured by Holland's Self-Directed Search – SDS) of a group of likely applicants for managerial jobs. Following factor analysis of the biodata, regression models were developed to predict individuals' scores on the six SDS scales. Tested on a sample of male and female students, biodata measures proved to be powerful predictors of vocational interest.

Women's Managerial Advancement

Biodata have been implicated as predictors of women's occupational advancement, especially to management positions. Although theories of women's promotional prospects and progression into management positions have identified a variety of factors that influence this process, background variables are frequently included as being among the most important (Fagenson, 1990; Tharenou, 1990; Tharenou, Latimer and Conroy, 1994).

Organizational structure and culture are known to play a significant part in affecting the kinds of opportunities that are provided to women to enter higher levels of the hierarchy. Organizational attitudes may vary towards the degree of career encouragement and training opportunities that are opened up specifically to female employees. In addition to these factors, however, women's managerial advancement has also been linked to personal characteristics such as self-confidence, which in turn stem from early developmental experience as children (Fagenson, 1990; Tharenou, 1990). Self-confidence is important if female employees are to obtain management positions in often male-dominated organizations (Kanter, 1977). Organizational encouragement to women to reach executive levels is very important (Morrison, White and Von Velsor, 1987).

Home life can make a significant difference to women's career advancement, and degree of attachment to domestic affairs has been negatively linked to salary and organizational level achieved for both male and female managers (Gattiker and Larwood, 1988, 1989). There are gender-related differences, however. Evidence has emerged, for instance, that women who advance as managers are less likely to be spouses or parents than men who advance as managers (Davidson and Cooper, 1987). Getting married and having children is more disruptive to a woman's work experience and this in turn reduces career advancement prospects (Ragins and Sundstrom, 1989). Consistent with this view is further evidence that female managers are more likely to be unmarried and childless than are male managers (Davidson and Cooper, 1983; Tharenou and Conroy, 1988; Rowney and Cahoon, 1990). Women are more likely to move from full-time to part-time employment because of young children (Felmlee, 1984) and women managers may leave jobs because of heavy demands pre-school children pose (Rosin and Korabik, 1990).

For women who do advance to executive positions and who enter jobs not usually associated with their gender, parental encouragement, particularly in relation to educational attainment, is believed to be important (Betz and

Fizgerald, 1987). Such parental encouragement has, once again, been associated with instilling self-confidence. This disposition underpins an individual's expectation of success. This trait seems to be especially important to women's managerial advancement (Lemkau, 1983; Ragins and Sundstrom, 1989; Tharenou, Latimer and Conroy, 1994).

One important aspect of background experience is the training an individual has received and skills they have acquired in their working life. Career encouragement seems to increase women's training and development, which in turn enhances managerial advancement. An active and demanding home life can reduce the amount of training completed by women. This reduces career advancement prospects (Tharenou, Latimer and Conroy, 1994). Self-confidence alone may not be enough to ensure managerial enhancement. Much depends on how self-confidence is used in the organizational framework. Higher self-confidence seems to be associated with obtaining more training opportunities, which can contribute towards promotion and advancement. It is also associated with overcoming obstacles to advancement. Training increases the probability of managerial advancement but may have a more positive effect on men than on women. Men are more likely to attend training courses than women and to participate in more industry meetings. Yet, it is often women who need greater encouragement to go on training courses and to seek advancement. Women are at a disadvantage compared with men because of both the less positive impact of training on advancement and the less positive, indirect impact of work experience and education. Women's advancement is furthered by the indirect impact of career encouragement (through training), but is hindered indirectly by the negative impact of home roles on work experience.

Conclusion

This chapter has discussed various applications of biodata and the criteria relating to employment, performance, commitment and career progression with which biographical information has been linked. For practical reasons biodata have been used to see whether they can predict work-related criteria as different as career choice, job success (which is rather differently operationalized and measured), staff turnover, absenteeism and various aspects of job performance. Thus, specific and general, and positive and negative elements of employee potential have been examined. The application of biodata in the process of selection of employees to fill particular positions has proved to be useful at varying levels of hierarchical seniority in an organization. Thus, biodata not only enhance employee recruitment procedures at lower levels in the organization, but can also have value for selection of personnel to fill high-level positions in senior management (Wilkinson, 1995; Wilkinson, Anderson, van Zwanenberg, Erdos and Harvey, 1997) and even for top executive positions (Russell, 1990). With growing concerns about equal opportunities in employment, with much attention being given to equal opportunities across sexes especially in relation to managerial advancement, the use of biodata may place decision-making about promotional choices on a more objective footing. However, problems may arise, of a political nature, where biodata predictors reveal that career success may be achieved at the expense of family commitments (for example, Davidson and Cooper, 1983; Rowney and Cahoon, 1990; Rosin and Korabik, 1990). However, biodata research on women's career advancement may also reveal that although certain biographical attributes may be negative predictors of occupational success per se, such conflicts can be resolved with appropriate and sufficient employer training and support.

In sum, the accumulating research evidence has shown that carefully conceived and constructed biographical data collection instruments and procedures can yield valuable information for recruiters and assessors. Although some of the findings remain equivocal, and in need of further exploration and clarification, there is no doubt that current research has shown that selected biodata items can, and do, predict specific work-related behaviours.

Chapter 7:
The Predictors of
Business Success

Most organzations attempt, through the processes of recruitment, selection and training, to find, choose and develop the best people at all levels. Some organizations have other schemes such as mentoring, developmental workshops or a curriculum of educational opportunities to ensure that they get the best out of their staff. Most business people are conscious of the long-term cost of poor decision-making in the business of selection, but are not always eager to spend money so as to prevent serious mistakes from occurring.

This book has concentrated on the use of biographical information or biodata in the classification and assessment of individuals, an approach that has a long history (Owens, 1976). It is probably true to say that all employee selection implicitly involves a biodata approach since most of us make judgements about other people on the basis of their background experiences, which we regard as predictive of how those individuals are likely to behave in the future. The difference between the 'everyday' collection and interpretation of biographical data and the more formal, empirical biodata analysis used in employee selection contexts is the adoption of a more rigorous and systematic approach. Biodata indicators are empirically proven to be predictive of specific job performance behaviours through the use of statistical methods. These methods are used to discover the best predictors of job performance. The maintenance of biodata measures with predictive validity is a continuous, ongoing process that needs constant research (McManus and Masztal, 1999). Some approaches to the development of predictors of job performance or career success may go under different names, even though they nevertheless use considerable amounts of biographical data (Judge, Cable, Boudreau and Bretz, 1995). Thus, much of the information that managers and professional recruiters might obtain about job applicants or candidates for promotion in organizations can be regarded in a broad sense as 'biographical', including those measures that might more formally be considered measures of personality or aptitude.

It is surprising how many lay people express theories of job success grounded in biographical information about candidates. Anyone who has sat on a selection panel may have noted that many of the questions asked are, to all intents and purposes, concerned with biodata. When closely questioned, many selectors reveal a 'theory' about job applicants that is in a sense related to their biography. Thus, it is not uncommon to hear that playing team sports at school is believed to teach the individual to become a better team player, and may therefore be predictive of being a good team player at work. Some professional selectors for commercial enterprises may look out for early signs in candidates of childhood entrepreneurship such as trading with other children in the playground. Equally, the more wary may be particularly interested in a history of childhood illnesses, which some may see as potentially predictive of later absenteeism driven by hypochondriasis (Furnham, 2000a, 2000b).

One approach is to look for a particular 'set of experiences' in candidates. Thus, a private school education, a short-term commission in the military, or the experience of relatively lengthy travel abroad alone during a 'year out' may be seen as character-forming experiences that are highly predictive of later management success. An alternative view of this bundle of experiences would claim that such a history is the very opposite of what is required for success in a particular job or career. Yet, despite the fact that they are unlikely openly to admit it, many professional selectors do look for a range of particular life experiences that they think are highly predictive of certain jobs (Furnham, 2000a, 2000b).

Problems of political correctness, potential litigation and accusations of unfair discrimination, however, mean that many professional selectors are unhappy to admit their theories of biographical correlates of success. Take two examples, for instance: the first is religious observance. Religion is a difficult problem for selectors. They are partly embarrassed, partly ignorant, and almost certainly wary of being accused of discrimination if they enquire about the topic. Yet there is an extensive literature that suggests that those who have a fairly strict religious background have different attitudes to work than those who do not (Furnham, 1990; Berry, 1999). It is possible with biodata questions to enquire about religious service attendance in the past without too much difficulty, however. Religiousness, rather than religion, may be a powerful correlate of morality and conscientiousness, which are important predictors of work-related behaviour.

The issue of unfair discrimination is not unique to biographical ratings. Concerns about the risk of discrimination in psychometric testing, which are believed to unfairly disadvantage ethnic minority groups, have led to the development of aptitude tests that reduce this risk (Coles, 2000).

A second area of difficulty is mental and physical health. Although few recruiters would wish to discriminate those who, through no fault of their own, have experienced serious illness, some such problems may be highly prognostic of future behaviour. But, once again, this area is fraught with problems. Do candidates over-report or under-report illness? What evidence is there that these problems do predict work behaviour?

In many ways the biodata approach may help to take the guess-work and prejudice out of lay attempts to investigate biographical predictors of behaviour. Inevitably, it will show that long-held 'pet theories' have little or no factual evidence to support them. Equally, the method may easily throw up important relationships between background characteristics of individuals and their future job performance that have not been previously considered. Lay theories of the biography of success will always be useful at the stage of hypothesis generation in biodata analysis. Precisely because the biodata method is not theoretically driven, it is possible to test specific lay hypotheses.

Changes in the World of Work

With social and technological developments, improved health and increased longevity, and greater education and affluence in developed societies, conceptions of work are changing. The world of work in the 21st century is likely to experience an evolution that will alter the way we work, when we work and where we work. If the nature of work changes, then it is not unlikely that the predictors of success at work might change as well. There are many speculations about the future of work in the new millennium. However, two are of central importance. These concern aspects of time and place – how long we work for an employer and how much time we actually spend at work; and then where we work.

Armstrong-Stassed (1998) has focused on five developments at work called 'alternative work arrangements'. She examines the definition and form of these alternative arrangements, their prevalence and predicted future status (exclusively in Canada) and the challenges they provide.

- *Part-time employment*, defined as working less than 30 hours a week. These jobs can be very varied and distinguished as permanent vs casual, good vs bad, voluntary vs involuntary. Nearly one-quarter of jobs in North America fell into this category. They clearly provide real challenges, which include establishing policies, practices and procedures for part-timers with their preferred work status if possible; promoting part-time work as a legitimate alternative to full-time work; and promoting part-time work for older workers.
- *Contingent employment*, defined as when an individual is working for an organization but is not considered a regular employee. These include temporary, casual and technical contingent workers. There are three specific challenges for this group: first, designing new ways of managing and motivating contingent workers; next, providing equitable treatment of contingent workers; and finally, protecting their interests.
- *Flexitime*, defined as when employees vary their starting and finishing times

but are required to work a standard number of hours within a specific time period. About one-quarter of Canadians reported having these arrangements, which most seemed to like and regard as a stress reliever. Challenges included: establishing selection and eligibility criteria and successful implementation procedures; promoting the use of flextime; and ensuring its compatibility with other organization initiatives.

- *Compressed work weeks*, defined as reallocating the work time by condensing the total hours in the traditional five-day working week into fewer days. This is popular, although its effects on productivity are unknown. Four challenges are specified: identifying jobs that are appropriate for compressed work weeks; identifying which form of compressed work week is best; preparing employees for compressed work weeks and preparing managers and supervisors to manage these workers.

- *Teleworking*, defined as working at a location away from the traditional place of work, full-time or part-time, and involving the use of telecommunications and the electronic processing of information. Again, four challenges of this type of work are identified: ensuring a supportive environment; identifying jobs that are appropriate for teleworking; establishing selection procedures and eligibility criteria; and training both telemanagers and teleworkers.

Four of the above five points are concerned with how long we work. The nine-to-five, five days a week job may become a thing of the past. The option to choose their own work routine may suit many people well, particularly those with odd chronobiological rhythms. The fifth point concerns *where* we work.

Developments in communications technology have led to the growth in teleworking, or working at a location remote from the central workplace, usually from home, in what has come to be known as the electronic cottage (Holland and Hogan, 1999). In the USA, teleworking is also known as *telecommuting*. A recent US study showed that 62% of companies encouraged telecommuting in 1996, up from 40% in 1994. In late 1997 more than 10 million Americans telecommuted and nearly 70% of 500 companies employed telecommuters (Holland and Hogan, 1999). European data are less reliable, although a similar growth pattern seems to show that the virtual workplace is reality now. Investors in People commissioned a British study, which showed that 73% of companies responding had 'arrangements for teleworking'.

Warner (1997) found that workers reported being 40% more productive while working away from the office, mainly because they had fewer distractions. Another study conducted by the telecommunications giant AT&T found that telecommuters were so happy that one said they would look for another job if they were forced back into the old office. Even more impressive, according to some reviewers, is that people could be virtual teams that may never meet but have total access to each other (Cascio, 1998).

The advantages of teleworking considered by Cascio (1998) include:

- teleworking eliminates lack of access to experts – everyone is online, all the time;
- intercontinental teams can be formed – proximity is not an issue;
- consultants can be hired and do not need to charge travel, lodging and downtime;
- one can hire the best people in the world to join that network at negligible cost;
- people can easily be part of different teams at the same time;
- because everything is online, swift responses to any event, including demands of the market, are possible.

Organizations are told that teleworking can lead to space savings, reduced absenteeism, greater retention. Because of such changes, employee satisfaction may improve, leading to increased productivity. Indeed, teleworkers may even become independent of other cost elements for businesses such as occupational pension plans and essentially become self-employed.

There is, however, little empirical evidence for these claims (Furnham, 2000a). Teleworkers cannot be expected to carry the cost of their work-related equipment. Effective teleworking requires state-of-the-art computer hardware and software that needs to be continually upgraded. To send and receive large amounts of data and to facilitate audio-visual forms of communication such as videoconferencing and the transmission of multimedia data require high-quality digital telephone links with relatively high running costs. These costs are often forgotten in the calculations.

There are other factors relating to the employees themselves that need to be borne in mind. Tele-employees are difficult to monitor. Are they at work? Are they out shopping or playing with the children? Are they producing anything? Teleworking may be best suited to those individuals who do not need close supervision or regular feedback, and who can be trusted as self-motivators. Telecommuting only really makes sense with the right job, the right person, the right reason and the right manager (Holland and Hogan, 1999). Not all employees have a suitable alternative, home-based location for teleworking – the quiet, spacious 'spare bedroom'. In fact, surprisingly few ordinary workers have a home environment conducive to any sort of work, let alone high-tech work.

Many important questions remain unanswered. How frequently should manager and teleworker be in touch? Who is responsible for maintaining and insuring business equipment? What are the conditions of work? What are the measurable outputs of work? What is the attitude of clients or customers to dealing with teleworkers? And, more importantly, what are the psychological needs of the employees themselves and are these satisfied by working in a remote, satellite telecottage? Work is not just about earning money or achieving professional esteem. It also has a social function. At the office, the individual can mix with colleagues, engage in conversation and gossip. Working from home can be lonely and isolating. It is necessary, from time to time, to meet with other people in person in order to gauge fully what is happening at work. An important aspect of employment is having a sense of identity with the employing organization. Without this, the employee may feel that he or she does not belong. This, in turn, could have implications for longer-term loyalty and commitment to the business.

Somewhat paradoxically, it also seems that teleworkers need to be ambitious, self-disciplined, conscientious individuals. Yet, because they are so often forgotten, those types do not want to work away from the office. Often, the less ambitious, the near-to-retirement and the 'quality-of-life' brigade drift into teleworking – precisely the type who are not really suited to it. Thus, in the short term, telecommuting cuts costs. But the longer-term issues may be serious because, by neglecting the psychological consequences of telecommuting, the short-term gains may easily turn into long-term losses (Furnham, 2000a).

Changes in when and where we work inevitably have important consequences for employee selection. If people are to be 'trusted' to work unsupervised, they may need different qualities from those who work less efficiently under these conditions. The biodata approach is well suited to investigating these problems. As long as one has good success criteria and data on a sufficient number of people, it is a relatively simple task to determine which biographical factors relate to productivity and satisfaction in the 'new workplace'.

The End of the 'Career'

Until comparatively recently, the 'long-service-in-one-organization' career still existed. It was based on the precepts of personal loyalty and identification with an organization (its service, brand image and product). Individuals moved around within rather than between organizations. Hence, it was important for an employer to choose and develop the right people. Today, this position is changing. Organizations are increasingly giving out the message: don't count on us for continued employment. In countries such as the USA, for example, about one-third of all workers are self-employed or in contingent employment.

According to Hall, Briscoe and Kram (1997), the old career idea meant that the individual had a contract with the organization, whereas the new career idea means individuals have contracts with themselves. These writers refer to the *Protean* career, which is primarily concerned with the ability for lifelong learning, adaptation and reinvention of the self. Hence, they point out that certain characteristics that predict learning – such as feedback-seeking and personality factors such as hardiness, flexibility, tolerance of ambiguity and uncertainty, dominance and independence – are advantageous. They maintain that 'organizational factors are becoming less important in determining individual career outcomes; intrapersonal (especially relational connection) factors are becoming more important in shaping career directions and rewards' (Hall, Briscoe and Kram, 1997: 332).

Other writers have envisaged a future in which firms have a small core work-force and a much larger group of non-core employees who will have led trad-itional careers (Feldman, 1997). Clearly, the latter will need opportunities for skill development and career advancement. Feldman proposed four factors that related to career advancement for those non-core workers.

1. Opportunities for career advancement for non-core workers will be: (a) positively related to criticality of the services they provide; (b) negatively related to their replaceability and substitutability.
2. Opportunities for career advancement for non-core workers will be: (a) positively associated with industry growth; and (b) negatively associated with firm or sub-unit decline.
3. Opportunities for career advancement for non-core employees will be: (a) nega-tively associated with rigidity of opportunity structures in an occupation; and (b) positively associated with ability to practice an occupation outside formal organizational boundaries.
4. Loss of subsequent career advancement opportunities due to non-core employ-ment will be greater for individuals in early-career stages. (Feldman, 197: 340)

Frese (1997) has argued that self-reliance is the key to being a success in a job in the new millennium. The successful worker will have to be good at learning by himself or herself, good at communication with co-workers, good at interdisci-plinary and group work and be self-initiating.

What does the end of the traditional career mean for the assessment of potential through biodata? In many ways this should be good news for biodata technology. First, biodata will need to be 'refreshed' every three to five years – that is, the factors that predicted job performance in the past may not always do so in the future. Nevertheless, if one is asked to predict success over a five-year period as opposed to a 25-year period, the chances of doing so with continually renewed biodata are probably increased.

Next, the 'portfolio' employee (Handy, 1995) would no doubt have a wider range of occupational experiences than in previous times, *and* will expect to provide biodata about them. In other words, the onus will be on individuals to keep accurate and comprehensive records of their own background that prospective employers can plug into wider biographical databanks in which a wide range of biodata indices will have been empirically linked to a wide range of working competencies and performance criteria. This should provide a richer set of data for the biodata expert. On the other hand, it may be more difficult to establish a good criterion group because people will be so mobile.

The end of the career and increased job mobility will lead to more selection decisions having to be made. The selection of potential may have a shorter time horizon (that is, three to five years), but this is well suited to the biodata approach. If anything, then, changes in the traditional career are good news for biodata researchers.

Habits, Traits and Practices of Successful People

An essentially biographical approach to establishing the predictors of success is to find 'known groups' of successful people and to try to establish what characteristics or behaviours distinguished them from those who were less successful. The 1980s saw enormous sales (10 million) of a book entitled, *The Seven Habits of Highly Effective People* by Stephen Covey (1989). He claimed to have identified a number of specific 'habits' of those individuals who did well. They were to be proactive, begin with the end in mind, put first things first, think win/win, seek first to understand then be understood, synergize and finally sharpen the saw. As before, there was little that was surprising or counter-intuitive about the list, save perhaps the idea that the distinguishing factors between the most successful and the majority were habits, as opposed to traits, abilities or values. Cramer (1999) noted of Covey's work:

> People like its sugary admonitions to self-improvement. They appear to thrive on its mixture of old-fashioned common sense (vintage 1950s) and holistic self-help (vintage 1990s). It makes them feel good. Of course whether this makes them better managers or better people is difficult, if not impossible, to determine.

Habits are customary manners of acting, rather than uncontrollable compulsions. Most people think of bad habits like smoking, nail biting and so on, but Covey focused on good habits. It is unclear why the book proved so successful, save one fundamentally important point: habits, unlike abilities or traits, can be learnt (or unlearnt). In this sense, the book was inspirational and this may be a central facet of its success. But little was said about how, when or why these habits were acquired or whether they are related to other systematic and less changeable individual differences.

This emphasis on habits reflects a very old tradition in trying to understand high-flyers of different sorts. There remains an abiding interest in the old-fashioned trait approach to success – particularly leadership. Over the years, a considerable amount of effort went into identifying traits associated with successful leaders. Inevitably, the list got ever longer. By the 1980s Yukl (1980) had more than two dozen factors:

Traits expected to characterize good leaders

Pleasant appearance	Intelligence	Good grooming
Self-confidence	Moderate weight	Interpersonal sensitivity
Adaptability	Tactfulness	Alertness
Persuasiveness	Assertiveness	Fluency
Co-operativeness	Creativity	Ambition
Dependability	Aggressiveness	Judgement
Enthusiasm	Achievement orientation	Persistence
Extroversion	Stress tolerance	Integrity
Responsibility		

But Furnham (1997) has been very critical of this speculation trait approach to identify (leadership) success:

> The research in this tradition is inconsistent and non-replicable. The list of traits simply grows over time, leading to confusion, disputes and little insight into why leadership traits operate as they do. The trait approach identifies people in leadership roles after they have been seen as successful. It is not certain therefore whether these traits make the leader or whether the leadership role shapes the traits. The trait approach may also be thought of as fundamental attribution error: that is, explaining the behaviour (success or failure) almost exclusively in terms of the internal traits and motives of leaders, while ignoring or underplaying organizational, social and economic factors that clearly play a large part. Lay people remain trait theorists when it comes to explaining leadership, which means that this school of thought is still alive and well. Indeed, it can be observed today in those business managers who have replaced the term 'trait' with 'competency' and who believe a particular combination or profile of competencies predicts leadership success. Yet at all levels, the trait approach is never more than descriptive because very rarely do the trait theorists explain how, when and why the traits they stipulate are necessary and sufficient for the leadership process to be successful. They also do not stipulate how much of a trait or ability one needs, or, indeed, what occurs if that ability is missing. (Furnham, 1997: 521)

Recent studies, however, have attempted to categorize the abilities of successful people. Locke (1997), in his retrospective attempt to understand the traits of successful business men and women, divided them into three groupings.

1. Cognition:
   Reality focus
   Honesty
   Independence and Self-confidence
   Active mind
   Competence/ability
   Vision
2. Motivation:
   Egotistic passion for the work
   Commitment to action
   Ambition
   Effort and tenacity
3. Attitude toward employees:
   Respect for ability
   Commitment to justice
   Rewarding merit.

Locke (1997) speculated on various related questions.

1. What methods could be used to infer the quantity of a trait possessed by a

deceased business leader based on biographical and autobiographical material? Can trait measurements of such people be made reliably?

2. How well can these traits be measured in existing business leaders (e.g. assessment centers, tests, interviews, peer ratings)? Howard and Bray (1988) found that intelligence and ambition, measured by tests and interviews, were the best predictors of advancement of AT&T managers over a 25 year period.

3. Could such traits be measured early in a person's career as a way of identifying 'prime mover' potential? Howard and Bray's results suggest that they could, but their dependent variable was promotion rather than wealth creation.

4. Would quantitative analysis support 12 distinct traits, or could they be grouped into a smaller number without loss of important information? My prediction is that they can be combined into a smaller number.

5. Do the traits operate independently (e.g. in additive fashion) or are there interactions between them? I have one prediction here: I think dishonesty negates all a person's other virtues in that it divorces a person from reality in principle. A complicating factor, however, is that people are not always consistent in their honesty or dishonesty.

6. Do the same traits produce wealth creation in all cultures? I would say yes, although there may be culture-specific traits as well.

7. Do prime movers and (lower-level) managers differ in their traits only in degree, or are there more fundamental differences? I would predict big difference in degree on some traits (e.g. ability, ambition). In the case of vision, on the other hand, some managers may not have any at all. (Locke, 1997: 92)

The quest for listing and understanding those personal factors that predict business success will never end. Although different methodologies will be used – historical, biodata longitudinal studies – they all attempt to answer the same question. It may be expected, therefore, that their findings should converge. The question remains as to which method is most efficient and effective. It is the contention of this book that the biodata method is among the best.

Biographical Correlates of Emotional Intelligence

Every so often a new, or at least re-branded, concept appears that 'explains' success at work. The idea that seemed to be the 'silver bullet' of the last decade of the twentieth century was Emotional Intelligence, an idea popularized by Goleman (1995). The idea, which seemed to echo many people's personal experience, was that emotional intelligence is more important than conventional intelligence in the workplace. The argument is that it is no accident that motive and emotion share the same Latin root meaning to move. Great work starts with understanding feeling, and failed managers fail not because of lack of ability, but rather because of poor social skills, poor self-control and poor relationship building.

It is presumed that technical skills apposite to a job are of secondary importance to 'emotional' or relationship building skills. It is argued, probably correctly, that technical training is easy compared with teaching emotional skills.

Soft, people skills are *more* important than hard, technical skills in predicting job success.

However, there is much disagreement about the precise meaning of the 'Emotion Quotient' (EQ). Salovey and Mayer (1990), who first used the term 'emotional intelligence', thought that it consisted of three categories of adaptive abilities: appraisal and expression of emotion, regulation of emotion, and utilization of emotions in solving problems. The first category consisted of the components of appraisal and expression of emotion in the self and appraisal of emotion in others. The component of appraisal and expression of emotion in the self was further divided into the subcomponents of verbal and non-verbal and, as applied to others, was broken into the subcomponents of non-verbal perception and empathy. The second category of emotional intelligence was regulation of emotions in others. The third category, utilization of emotion, included the components of flexible planning, creative thinking, redirected attention and motivation. Even though emotions are at the core of this model, it also encompasses social and cognitive functions related to the expression, regulation and utilization of emotions.

Mayer and Salovey (1997) provided a revised model of emotional intelligence that gave more emphasis to the cognitive components of the concept and conceptualized emotional intelligence in terms of the potential for intellectual and emotional growth. The model consisted of four branches of emotional intelligence: perception, appraisal and expression of emotion; emotional facilitation of thinking; understanding, analysing and using emotional knowledge; and reflective regulation of emotions to further emotional and intellectual growth. The perception, appraisal and expression of emotion were viewed as the most basic processes, while the reflective regulation of emotions requires the most complex processing.

Can these 'competencies' be measured, learnt and trained? Certainly, once they have been clearly operationalized, they can be measured. Indeed, psychometrically sophisticated measures exist for nearly all of the above measures. The question of learning and training is more difficult. Most research on the topic of intelligence would probably argue that, although people can be trained to do IQ tests more effectively and raise their score by, say, half a standard deviation, you cannot teach intelligence. People can, however, be taught to think more laterally. Introverts can be taught to behave more like extroverts, but this does not mean they actually become extroverts. In this sense, it seems unlikely that EQ skills or competencies may be easily acquired.

The central and highly topical question for this book is whether biodata can be used to select people with high EQ? In principle, the answer is 'yes', supposing, of course, that EQ can be properly defined. This could be done on a competence-by-competence procedure. Thus, for a range of 'emotional' competencies such as self-confidence, self-control or optimism, it would be possible to obtain groups of individuals agreed to be high or low on this competence and to look for their biographical correlates. A great deal of this research has already been done with respect to a few of these competencies such as self-confidence or self-esteem. There are known demographic correlates of self-esteem, such as sex, age and education. Others such as trustworthiness are currently of great interest to many people in business.

Goleman (1998) tried to be more specific with regard to EQ at work and specified five competencies, grouped under two areas:

Personal competence ⇒ *competencies that determine how we manage ourselves*

Self-awareness: *Knowing one's internal states, preferences, resources and intuitions*
- Emotional awareness: recognizing emotions and their effects
- Accurate self-assessment: knowing own strengths and limits
- Self-confidence: strong sense of self-worth and capabilities

Self-regulation: *Managing one's internal states, impulses and resources*
- Self-control: keeping disruptive emotions and impulses in check
- Trustworthiness: maintaining standards of honesty and integrity
- Conscientiousness: taking responsibility for personal performance
- Adaptability: flexibility in handling change
- Innovation: being comfortable with novel ideas, approaches and new information

Motivation: *Emotional tendencies that guide or facilitate reaching goals*
- Achievement drive: striving to improve or meet a standard of excellence
- Commitment: aligning with the goals of the group or organization
- Initiative: readiness to act on opportunities
- Optimism: persistence in pursuing goals despite obstacles or setbacks

Social competence ⇒ competencies that determine how we handle relationships

Empathy: *Awareness of others' feelings, needs and concerns*
- Understanding others: sensing others' feelings and perspectives and taking an active interest in their concerns
- Developing others: sensing others' developmental needs and bolstering their abilities
- Service orientation: anticipating, recognizing and meeting customer needs
- Leveraging diversity: cultivating opportunities through different kinds of people
- Political awareness: reading a group's emotional currents and power relationships

Social skills: *Adeptness at inducing desirable responses in others*
- Influence: wielding effective tactics for persuasion
- Communication: listening openly and sending convincing messages
- Conflict management: negotiating and resolving disagreements
- Leadership: inspiring and guiding individuals and groups
- Change catalyst: initiating or managing change
- Building bonds: nurturing instrumental relationships
- Collaboration and co-operation: working with others towards shared goals
- Team capabilities: creating group synergy in pursuing collective goals.

To the psychometrician the above list looks muddled and complex. Some 'competencies' such as conscientiousness have been conceived of as personal traits. Others like conflict management or team capabilities are unclear. But unless the many subfactors can be satisfactorily combined, it is quite likely that research would show the biodata correlates of one factor (conscientiousness) may be unrelated to, even opposite to, those for another factor (initiative). Nevertheless, the above list could easily serve as a source of hypotheses to be tested by the biodata method.

Searching Out Creativity

Just as with EQ, many selectors talk about the importance of selecting creative employees – is it worth asking whether biodata could be useful here? Psychological research on the causes, consequences and predictors of human creativity remains something of a backwater. There are various reasons for this state of affairs, but perhaps the most fundamental is the problem of how to define it.

There seem to be four approaches to the topic: those that examine the creative process (cognitive factors underlying creativity); those that look at the creative person (personality correlate); those looking at the creative product (the output process); and those that consider the creative situation (environmental, situational and cultural factors associated with creativity). Most researchers have agreed that at least three sorts of factors are relevant to creative achievement. They are cognitive variables (intelligence, knowledge, technical skills and special talent), environmental variables (political-religious, socioeconomic factors) and personality variables (particularly, tough-mindedness) (Eysenck, 1995).

It has been known for a long time that both highly creative and psychotic people share the 'ability' to produce more unusual associations between words and ideas than 'normal' people. They seem unable to inhibit irrelevant information from entering consciousness. Hence unrelated ideas become interconnected and there is a widening of associative horizon (Eysenck, 1995).

Stravidou and Furnham (1996) noted that there is considerable evidence that psychoticism or tough-mindedness is linked to creativity. There seem to be at least five types of evidence to support this finding. First, people genetically related to psychotics are often creative. Next, psychoticism or tough-mindedness is related to tested creativity or originality. Third, psychoticism is clearly related to various forms of creative achievement. Next, creative persons often suffer from mental illness. Finally, psychotics and creative people seem to share cognitive styles.

One recent study compared a group of advertising and design creatives with a comparable group of professional managers in occupations that are not evidently creative. Gelado (1997) found, as predicted, that the creatives were significantly more neurotic, extroverted and open to experience, but were also less conscientious. Some of the biggest differences were on subfacets of openness, especially fantasy.

But there are fewer studies on the biography of creative people. Berry (1999) has pointed out that a popular method to try to understand creativity has been to identify common features in samples of past achievers (such as social class, childhood loss, ill health). This is essentially the biodata method. However, problems with sampling lead to inconsistent, even contradictory, conclusions.

More than 125 years ago, Galton (1874) showed that notable British scientists tended to derive disproportionately from middle-class, Protestant (non-dogmatic, reformed traditions) backgrounds. Others, such as Merton (1936), borrowed ideas from Weber and argued that Protestant 'core values' led them to be great achievers, particularly in science. These values included utilitarianism, disinterested enquiry into nature and postponement of gratification. Berry (1999), in a study of 1400 notable achievers in the past two centuries, found Protestant fruitfulness to be greater in the sciences, whereas for Catholics it has been greater in the arts. He also noted the importance of 'concealed factors' transmitted through family tradition, which refers to the pattern of values inculcated by parents. Certainly the extent of the literature on creativity points to the fact that experiences in childhood and early adulthood are likely to have a major impact on later creativity. It is therefore ideally suited to the biodata approach, which seeks to link historical and biographical details with current success.

Conclusion

This book has focused on one particular method of assessing human potential in the workplace and has tried to uncover the predictors of work success. The basic idea is that a person's unique lifetime experiences as summarized in a biographical portfolio is highly salient to understanding them and perhaps to predicting their future job performance. This is not a new idea. Biographical information has traditionally been collected from job applicants over many years. Nearly all application forms require biographical details. What is different about the biodata method is that it is empirical in that it seeks to establish robust and reliable statistical relationships between biographical events and success outcomes.

Many people enjoy reading biographies and autobiographies to try to understand what makes certain people tick. Historians, sociologists and even psychologists try to get a deeper understanding of the motives, conflicts and drives of famous people through understanding the particularities of an individual life. Some are 'theory-driven' in the sense that they believe that particular types of experience have specific outcomes, but most are happy to explore the patterns they see.

Biodata methods have been criticized for being atheoretical. This criticism centres on the view that purely empirically demonstrated relationships may not assist with explaining and understanding why some individuals succeed and others fail in their jobs or careers. This criticism is probably a little harsh. It is often the case that the generation of biodata items is grounded in theory. Thus, if one is a follower of Weber's work ethic hypothesis, one may be inclined to include questions on religious experience and parental rules. Freudians may be inclined to ask questions appertaining to childhood memories around the major psychosexual stages set out in the theory. Approaches that are powerfully theoretically driven may often be dependent on one particular approach and they may also be open to empirical testing.

The biodata approach allows, even encourages, the testing of many theoretically derived hypotheses. Indeed, it is often frustrating to find that 'pet theories' cannot be substantiated – in fact, selectors often have implicit, occasionally explicit, theories about how certain life experiences (coming from a divorced family, being first born, having served in the army and so on) have an impact on business success. What is attractive about biodata is that these theories can be put to the test.

Changes to the world of work are probably going to increase the usefulness of the biodata approach. A more heterogeneous workforce with personal portfolios rather than unidirectional career paths may be more difficult to understand and select than was the case in the past. Indeed, we predict a renaissance of the biodata method to assess business potential.

References

Albright, L.E. and Glennon, J.R. (1961) Personal history correlates of physical scientists' career aspirations. *Journal of Applied Psychology* 45: 281–4.

Alderfer, C.P. and McCord, C.G. (1970) Personal and situational factors in the recruitment interview. *Journal of Applied Psychology* 54: 377–85.

Allport, G. (1942) The use of personal documents in psychological science. *Social Science Research Council Bulletin* No. 49.

Amabile, T.M., Hill, K.G., Hennessey, B.A. and Tighe, E.M. (1994) The work preference inventory: Assessing intrinsic and extrinsic motivational orientations. *Journal of Personality and Social Psychology* 66: 950–67.

Ames, S.D. (1983) Prediction of research vs applied interests in veterinarians. Unpublished master's thesis, University of Georgia, Athens, Ga.

Anderson, N.R. and Shackleton, V.J. (1986) Recruitment and selection: A review of development in the 1980s. *Personnel Review* 15: 19–26.

Annis, A. (1967) The autobiography: Its use and value. *Professional Psychology* 14: 9–17.

Archer, R., Gordon, R. and Kirchner, F. (1987) MMPI response-set characteristics among adolescents. *Journal of Personality Assessment* 51: 506–16.

Armstrong-Stassed, M. (1998) Alternative work arrangements: Meeting the challenge. *Canadian Psychology* 39: 108–23.

Arvey, R., Passino, E. and Lansbury, J. (1977) Job analysis results as influenced by sex of incumbent and sex of analyst. *Journal of Applied Psychology* 62: 411–16.

Asher, J.J. (1972) The biographical item: Can it be improved? *Personnel Psychology* 25: 251–69.

Ashforth, B.E. and Mael, F. (1989) Social identity theory and the organisation. *Academy of Management Review* 14: 20–39.

Atwater, D.C., Abrahams, N.M., Wiskoff, M.F. and Sands, M.M. (1984) Evaluation and control of faking in biodata instruments. In B. Means (chair) *Recent Developments in Military Suitability Research*, 25th Annual Conference of the Military Testing Association, Munich.

Baehr, M.E. and Williams, G.B. (1967) Underlying dimensions of personal background data and their relationships to occupational classification. *Journal of Applied Psychology* 51: 481–90.

Baehr, M.E. and Williams, G.B. (1968) Prediction of sales success from factorially determined dimensions of personal background data. *Journal of Applied Psychology* 52(2): 98–103.

Bandura, A. (1986) *Social Foundations of Thoughts and Action: A Social Cognitive Theory*. Englewood Cliffs, NJ: Prentice-Hall.

Bandura, A. (1989) Human agency in social cognitive theory. *American Psychologist* 44: 1175–84.

Banks, M., Jackson, P., Stafford, E. and Warr, P. (1983) The Job Components Inventory and the analysis of jobs requiring limited skill. *Personnel Psychology* 36: 57–60.

Barrick, M. and Mount, M. (1991) The Big Five personality dimensions and job performance: A meta analysis. *Personnel Psychology* 44: 1–26.

Bellak, R.N., Madsen, R., Sullivan, W.M., Swidler, A. and Tipton, S.M. (1985) *Habits of the Heart*. New York: Harper and Row.

Berkeley, M.H. (1953) *A Comparison between Empirical and Rational Approaches for Keying a Heterogeneous Test*. Research Bulletin 53–24. Lackland Airforce Base, Texas.

Berry, C. (1999) Religious traditions as contexts for historical creativity. *Personality and Individual Differences* 26: 1125–35.

Betz, N. and Fitzgerald, L. (1987) *The Career Psychology of Women*. New York: Wiley.

Bittner, R. (1945) Quantitative predictions from qualitative data: Predicting college entrance from biographical information. *Journal of Psychology* 19: 97–108.

Blum, M. and Naylor, J. (1968) *Industrial Psychology: Its Theoretical and Social Foundations*. New York: Harper.

Booth, R., McNally, M. and Berry, N. (1978) Predicting performance effectiveness in paramedical occupations. *Personnel Psychology* 31: 581–93.

Bowditch, J. (1969) Biographical similarity and interpersonal choice. Unpublished doctoral dissertation, Purdue University, Lafayette, Ind.

Bowers, K.S. (1973) Situationism in psychology: An analysis and critique. *Psychological Review* 80: 307–36.

Breaugh, J.A. (1981) Relationships between recruiting sources and employee tenure, absenteeism and work attitudes. *Academy of Management Journal* 24: 142–7.

Brown, B.K. and Campion, M.A. (1994) Biodata phenomenology: Recruiters' perceptions and use of biographical information in résumé screening. *Journal of Applied Psychology* 79(6): 897–908.

Brown, S.H. (1978) Long-term validity of personal history item scoring procedure. *Journal of Applied Psychology* 63: 673–6.

Brown, S.H. (1981) Validity generalisation and situational moderation in the life insurance industry. *Journal of Applied Psychology* 66: 664–70.

Brown, S.H. (1994) Validating biodata. In G.S. Stokes, M.D. Mumford and W.A. Owens (eds) *Biodata Handbook: Theory, Research and Use of Biographical Information in Selection and Performance Prediction*. Palo Alto, Calif.: CPP Books, pp. 199-236.

Brush, D.H. and Owens, W.A. (1979) Implementation and evaluation of an assessment classification model for manpower utilisation. *Personnel Psychology* 32: 369–83.

Buel, W.D. (1964) Voluntary female clerical turnover: The concurrent and predictive validity of a weighted application blank. *Journal of Applied Psychology* 48(3): 180–2.

Burbeck, E. and Furnham, A. (1984) Personality and police selection: Trait differences in successful and non-successful applicants to the Metropolitan Police. *Personality and Individual Differences* 5: 257–63.

Burrington, D.D. (1982) A review of state government employment application forms for suspect inquiries. *Public Personnel Management Journal* 11: 55–60.

Byrne, D. (1971) *The Attraction Paradigm*. New York: Academic Press.

Campbell, J.P., Dunnette, M.D., Lawler, E.E. and Weick, K.E. (1970) *Managerial Behaviour, Performance and Effectiveness*. New York: McGraw-Hill.

Campion, M.A. (1978) Identification of variables most influential in determining interviewers' evaluations of applicants in a college placement centre. *Psychological Reports* 42: 947–52.

Caplan, J.R. and Schmidt, F.L. (1977) The validity of education and experience ratings. Paper presented to the International Personnel Management Association Assessment Council, 19 April.

Carlson, A.F. (1971) The effect of interview information in altering valid impressions. *Journal of Applied Psychology* 55: 66–72.

Carroll, S.J. (1966) Relationship of various college graduate characteristics to recruiting decisions. *Journal of Applied Psychology* 50: 421–3.

Cascio, W.F. (1975) Accuracy of verifiable biographical information blank responses. *Journal of Applied Psychology* 60: 767–9.

Cascio, W.F. (1976) Turnover, biographical data, and fair employment practice. *Journal of Applied Psychology* 61: 576–80.

Cascio, W. (1998) The virtual workplace: A reality now. *The Industrial-Organizational Psychologist* 35: 32–6.

Caspi, A., Bem, D.J. and Elder, G.H. (1989) Continuities and consequences of interactional styles across the life course. *Journal of Personality* 57: 375–406.

Casson, M. (1982) *The Entrepreneur: An Economic Theory*. Oxford: Martin Robertson.

Chaney, F.B. and Owens, W.A. (1964) Life history antecedents of sales, research, and general engineering interests. *Journal of Applied Psychology* 48: 101–5.

Chell, E. (1986) The entrepreneurial personality: A few ghosts laid to rest. *International Small Business Journal* 3: 43–53.

Childs, A. and Klimoski, R.J. (1986) Successfully predicting career success: An application of the biographical inventory. *Journal of Applied Psychology* 71(1): 3–8.

Clifton, T.C., Kilculan, R.N., Reiter-Palmon, R. and Mumford, M.D. (1992) Comparing different background data scaling procedures using triple cross-validation. Paper presented at the Annual Convention of the American Psychological Association, Washington, DC, August.

Coles, M. (2000, 16 January) New tests will end recruitment bias. *The Sunday Times*, Appointments Section, p.32.

Conley, J. (1984) The hierarchy of consistency: A review and model of longitudinal findings on adult individual differences in intelligence, personality and self-opinion. *Personality and Individual Differences* 5: 11–26.

Cook, M. (1998) *Personnel Selection*. Chichester: John Wiley & Sons.

Costa, P. and McCrae, R. (1994) Set like plaster? Evidence for the stability of adult personality. In T. Heatherton and J. Weinberger (eds) *Can Personality Change?* Washington, DC: American Psychological Association.

Covey, S. (1989) *The Seven Habits of Highly Effective People*. New York: Simon & Schuster.

Cox, C. and Cooper, C. (1988) *High Flyers: An Anatomy of Management Success*. Oxford: Blackwell.

Cox, M.C. (1985) The effectiveness of Black identification and organizational identification on communication supportiveness. Unpublished doctoral dissertation, Purdue University, Lafayette, Ind.

Cramer, S. (1999) The seven habits of highly inefficient people. *Human Resources* 118: 49–52.

Crosby, M.M. (1990) Social desirability and biodata: Predicting sales success. Poster presented at the Annual Conference for Industrial and Organizational Psychology, Miami Beach, Fla., April.

Crosby, M.M., Dalessio, A.T. and McManus, M.A. (1990) Stability of biodata dimensions across English-speaking cultures: A confirmatory investigation. Paper presented at the annual meeting of the American Psychological Association, Boston, Mass.

Crowne, D.P. and Marlowe, D. (1960) *The Approval Motive*. New York: Wiley.

Crowne, D.P. and Marlowe, D. (1964) *The Approval Motive: Studies in Evaluation Dependence*. New York: Wiley.

Cureton, E. (1950) Validity, reliability, and baloney. *Educational and Psychological Measurement* 10: 94–6.

Dalessio, A.T. and Silverhat, T.A. (1994) Combining biodata test and interview information: Predicting decisions and performance criteria. *Personnel Psychology* 47: 303–15.

Davidson, M. and Cooper, C. (1983) *Stress and the Woman Manager*. Oxford: Martin Robertson.

Davidson, M. and Cooper, C. (1987) Managers in Britain – A comparative perspective. *Human Resource Management* 26: 217–42.

Davis, K.R. (1984) A longitudinal analysis of biographical sub-groups using Owens' Development-Integration model. *Personnel Psychology* 37: 1–14.

De Waele, J.-P. and Harré, R. (1979) Autobiography as a psychological method. In G. Ginsberg (ed.) *Emerging Strategies in Psychological Research*. Chichester: Wiley, pp. 177-224.

Decker, P.J. and Cornelius, E.T. (1979) A note on recruiting sources and job survival rates. *Journal of Applied Psychology* 64: 463–6.

Doll, R.E. (1971) Item susceptibility to attempted faking as related to item characteristics and adopted fake set. *Journal of Psychology* 77: 9–16.

Drakeley, R. (1988) Achievement, background and commitment: classification of biographical data in personnel selection. Unpublished doctoral dissertation, University of London.

Drakeley, R.J. (1989) Biographical data. In P. Herriott (ed.) *Assessment and Selection in Organizations*. Chichester: John Wiley & Sons, pp. 439–53.

Drakeley, R.J., Herriott, P. and Jones, A. (1988) Biographical data, training success and turnover. *Journal of Occupational Psychology* 61: 145–52.

Dunnette, M.D. (1962) Personnel Management. *Annual Review of Psychology* 13: 285–313.

Dunnette, M.D. and Maetzold, J. (1955) Use of a weighted application blank in hiring seasonal employees. *Journal of Applied Psychology* 39: 308–10.

Dunnette, M., Kirchner, W., Erickson, J. and Banas, P. (1960) Predicting turnover among female office workers. *Personnel Administration* 23: 45–50.

Duttoon, J.E., Dukerich, J.M. and Harquail, C.V. (1994) Organisational images and member identification. *Administrative Science Quarterly 39*: 239–63.

Dyer, E.D. (1987) Can university success and first-year job performance be predicted from academic achievement, vocational interest, personality and biographical measures? *Psychological Reports* 61: 655–71.

Eberhardt, B.J. and Muchinsky, P.M. (1982a) An empirical investigation of the factor stability of Owens' biographical questionnaire. *Journal of Applied Psychology* 67: 138–45.

Eberhardt, B.J. and Muchinsky, P.M. (1982b) Biodata determinants of vocational typology: An integration of two paradigms. *Journal of Applied Psychology* 67: 714–27.

Eberhardt, B.J. and Muchinsky, P.M. (1984) Structured validation of Holland's exagonal model: Vocational classification through the use of biodata. *Journal of Applied Psychology* 69: 174–81.

Endler, N.S. and Magnussen, D. (1976) *Interactional Psychology and Personality*. Washington, DC: Hemisphere.

England, G.W. (1971) *Development and Use of Weighted Application Blanks*. International Relations Centre, University of Minnesota.

Erikson, E. (1958) *Young Man Luther: A Study in Psychoanalysis and History*. New York: Norton.

Erikson, E. (1975) *Life History and the Historical Movement*. New York: Norton.

Eysenck, H. (1952) The effects of psychotherapy: An evaluation. *Journal of Consulting Psychology* 16: 319–24.

Eysenck, H. (1995) *Genius: The Natural History of Creativity*. Cambridge: Cambridge University Press.

Eysenck, H.J. and Eysenck, M.W. (1985) *Personality and Individual Differences*. New York: Plenum.

Fagenson, E.A. (1990) At the heart of women in management research. *Journal of Business Ethics* 9: 1–8.

Federico, J.M., Federico, P. and Lundquist, G.W. (1976) Predicting women's turnover as a function of extent of net salary expectations and biodemographics. *Personnel Psychology* 29: 559–66.

Feldman, D. (1997) Career issues facing contingent and self-employed workers. In C. Cooper and S. Jackson (eds) *Creating Tomorrow's Organisations*. Chichester: Wiley. pp. 337–358.

Felmlee, D.H. (1984) The dynamics of women's job mobility. *Work and Occupation* 11: 259–81.

Ferguson, L. (1961) The development of industrial psychology. In B. Gilmer (ed.) *Industrial Psychology*. New York: McGraw-Hill, pp. 18–37.

Ferguson, L.W. (1967) Economic maturity. *Personnel Journal* 46: 22–6.

Flanagan, J. (1954) The critical incident technique. *Psychological Bulletin* 51: 327–58.

Fleishman, E. and Berniger, J. (1967) Using the application blank to reduce office turnover. In E. Fleishman (ed.) *Studies in Personnel and Industrial Psychology*. Homewood, IL: Dorsey Press, pp. 39–46.

Frese, M. (1997) Dynamic self-reliance: An important concept for work in the twenty-first century. In C. Cooper and S. Jackson (eds) *Creating Tomorrow's Organisations*. New York: Wiley, pp. 399–416.

Furnham, A. (1986a) The social desirability of Type A behaviour pattern. *Psychological Medicine* 16: 805–11.

Furnham, A. (1986b) Response bias, social desirability, and dissimulation. *Personality and Individual Differences* 7: 385–406.

Furnham, A. (1990) *The Protestant Work Ethic*. London: Routledge.

Furnham, A. (1997) *The Psychology of Behaviour at Work*. Hove: Psychologists Press.

Furnham, A. (2000a) Work in 2020. *Journal of Managerial Psychology* in press.

Furnham, A. (2000b) *The Hopeless, Hapless and Helpless Manager*. London: Whurr.

Furnham, A. and Craig, S. (1987) Fakeability and correlates of the Perception and Preference Inventory. *Personality and Individual Differences* 8: 459–70.

Furnham, A. and Heaven, P. (1999) *Personality and Social Behaviour*. London: Arnold.

Furnham, A. and Henderson, M. (1982) The good, the bad, and the mad: Response bias in self-report measures. *Personality and Individual Differences* 3: 311–20.

Galton, F. (1874) *English Men of Science*. London: Macmillan.

Gandy, J.A., Outerbridge, A.N., Sharf, J.C. and Dye, D.A. (1989) *Development and Initial Validation of the Individual Achievement Record (IAR)* . Washington, DC: US Office of Personnel Management.

Gattiker, U.E. and Larwood, L. (1988) Predictors for managers' career mobility success and satisfaction. *Human Relations* 8: 569–91.

Gattiker, U.E. and Larwood, L. (1989) Career success, mobility and extrinsic satisfaction of corporate managers. *Social Science Journal* 28: 75–92.

Gelado, G. (1997) Creativity in conflict: The personality and the commercially creative. *Journal of Genetic Psychology* 158: 67–78.

Ghiselli, E. (1966) *The Validity of Occupational Aptitude Tests*. New York: John Wiley & Sons.

Ghiselli, E. and Barthol, R. (1953) The validity of personality inventories in the selection of employees. *Journal of Applied Psychology* 37: 18–20.

Ghiselli, E. and Brown, C. (1955) *Personnel and Industrial Psychology*. New York: McGraw-Hill.

Glennon, J.R., Albright, L.E. and Owens, W.A. (1966) *A Catalogue of Life History Items*. Greensboro, NC: Richardson Foundation.

Goldsmith, D.B. (1922) The use of personal history blanks as a salesmanship test. *Journal of Applied Psychology* 6: 149–55.

Goldstein, I.L. (1971) The application blank: How honest are the responses? *Journal of Applied Psychology* 55: 491–2.

Goleman, D. (1995) *Emotional Intelligence*. New York: Bantam Books.

Goleman, D. (1998) *Working with Emotional Intelligence*. London: Bloomsbury.

Golembiewski, R.T., Billingsley, K. and Munzenrider, R. (1970) Electoral choice and individual characteristics: Towards a biodata approach. Unpublished manuscript, Institute for Behavioral Research, University of Georgia.

Gordon, and Fitzgibbons, W. (1982) Empirical test of the validity of seniority as a factor in staffing decisions. *Journal of Applied Psychology* 67: 311–19.

Gorsuch, R.L. (1974) *Factor Analysis*. Philadelphia, Pa.: W.B. Saunders.

Grinker, R.R. and Spiegel, J.P. (1945) *Men Under Stress*. Philadelphia, Pa.: Blakiston.

Gross, M. (1962) *The Brain Watchers*. New York: Random House.

Guion, R.M. (1965) *Personnel Testing*. New York: McGraw-Hill.

Guion, R. and Gottier, R. (1965) Validity of personality measures in personnel selection. *Personnel Psychology* 18: 135–64.

Guthrie, E. (1944) Personality in terms of associative learning. In J. Hunt (ed.) *Personality and Behaviour Disorders*, Vol. 1. New York: Ronald Press, pp. 49–68.

Hall, D., Briscoe, J. and Kram, K. (1997) Identity, values and learning in the Protean Career. In C. Cooper and S. Jackson (eds) *Creating Tomorrow's Organisations*. Chichester: Wiley. pp. 321–335.

Handy, C. (1995) *The Empty Raincoat*. London: Arrow.

Harrell, T.W. (1960) The validity of biographical data items for food company salesmen. *Journal of Applied Psychology* 44: 31–3.

Heneman, H.G. (1977) Impact of test information and applicant sex on applicant evaluations in a selection simulation. *Journal of Applied Psychology* 62: 524–6.

Heneman, H.G., Schwab, D.P., Fossum, J.A. and Dyer, L.C. (1983) *Personnel/Human Resource Management*. Homewood, Ill.: Richard D. Irwin.

Henry, E. (1966) Conference on the use of biographical data in psychology. *American Psychologist* 21: 247–9.

Herbert, R. and Link, A. (1988) *The Entrepreneur: Mainstream Views and Radical Critiques*. New York: Praeger.

Himmelstein, D. and Blaskovicks, T.L. (1960) Prediction of an intermediate criterion of combat effectiveness with a biographical inventory. *Journal of Applied Psychology* 44: 166–8.

Hirsch, W. and Bevan, S. (1988) What makes a manager – In search of a language for management skills. *IMA Report 144*. Institute of Manpower Studies, University of Sussex, Brighton.

Hoiberg, A. and Pugh, W. (1978) Predicting navy effectiveness: Expectations, motivation, personality, aptitude, and background variables. *Personnel Psychology* 31: 841–52.

Holland, B. and Hogan, R. (1999) Remodelling the electronic cottage. *The Industrial-Organisational Psychologist*, 36, 1–9.

Holland, J.L. (1973) *Making Vocational Choices: A Theory of Careers*. Englewood Cliffs, NJ: Prentice Hall.

Holland, J.L. (1975) *The Psychology of Vocational Choice*. Waltham, Mass.: Blaisdell.

Holland, J.L. (1985) *Making Vocational Choices: A Theory of Vocational Personalities and Work Environments*. Englewood Cliffs, NJ: Prentice-Hall.

Hornick, C.W., James, L.R. and Jones, A.P. (1977) Empirical item keying versus a rational approach to analysing a psychological climate questionnaire. *Applied Psychological Measurement* 1: 489–500.

Hough, L. (1998) Personality at work: Issues and evidence. In M. Hakel (ed.) *Beyond Multiple Choice: Evaluating Alternatives to Traditional Testing for Selection*. Hillsdale, NJ: Lawrence Erlbaum, pp. 131–59.

Hough, L.M., Eaton, N.K., Dunnette, M.D., Kamp, J.D. and McCloy, R.A. (1990) Criterion-related validities of personality constructs and the effect of response distortion on those validities. *Journal of Applied Psychology* 75: 581–95.

Howard, A. and Bray, D. (1988) *Managerial Lives in Transition: Advancing Age and Changing Times*. New York: Guilford Press.

Hughes, J., Dunn, J. and Baxter, B. (1956) The validity of selection instruments under operating conditions. *Personnel Psychology* 9: 321–4.

Hunter, J.E. and Hunter, R.F. (1984) Validity and utility of alternative predictors of job performance. *Psychological Bulletin* 96: 72–98.

Hunter, J.E., Schmidt, F.L. and Jackson, G.B. (1982) *Meta-analysis: Cumulating Research Findings Across Studies*. Beverly Hills, Calif.: Sage.

Iles, P. and Foster, W. (1994) Developing organizations through collaborative development centres. *Organization Development Journal* 12: 45–51.

Jackson, S.E., Brett, J.F., Sessa, V.I., Cooper, D.M., Julan, J.A. and Peyronnin, K. (1991) Some differences make a difference: Individual dissimilarity and group heterogeneity as correlates of recruitment, promotions and turnover. *Journal of Applied Psychology* 76: 675–89.

Jennings, R., Cox, C. and Cooper, C. (1994) *Business Elites: The Psychology of Entrepreneurs*. London: Routledge.

Jones, E.L. (1971) The relationship among biographical similarity, perceived similarity and attraction in the roommate situation. Unpublished Master's thesis, Institute for Behavioral Research, University of Georgia.

Judge, T., Cable, D., Boudreau, J. and Bretz, R. (1995) An empirical investigation of the predictors of executive career success. *Personnel Psychology* 48: 485–519.

Kanter, R.M. (1977) *Men and Women of the Corporation*. New York: Basic Books.

Keating, E., Paterson, D.C. and Stones, H.C. (1950) Validity of work histories obtained by interview. *Journal of Applied Psychology* 36: 365–9.

Keenan, A. (1976) Interviewers' evaluation of applicant characteristics: Differences between personnel and non-personnel managers. *Journal of Occupational Psychology* 49: 223–30.

Keenan, A. and Scott, R.S. (1985) Employment success of graduates: Relationships to biographical factors and job-seeking behaviours. *Journal of Occupational Behaviour* 6: 305–11.

Kirchner, W. and Dunnette, M. (1957) Applying the weighted application blank technique to a variety of office jobs. *Journal of Applied Psychology* 41: 206–9.

Klein, H.A. (1972) Personality characteristics of discrepant academic achievers. Unpublished doctoral dissertation, Institute for Behavioral Research, University of Georgia.

Klein, S.P. and Owens, W.A. (1965) Faking of a scored life history blank as a function of criterion objectivity. *Journal of Applied Psychology* 49: 452–4.

Klimoski, R.J. (1973) A biographical data analysis of career patterns in engineering. *Journal of Vocational Behaviour* 3: 103–13.

Klinger, D. (1979) When the traditional job description is not enough. *Personnel Journal* 58: 243–8.

Kluckholn, C. (1949) *Mirror for Man: The Relation of Anthropology to Modern Life.* New York: McGraw Hill.

Kluger, A.N. and Colella, A. (1993) Beyond the mean bias: The effect of warning against faking on biodata item variances. *Personnel Psychology* 46: 763–80.

Kluger, A., Reilly, R. and Russell, C. (1991) Faking biodata tests: Are option-keyed instruments more resistant? *Journal of Applied Psychology* 76: 889–96.

Korman, A.K. (1968) The prediction of managerial performance: A review. *Personnel Psychology* 21: 299–322.

Kuhnert, K.W. and Lewis, P. (1987) Transactional and transformational leadership: A constructive developmental analysis. *Academy of Management Review* 12: 648–51.

Kuhnert, K.W. and Russell, C.J. (1990) Using constructive developmental theory and biodata to bridge the gap between personnel selection and leadership. *Journal of Management* 16(3): 595–607.

Kulberg, G. and Owens, W.A. (1960) Some life history antecedents of engineering interests. *Journal of Educational Psychology* 51: 26–31.

Laurence, J.H. and Means, B. (1985) *A Description and Comparison of Biographical Inventories for Military Selection.* Alexandria, Va.: Human Resources Research Organisation.

Laurent, H.A. (1951) A study of the developmental backgrounds of men to determine by means of the biographical information blank the relationship between factors in their early background and their choice of profession. Unpublished doctoral dissertation, Western Reserve University.

Laurent, H.A. (1962) Early identification of management talent. *Management Record* 24: 33–8.

Laurent, H.A. (1970) Cross-cultural cross-validation of empirically validated tests. *Journal of Applied Psychology* 54: 417–23.

Lautenschlager, G.J. (1985) Within subject measures for the assessment of individual differences in faking. *Educational and Psychological Measurement* 46: 309–16.

Lautenschlager, G.J. and Atwater, D. (1986) Controlling response distortion on an empirically keyed biodata questionnaire. Unpublished manuscript, University of Georgia, Athens, Ga.

Lautenschlager, G. and Shaffer, G.S. (1987) Re-examining the component stability of Owens' biographical questionnaire. *Journal of Applied Psychology* 72: 149–52.

Lemkau, J.P. (1983) Women in male-dominated occupations. *Psychology of Women Quarterly* 8: 144–65.

Levine, A.S. and Zachert, V. (1951) Use of biographical inventory in the Air Force classification program. *Journal of Applied Psychology* 35: 241–4.

Lindsey, E.H., Homes, V. and McCall, M.W. (1987) *Key Events in Executives' Lives.* Report No. 32, Center for Creative Leadership, Greensboro, NC.

Locke, E. (1997) Prime movers: The traits of great business leaders. In C. Cooper and S. Jackson (eds) *Creating Tomorrow's Organisations.* Chichester: Wiley.

Loenvinger, J., Gleser, G.C. and Dubois, P.H. (1953) Maximizing the discriminating power of a multiple-score set. *Psychometrika* 18: 309–11.

Long, J.A. and Sandiford, P. (1935) *The validation of test items.* Research Bulletin No. 3. Toronto, Canada: University of Toronto Department of Education.

Lowell, R.S. and De Loach, J.A. (1982) Equal employment opportunity: Are you overlooking the application form? *Personnel* 59: 49–55.

Lumsden, H. (1967) The plant visit: A crucial area of recruiting. *Journal of College Placement* 27: 74–84.

Lykken, D.T. and Rose, R. (1963) Psychological prediction from actuarial tables. *Journal of Clinical Psychology* 29: 136–56.

Macan, T.H. and Dipboye, R.L. (1990) The relationship of interviewers' preinterview impressions to selection and recruitment outcomes. *Personnel Psychology* 43: 745–68.

Mael, F.A. (1988) Organisational identificaiton: Construct redefinition and a field application with organisational alumni. Unpublished doctoral dissertation, Wayne State University, Detroit, Mich.

Mael, F.A. (1991) A conceptual rationale for the domain and attributes of biodata items. *Personnel Psychology* 44: 363–92.

Mael, F.A. and Ashforth, B.E. (1992) Alumni and their alma mater: A practical test of the reformulated model of organizational identification. *Journal of Organisational Behaviour* 13: 101–23.

Mael, F.E. and Ashforth, B.E. (1995) Loyal from day one: Biodata, organizational identification and turnover among newcomers. *Personnel Psychology* 48: 309–33.

Mael, F.A. and Hirsch, A.C. (1993) Rainforest empiricism and quasi-rationality: Two approaches to objective biodata. *Personnel Psychology* 46: 719–38.

Mael, F.A. and Tetnik, L.E. (1992) Identifying organisational identification. *Educational and Psychological Measurement* 52: 813–24.

Malloy, J. (1955) The prediction of college achievement with the life experience inventory. *Educational and Psychological Measurement* 15: 170–80.

Manning, F.S. (1991) Morale, cohesion and esprit de corps. In R. Galo and A.D. Mangelsdorff (eds) *Handbook of Military Psychology*. New York: Wiley, pp. 453–70.

Markowitz, J. (1981) Four methods of job analysis. *Training and Development Journal* 35: 112–18.

Matteson, M.G. (1978) An alternative approach using biographical data for predicting job success. *Journal of Occupational Psychology* 51: 155–62.

Matteson, M.G., Osborn, H.G. and Sparks, C.P. (1969) *A Computer-based Methodology for Constructing Homogeneous Keys with Applications to Biographical Data*. Report 1. Houston, TX: University of Houston Personnel Psychology Services Center.

Matthews, G. and Deary, I. (1998) *Personality Traits*. Cambridge: Cambridge University Press.

Mayer, J. and Salovey, P. (1997) What is emotional intelligence? In P. Salovey and D. Sluyter (eds) *Emotional Development and Emotional Intelligence: Educational Implications*. New York: Basic Books.

McCall, M. (1994) Identifying leadership potential in future international executives: Developing a concept. *Consulting Psychology Journal* 46: 49–63.

McCall, M. (1998) *High Flyers: Developing the Next Generation of Leaders*. Boston, Mass.: Harvard Business School Press.

McCall, M., Lombardo M. and Morrison, A. (1990) *The Lessons of Experience: How Successful Executives Develop on the Job*. Lexington, Mass.: Lexington Books.

McCall, M., Spreitzer, G. and Mahoney, J. (1994) *Identifying Leadership Potential in Future International Executives: A Learning Resource Guide*. Lexington, Mass.: International Consortium for Executive Development Research.

McCormick, E.J. (1976) Job and task analysis. In M. Dunnette (ed.) *Handbook of Industrial and Organizational Psychology*. Chicago, Ill.: Rand McNally, pp. 651–96.

McCormick, E., Jeanneret, P. and Mecham, R. (1972) A study of job characteristics and job dimensions based on the Position Analysis Questionnaire (PAQ) *Journal of Applied Psychology* 56: 347–68.

McCrae, R.H. and Costa, P.T. (1987) Validation of the full factor model across instruments and observers. *Journal of Personality and Social Psychology* 52: 81–90.

McDaniel, M.A. (1988) Does pre-employment drug use predict on-the-job suitability? *Personnel Psychology* 41: 717–29.

McDaniel, M.A. (1989) Biographical constructs for predicting employee suitability. *Journal of Applied Psychology* 74(6): 964–70.

McManus, M. and Masztal, J. (1999) The impact of biodata item attributes on validity and socially desirable responding. *Journal of Business and Psychology* 13: 437–50.

McQuitty, L.L. (1957) Isolating predictor patterns associated with major criteria patterns. *Educational and Psychological Measurement* 17: 3–42.

Means, B. and Heisey, J.G. (1986) *Educational and Biographic Data as Predictors of Early Attrition. Report No. FR-PRD-84-14*. Alexandria, Va.: Human Resources Research Organization.

Means, B. and Laurence, J.H. (1986) Improving the prediction of military suitability through educational and biographic information. Technical Memorandum 86-1. In W.S. Sellman (Chair) *Recent Developments in Military Suitability Research*. Symposium conducted at the 26th Annual Conference of Military Testing Association, Munich. Alexandria, VA: Human Resources Research Organisation.

Means, B. and Perelman, L.S. (1984) The Development of the Educational and Background Information Survey (Report No. FR-PRD-84-3). Alexandria, Va.: Human Resources Research Organization.

Means, B., Laurence, J.W. and Waters, B.K. (1984) Pre-Service Experiences of Military Applicants and Recruits. Report No. FR-PRD-84-17. Alexandria, Va.: Human Resources Research Organization.

Meehl, P.E. (1950) Configural scoring. *Journal of Consulting Psychology* 14: 165–71.

Merton, R. (1936) Puritanism, pietism and science. *Sociological Review* 28: 1–15.

Michaelis, W. and Eysenck, H.J. (1971) The determination of personality inventory factor patterns and intercorrelations by changes in real life motivation. *Journal of Genetic Psychology* 118: 223–34.

Miller, E.C. (1980) An EEO examination of employment applications. *The Personnel Administrator* 25: 63–81.

Mitchell, T.W. (1986) Specialized job analysis for developing rationally oriented biodata prediction systems. Paper presented at the meeting of the Society for Individual and Organizational Psychology, Chicago, Ill.

Mitchell, T.W. and Klimoski, R.J. (1982) Is it rational to be empirical? A test of methods for scoring biographical data. *Journal of Applied Psychology* 67: 411–18.

Mitchell, T.W. and Klimoski, R.J. (1986) Estimating the validity of cross-validity estimates. *Journal of Applied Psychology* 71: 311–17.

Mobley, W.H. (1982) Employee Turnover: Causes, Consequences and Control. Reading, Mass.: Addison-Wesley.

Mobley, W.H., Griffith, R.W., Hand, H.H. and Meglino, B.M. (1979) Review and conceptual analysis of the employee turnover process. *Psychological Bulletin* 86: 493–522.

Mokesel, R.H. and Tesser, A. (1971) Life history antecedents of authoritarianism: A quasi-longitudinal approach. *Proceedings of the 74th Convention of the American Psychological Association* 6: 136–7.

Morrison, R.F., Owens, W.A., Glennon, J.R. and Albright, L.E. (1962) Factored life history antecedents of industrial research performance. *Journal of Applied Psychology* 46: 281–4.

Morrison, A.M., White, R.P. and Von Velsor, E. (1987) *Breaking the Glass Ceiling*. Reading, Mass.: Addison-Wesley.

Mosel, J.N. (1951) Prediction of department store sales performance from personal data. *Journal of Applied Psychology* 36: 8–10.

Mosel, J.N. and Cozan, C.W. (1952) The accuracy of application blank work histories. *Journal of Applied Psychology* 36: 365–9.

Muchinsky, P. and Tuttle, M. (1979) Employee turnover: An empirical and methodological assessment. *Journal of Vocational Behaviour* 14: 43–77.

Mumford, M.D. and Owens, W.A. (1984) Individuality in a developmental context: Some empirical and theoretical considerations. *Human Development* 27: 84–108.

Mumford, M.D. and Owens, W.A. (1987) Methodology review: Principles, procedures and findings in the application of background data measures. *Applied Psychological Measurement* 11: 1–31.

Mumford, M.D. and Stokes, G.S. (1982) Life history correlates of positive and negative emotionality. Paper presented at the annual meeting of the Southeastern Psychological Association, Atlanta, Ga.

Mumford, M.D., Cooper, M. and Schwimmer, F.M. (1983) *Development of a Content Valid Set of Background Data Measures*. Bethesda, Md.: Advanced Research Resources Organization.

Mumford, M.D., Snell, A.F. and Reiter-Palmon, R. (1994) Personality and background data: Life history and self-concepts in an ecological system. In G.S. Stokes, M.D. Mumford and W.A Owens (eds) *Biodata Handbook: Theory, Research and Use of Biographical Information in Selection and Performance Prediction*. Palo Alto, Calif.: CPP Books, pp. 583–625.

Mumford, M.D., Stokes, G.S. and Owens, W.A. (1990) *Patterns of Life Adaptation: The Ecology of Human Individuality*. Hillsdale, NJ: Lawrence Erlbaum.

Nachman, B. (1960) Childhood experience and vocational choice in law, dentistry, and social work. *Journal of Counselling Psychology* 7: 243–50.

Naylor, J. and Vincent, N. (1959) Predicting female absenteeism. *Personnel Psychology* 12: 81–4.

Nevo, B. (1976) Using biographical information to predict success of men and women in the army. *Journal of Applied Psychology* 61(1): 106–8.

Nickels, B.J. (1994) The nature of biodata. In G.S. Stokes, M.D. Mumford and W.A. Owens (eds) *Biodata Handbook: Theory, Research and Use of Biographical Information in Selection and Performance Prediction*. Palo Alto, Calif.: CPP Books, pp. 1–16.

Niener, A.G. and Owens, W.A. (1982) Relationships between two sets of biodata with 7 years separation. *Journal of Applied Psychology* 67: 146–50.

Niener, A.G. and Owens, W.A. (1985) Using biodata to predict job choice among college graduates. *Journal of Applied Psychology* 70: 127–30.

Nutt, J.J. (1975) An examination of student attrition using life experience subgroups. Unpublished master's thesis, Institute for Behavioral Research, University of Georgia.

Ones, D., Mount, M., Barrick, J. and Hunter, J. (1994) Personality and job performance. *Personnel Psychology* 47: 147–56.

Owens, W.A. (1968) Toward one discipline of scientific psychology. *American Psychologist* 23: 782–5.

Owens, W.A. (1971) A quasi-actuarial prospect for individual assessment. *American Psychologist* 26: 992–9.

Owens, W.A. (1976) Background data. In M.D. Dunnette (ed.) *Handbook of Industrial and Organizational Psychology*. Chicago, Ill.: Rand McNally, pp. 609–46.

Owens, W.A. and Schoenfeldt, L.F. (1979) Toward a classification of persons [monograph]. *Journal of Applied Psychology* 63: 569–604.

Owens, W.A., Glennon, J.R. and Albright, L.E. (1966) *A Catalog of Life History Items*. Greensboro, NC: Richardson Foundation.

Pace, L.A. and Schoenfeldt, L.F. (1977) Legal concerns in the use of weighted applications. *Personnel Psychology* 30: 159–66.

Pannone, R.D. (1984) Predicting test performance: A content valid approach to screening applicants. *Personnel Psychology* 37: 507–14.

Paulhus, D.L. (1984) Two-component models of socially desirable responding. *Journal of Personality and Social Psychology* 46: 598–609.

Paulhus, D.L. (1986) Self-deception and impression management in test responses. In A. Angleitner and J.S. Wiggins (eds) *Personality Assessment via Questionnaires*. Berlin: Springer-Verlag, pp. 143–65.

Popovich, R. and Wanous, J.P. (1982) The realistic job preview as a persuasive communication. *Academy of Management Review*, 7: 570–8.

Porter, L.W. and Steers, R.M. (1973) Organisational, work and personal factors in employee turnover and absenteeism. *Psychological Bulletin* 80: 151–76.

Quaintance, M.L. (1981) Development of a weighted application blank to predict managerial assessment centre performance. Unpublished doctoral dissertation, George Washington University, Washington, DC.

Ragins, B.R. and Sundstrom, E. (1989) Gender and power in organisations. *Psychological Bulletin* 105: 51–88.

Reilly, R.R. and Chao, G.T. (1982) Validity and fairness of some alternative selection procedures. *Personnel Psychology* 35: 1–61.

Richardson, Bellows, Henry, and Co. (1981) *Supervisory Profile Record*. (Technical Reps, Vols 1, 2 and 3). Washington, DC: Author.

Ritchie, R.J. and Boehm, V.R. (1977) Biographical data as a predictor of women's and men's management potential. *Journal of Vocational Behaviour* 11: 363–8.

Roach, D.E. (1971) Double cross-validation of a weighted application blank over time. *Journal of Applied Psychology* 55: 157–60.

Robertson, I. and Kinder, A. (1993) Personality and job competency. *Journal of Occupational and Organizational Psychology* 66: 225–46.

Robertson, I. and Smith, M. (1987) Personnel selection methods. Paper presented at the International Conference on Advances in Selection and Assessment, Buxton. June.

Robinson, P. (1981) Content-oriented personnel selection in a small business setting. *Personnel Psychology* 34: 77–87.

Rose, H.A. and Elton, C.G. (1982) The relation of congruence, differentiation and consistency to interest and aptitude scores in women with stable and unstable vocational choices. *Journal of Vocational Psychology* 20: 162–74.

Rosin, H.M. and Korabik, K. (1990) Marital and family correlates of women managers' attention from organisations. *Journal of Vocational Behaviour* 37: 104–20.

Rothstein, M., Paunonen, S., Rush, J. and King, G. (1994) Personality and cognitive ability predictors of performance in graduate business school. *Journal of Eductional Psychology* 86: 516–36.

Rothstein, H.R., Schmidt, F.L., Erwin, F.W., Owens, W.A. and Sparks, C.P. (1990) Biographical data in employment selection: Can validities be made generalizable? *Journal of Applied Psychology* 75: 175–84.

Rotondi, T. (1975) Identification, personality needs and managerial position. *Human Relations* 29: 507–15.

Rowney, J.I.A. and Cahoon, A.R. (1990) Individual and organizational characteristics of women in managerial leadership. *Journal of Business Ethics* 9: 293–316.

Ruch, F.L. and Ruch, W.W. (1967) The K factor as a (validity) suppressor variable in predicting success in selling. *Journal of Applied Psychology* 51: 201–4.

Russell, C.J. (1990) Selecting top corporate leaders: An example of biographical information. *Journal of Management* 16: 73–86.

Russell, C.J., Devlin, S.E., Mattson, J. and Atwater, D. (1990) Predictive validity of biodata items generated from retrospective life experience essays. *Journal of Applied Psychology* 75(5): 569–80.

Russell, C.J., Mattson, J., Devlin, S.E. and Atwater, D. (1988) Predictive validity of biodata items generated from retrospective life experience essays. Paper presented at the Third Annual Meeting of the Society for Industrial and Organisational Psychology, Dallas, TX, April.

Rychlak, J.F. (1982) *Personality and Lifestyle of Young Male Managers: A Logical Learning Theory Analysis.* New York: Academic Press.

Rynes, S.L. (1993) Who's selecting whom? Effects of selection practices on applicant attitudes and behavior. In N. Schmitt, W.C. Borman and associates (eds) *Personnel Selection in Organisations.* San Francisco, Calif.: Jossey-Bass, pp. 240–74.

Rynes, S.L. and Barber, A.E. (1990) Applicant attraction strategies: An organisational perspective. *Academy of Management Review* 15: 286–310.

Saks, A.M., Leck, J.D. and Saunders, D.M. (1995) Effects of application blanks and employment equity on applicant reactions and job pursuit intentions. *Journal of Organisational Behaviour* 16: 415–30.

Salgado, J. (1999) Personnel selection methods. In C. Cooper and I. Robertson (eds) *International Review of Industrial and Organizational Psychology* 12: 1–63.

Salovey, P. and Mayer, J. (1990) Emotional intelligence. *Imagination, Cognition and Personality* 9: 185–211.

Sands, W. (1978) Enlisted personnel selections for the US Navy. *Personnel Psychology* 31: 63–70.

Saunders, D.M., Leck, J.D. and Marcil, L. (1992) What predicts employer propensity to gather protected group information from job applicants? In D.M. Saunders (ed.) *New Approaches to Employee Management: Fairness in Employee Selection*, Vol. 1. Greenwich, Conn.: JAI Press, pp. 105–30.

Saunders, D.M., Leck, J.D. and Vitins, G. (1989) Human rights legislation and employment in Canada. Paper presented at the Council on Employee Responsibilities and Rights, Orlando, FL.

Saville, P. and Holdsworth, R. (1984) *Occupational Personality Questionnaire Manual.* Esher: Saville & Holdsworth.

Schmitt, N., Gooding, R.Z., Noe, R. and Kirsch, M. (1984) Meta-analysis of validity studies published between 1964 and 1986 and the investigation of study characteristics. *Personnel Psychology* 27: 407–22.

Schmitt, N.W. and Pulakos, E.D. (1998) Biodata and differential prediction: Some reservations. In M.D. Hakel (ed.) *Beyond Multiple Choice: Evaluating Alternatives to Traditional Testing for Selection.* Hillsdale, NJ: Lawrence Erlbaum.

Schneider, B. (1987) The people make the place. *Personnel Psychology* 40(3): 437–53.

Schneider, B. and Schneider, J.L. (1994) Biodata: An organisational focus. In G.S. Stokes, M.D. Mumford and W.A. Owens (eds) *Biodata Handbook: Theory, Research and Use of Biographical Information in Selection and Performance Prediction.* Palo Alto, Calif.: CPP Books, pp. 423–50.

Schoenfeldt, L.F. (1992) Biographical data as the new frontier in employee selection research. Paper presented at the annual meeting of the American Psychological Association, New Orleans, La.

Schrader, A.D. and Osburn, H.G. (1977) Biodata faking: Effects of induced subtlety and position specificity. *Personnel Psychology* 30: 395–404.

Schuh, A.J. (1967) The prediction of employee tenure: A review of the literature. *Personnel Psychology* 20: 133–52.

Schwab, D.P. and Oliver, R.L. (1974) Predicting tenure with biographical data: Exhuming buried evidence. *Personnel Psychology* 27: 125–8.

Scott, R.D. and Johnson, R.W. (1967) Use of the weighted application blank in selecting unskilled employees. *Journal of Applied Psychology* 51(5): 393–5.

Segal, D.R. (1985) Management, leadership and the future battlefield. In J.G. Hunt and J.D. Blair (eds) *Leadership on the Future Battlefield*. Washington, DC: Pergamon Brassey's, pp. 201–13.

Seibert, S., Grant, J. and Kraimer, M. (1999) Proactive personality and career success. *Journal of Applied Psychology* 84: 416–27.

Shaffer, G.S., Saunders, V. and Owens, W.A. (1986) Additional evidence for the accuracy of biographical data: Long term retest and observer ratings. *Personnel Psychology* 39: 791–809.

Shapiro, D. (1995) Finding out how psychotherapies help people change. *Psychotherapy Research* 5: 1–21.

Sheridan, J.E. (1992) Organizational culture and employee retention. *Academy of Management Journal* 35: 1036–56.

Sides, E.H., Field, H.S., Giles, W.E., Holley, W.H. and Aronenakis, A.A. (1984) *Human Resource Planning* 7: 151–6.

Smernou, L.E. and Lautenschlager, G.J. (1991) Autobiographical antecedents and correlates of neuroticism and extraversion. *Personality and Individual Differences* 12(1): 49–59.

Smith, M., Glass, G. and Miller, T. (1980) *The Benefits of Psychotherapy*. Baltimore, Md.: Johns Hopkins University Press.

Smith, W.J., Albright, L.E., Glennon, J.R. and Owens, W.A. (1961) The prediction of research competence and creativity from personal history. *Journal of Applied Psychology* 45: 59–62.

Smither, J.W., Reilly, R.R., Millsap, R.E., Pearlman, K. and Stoffey, R.W. (1993) Applicant reactions to selection procedures. *Personnel Psychology* 46: 49–76.

Soldz, S. and Vaillant, G. (1999) The big five personality traits and the life course: A 45 year longitudinal study. *Journal of Research in Personality* 33: 208–32.

Spreitzer, G., McCall, M. and Mahoney, J. (1997) Early identification of international executive potential. *Journal of Applied Psychology* 82: 6–29.

Steinhouse, S.D. (1988) Predicting Military Attribution from Educational and Biographical Information. Report No. FR-PRD-88-06. Alexandria, Va.: Human Resources Research Organization.

Stokes, G.S. and Reddy, B. (1992) Use of background data in organisation decisions. In C. Cooper and I.T. Robertson (eds) *International Review of Industrial and Organisational Psychology*. Chichester: John Wiley & Sons, pp. 285–322.

Stokes, G.S., Hogan, J.B. and Snell, A.F. (1993) Comparability of incumbent and applicant samples for the development of biodata keys: The influence of social desirability. *Personnel Psychology* 46: 739–62.

Stokes, G.S., Jackson, K.E. and Owens, W.A. (1990) Sequential study. In M.D. Mumford, G.S. Stokes and W.A. Owens (eds) *Patterns of Life Adaptation: The Ecology of Human Individuality*. Hillsdale, NJ: Lawrence Erlbaum.

Stokes, G.S., Lautenschlager, G.J. and Blakley, B. (1987) *Sex Differences in the Component Structure of a Biographical Questionnaire*. Athens, Ga.: Institute for Behavioral Research.

Stokes, G.S., Meechan, R.C., Block, L.K. and Hogan, J.E. (1989a) Classification of persons and jobs. Paper presented at the meeting of the Society for Industrial and Organisational Psychology, Boston, Mass.

Stokes, G.S., Mumford, M.D. and Owens, W.A. (1989b) Life history prototypes in the study of human individuality. *Journal of Personality* 57: 509–45.

Stravidou, A. and Furnham, A. (1996) The relationship between psychoticism, trait-creativity and the attentional mechanism of cognitive inhibition. *Personality and Individual Differences* 21: 143–53.

Strebler, A. (1991) *Biodata in Selection: Issues in Practice*. IMS Paper No. 160. Institute of Manpower Studies. Sussex University, Brighton.

Strimbu, J.L. and Schoenfeldt, L.F. (1973) Life history subgroups in the prediction of drug usage patterns and attitudes. *JSAS Catalog of Selected Documents in Psychology*, 3: 83.

Tajfel, H. and Turner, J.C. (1986) The social identity theory of intergroup behaviour. In S. Worchel and W.G. Austin (ed.) *Psychology on Intergroup Relations (2nd edition)*. Chicago, Ill.: Nelson-Hall, pp. 7–24.

Tarnoiwski, S. (1973) *The Changing Success Ethic*. New York: Amacom.

Taylor, M.S. and Schmidt, D.W. (1983) A process-oriented investigation of recruitment source effectiveness. *Personnel Psychology* 36: 343–54.

Taylor, M.S. and Sniezek, J.A. (1984) The college recruitment interview: Topical content and applicant reactions. *Journal of Occupational Psychology* 57: 157–68.

Taylor, C., Ellison, R. and Tucker, M. (1965) *Biographical Information and the Prediction of Multiple Criteria of Success in Science*. Salt Lake City: University of Utah.

Telenson, P.A., Alexander, R.A. and Barrett, G.V. (1983) Scoring the biographical information blank: A comparison of three weighting techniques. *Applied Psychological Measurement* 7: 73–80.

Tett, R., Jackson, D. and Rothstein, M. (1991) Personality measures as predictors of job performance: A meta-analytic review. *Personnel Psychology* 43: 701–35.

Tharenou, P. (1990) Psychological approaches for investigating women's career advancement. *Australian Journal of Management* 15: 363–78.

Tharenou, P. and Conroy, D.K. (1988) Opportunities for and barriers to managerial role attainment. In G. Palmer (ed.) *Readings in Australian Personnel Management*. Sydney: Macmillan, pp. 179–221.

Tharenou, P., Latimer, S. and Conroy, D. (1994) How do you make it to the top? An examination of influences on women's and men's managerial advancement. *Academy of Management Journal* 37(4): 899–931.

Thayer, P.W. (1977) Somethings old, somethings new. *Personnel Psychology*, 30, 513-524.

Therivel, W. (1998) Creative genius and the GAM theory of personality: Why Mozart and not Salieri. *Journal of Social Behaviour and Personality* 13: 201–31.

Thornton, G.C. and Gierasch, P.F. (1980) Fakeability of an empirically derived selection instrument. *Journal of Personality Assessment* 44: 48–51.

Tillema, H. (1998) Assessment of potential from assessment centres to development centres. *International Journal of Selection and Assessment* 6: 185–91.

Turner, J.C. (1984) Social identification and psychological group formation. In H. Tajfel (ed.) *The Social Dimension: European Development in Social Psychology, volume 2*. Cambridge: Cambridge University Press, pp. 518–38.

Villwock, J.D., Schnitzan, J.P. and Carbonari, J.P. (1976) Holland's personality constructs as predictors of stability of choice. *Journal of Vocational Behaviour* 9: 77–85.

Vincent, C. and Furnham, A. (1997) *Complementary Medicine*. Chichester: Wiley.

Vroom, V.H. (1966) Organizational choice: A study of pre- and post-decision processes. *Organizational Behaviour and Human Performance* 1: 212–26.

Walker, C.B. (1985) The fakeability of the army's Military Applicant Profile (MAP). Paper presented at the annual conference of the Association of Human Resources Management and Organizational Behaviour, Denver, Colo.

Walther, R. (1961) Self-description as a predictor of success or failure in foreign service clerical jobs. *Journal of Applied Psychology* 45: 16–21.

Wanous, J.P. (1977) Organisational entry: Newcomers moving from outside to inside. *Psychological Bulletin* 84: 601–18.

Warner, M. (1997) Working at home. *Fortune* 165–6.

Webb, S.C. (1960) The comparative validity of two biographical inventory keys. *Journal of Applied Psychology* 44: 177–83.

Webster, E. (1964) *Decision Making in the Employment Interview*. Montreal: Engle.

Weick, K.E. (1979) *The Social Psychology of Organizing (2nd edn)*. Reading, Mass.: Addison-Wesley.

Weiner, Y. and Vactenas, R. (1977) Personality correlates of voluntary midcareer change in enterprising occupation. *Journal of Applied Psychology* 62(6): 706–12.

Wernimont, P.F. (1962) Reevaluation of a weighted application blank for office personnel. *Journal of Applied Psychology* 46: 417–19.

Wernimont, P.F. and Campbell, J.P. (1968) Signs, samples, and criteria. *Journal of Applied Psychology* 52: 372–6.

Wesley, S.S. (1989) Background data subgroups and career outcomes: Some developmental influences on person job matching. Unpublished doctoral dissertation, Institute of Technology, University of Georgia.

Whitney, D.J. and Schmitt, N. (1997) Relationship between culture and responses to biodata employment items. *Journal of Applied Psychology* 82(1): 113–19.

Wilkinson, L.J. (1993) An alternative view of biodata: The model. *Recruitment, Selection and Retention* 2(3): 23–8.

Wilkinson, L.J. (1994) An alternative view of biodata: Some empirical evidence. *Recruitment, Selection and Retention* 3(1): 11–16.

Wilkinson, L.J. (1995) The development of an alternative biodata model for managerial selection. PhD thesis, University of Newcastle.

Wilkinson, L.J. (1997) Generalisable biodata? An application to the vocatonal interests of managers. *Journal of Occupational and Organisational Psychology* 70: 49–60.

Wilkinson, L.J., Anderson, A., van Zwanenberg, N., Erdos, G. and Harvey, J. (1997) A study of the characteristics of prospective engineers at different stages of development. *Proceedings of Professional Standards and Quality of Engineering Education*. Sheffield Hallam University, 24–27 March.

Wingrove, J., Glendinning, P. and Herriott, P. (1984) Graduate pre-selection: A research note. *Journal of Occupational Psychology* 57: 169–71.

Wrzesniewski, A., McComisky, C., Rozin, P. and Schwartz, B. (1997) Jobs, careers and callings: People's relations to their work. *Journal of Research in Personality* 31: 21–33.

Yukl, E. (1980) *Leadership in Organizations*. New York: Wiley.

Zedeck, S. (1971) Problems with the use of 'Merator' variables. *Psychological Bulletin* 76: 295–310.

Zuckerman, M., Kuhlman, D.M. and Camac, C. (1988) What lies beyond E and N? Factor analyses of scales believed to measure basic dimensions of personality. *Journal of Personality and Social Psychology* 54: 96–107.

Index